THE ADVENTURES OF SHADREK

THE ADVENTURES OF SHADREK

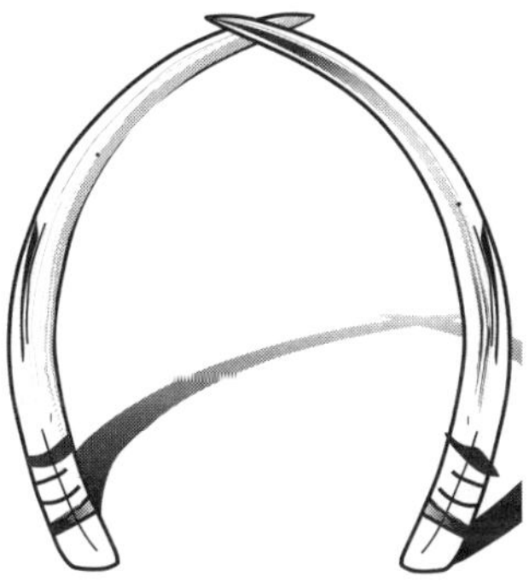

Southern Africa's Most Infamous Elephant Poacher

by
Ron Thomson

Safari Press Inc.

Thomson, Ron

Second edition

Safari Press Inc.

2014, Long Beach, California

ISBN 978-1-57157-440-4

Library of Congress Catalog Card Number: 00-105428

10 9 8 7 6 5 4 3 2 1

Printed in the United States of America

Readers wishing to receive the Safari Press catalog, featuring many fine books on big-game hunting, wingshooting, and sporting firearms, should write to Safari Press Inc., 15621 Chemical Lane, Huntington Beach, CA, 92649-1506, USA. Tel: (714) 894-9080 or visit our Web site at www.safaripress.com.

To Maggie

Preface

Twenty-three years have passed since I last saw Shadrek. Thirty-three years have gone by since I first heard of him—a lot of water has passed under the bridge of time since those faraway days.

I mention this because I must admit that I cannot now remember all the finer details surrounding this story, which happened so many years ago. I have forgotten, for example, many of the actual words spoken in the conversations I held with the people involved. I am now also no longer sure who told me what during the course of some of the events I relate.

I have, therefore, had to reconstruct, in a fictional or dramatic manner, many of those conversations in order to make the story readable. The gist of all those communications, however, is correct. There has been no fabrication in the substance of what they conveyed.

In all other respects this is an absolutely true story. The events that I describe actually happened. The people in the story are all real. This, then, is the true story of Shadrek—the most infamous black elephant poacher the continent of Africa has ever known.

PART I

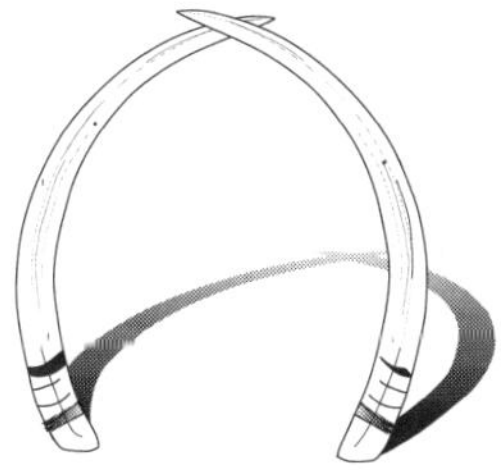

Chapter 1

Shadrek's elephant-poaching exploits in Zimbabwe's Gonarezhou National Park are legend. In his day there was nobody to touch him. He was indeed a poacher and hunter extraordinaire.

His name was on everybody's lips during the 1960s and 1970s. Every white resident in the towns, on the sugar plantations, and on the cattle ranches of the Zimbabwean lowveld knew about and spoke about Shadrek.

Between 1965 and 1975 he was particularly active—and very successful. No matter what our strategies, he ran rings around the game rangers and police who tried to catch him. When we asked the local black people about Shadrek, they denied any knowledge of this Scarlet Pimpernel of the African bush. Yet mention of his name brought enigmatic smiles to their faces.

Strangely, the white community, too, despite their disapproval of his plundering of the game reserve's great elephant bulls, had a grudging admiration for Shadrek. Everyone looked upon him as a swashbuckling pirate who dared to win—and he did!

He was not the only poacher who shot elephants in the Gonarezhou. There were many others to be sure, both black and white, but they were timid and overcautious, even fearful, by comparison. They were not such a permanent threat, and they never had anywhere near the same impact on the game reserve's big elephant bulls. None ever approached Shadrek's score, and most of them made mistakes that culminated in their arrest. Shadrek made very few mistakes.

During the late 1970s Shadrek became a very important figure in my life, because of the manner in which our lives came together and what followed as a consequence. All this happened, however, several years after I had left the Gonarezhou. For a very short time, we were kindred spirits who worked together for a common cause.

During his heyday as a poacher, Shadrek lived from time to time, or so we believed, on both sides of Zimbabwe's boundary with Mozambique, near the confluence of the Sabi and Lundi Rivers. As the pressure within the game reserve mounted against him, however, he seemed to reside more commonly in Mozambique. Nevertheless, irrespective of how intense our antipoaching efforts were at any time, he never stopped hunting. Our focused attempts to apprehend him merely caused him to gravitate toward living permanently across the border . . . or so we thought!

Among the black people of the region, Shadrek was looked upon as something of a Robin Hood. He stole elephants from the government, and he continually hoodwinked the various sheriffs of Nottingham who were employed to capture him. For five and a half years during the height of Shadrek's poaching career, I was one of those sheriffs—the game warden-in-charge of the Gonarezhou National Park.

Shadrek was elusive because, among other things, he had an effective and absorbing smokescreen in the local populace, within whose labyrinth of villages he could hide. For years he swam among the people and operated right under our noses.

The Rhodesia-Mozambique border was Shadrek's greatest asset, for he skipped across from one country to the other at will. This enabled him to carry out his poaching activities with absolute impunity. We would follow his tracks but had to stop at the boundary, for we had no jurisdiction in the Portuguese territory that lay beyond the fence line.

During the early and middle parts of Shadrek's life, Mozambique was governed as a province of Portugal. When Portugal capitulated to the FRELIMO guerrilla army in 1974 and Samora Machel took over the reins of government, the indigenous people of Mozambique ruled their own land for the first time in five centuries. That did not work to Shadrek's advantage—after 1974 his circumstances changed radically.

Nevertheless, around about 1970, so great had Shadrek's impact on the Gonarezhou's elephant bulls become that at my instigation the Department of National Parks and Wildlife Management officially appealed for help to the country's minister of law and order and to the minister of home affairs. This resulted in the police special branch in the lowveld's small capital town, Chiredzi, being tasked to visit Espungabera in Mozambique.

Espungabera is well to the north of the area in which Shadrek operated. Even so, it was the Portuguese administrative capital of the vast bush country that stretched from the Chimanimani Mountains in the north to the Rio Save in the south.

Rio Save (pronounced *Saahv*) is the name the Portuguese gave to the lower reaches of the combined Sabi and Lundi Rivers, which join just across the border inside the Gonarezhou. In Mozambique the river is a mile and a half wide. In the dry season, the Rio Save is a sheet of golden yellow sand fringed with green phragmites (reeds), over which meanders a broad but shallow stream of crystal-clear water. It becomes a raging, muddy torrent during the rains, but for the greater part of the year, the Rio Save is easily negotiable on foot.

At Espungabera, the special branch officers conferred with the Portuguese *chefe de posto* and the local chief of police. Under cordial and accommodating circumstances, they reached an agreement to set up a joint operation to arrest Shadrek.

Now that we had the cooperation of the Portuguese administration, we believed it would be only a matter of time before Shadrek was arrested. We increased our own efforts to capture him and, through the good offices of the police Special Branch in Chiredzi, worked hard at keeping the *chefe de posto* at Espungabera well informed of all our antipoaching endeavours.

Our cooperative efforts, however, were all to no avail. Nothing ever came of the joint operations because the jurisdiction of the chefe de posto at Espungabera stopped at the Rio Save, and Shadrek, the Portuguese told us, had moved his base to a secret place south of the river. It seemed that the *chefe de posto* at Espungabera could not, or would not, coordinate effectively with his counterpart south of the Rio Save. Whatever languid attempts the Portuguese ever made to bring Shadrek to justice quickly evaporated under the hot and soporific African sun.

Shadrek seemed to enjoy a charmed life. Not only was he able to use the international boundary adroitly to avoid arrest, he also used to his advantage the internal administrative boundary of the Rio Save in Mozambique. Much later I was to learn just how and why he was able to manipulate the Portuguese administration with such apparent ease. It was the key to his invulnerability.

Shadrek worked one yearlong contract in the gold mines of the Witwatersrand in South Africa during the time that I worked in the Gonarezhou. That accounted for a period when he appeared to be dormant. When the poaching stopped, my colleagues and I, not knowing what Shadrek was up to, patted ourselves on the back, thinking that our strenuous efforts were the cause. When Shadrek returned home from the mines, however, he hit us again like a bomb blast.

We were always very conscious of the support and empathy that Shadrek enjoyed from all the black people living on both sides of the border. Certainly, on our side we were never able to extract from local black communities any kind of information about his modus operandi, his whereabouts, or his circumstances. For a long time we had no idea what he even looked like—whether he was tall or short, thin or fat, dark-skinned or fair-skinned. Indeed, we could have employed the man and not known it. For years, therefore, Shadrek remained an enigma, a veritable will-o'-the-wisp. Despite all our efforts, we never caught Shadrek in the act of poaching. And over the years his tally mounted into many hundreds of the Gonarezhou's biggest and best elephant bulls.

I first heard of Shadrek when I was introduced to the results of his poaching in 1968. This was during the period of southern Africa's history when present-day Zimbabwe was known as Rhodesia. Therefore, the names Zimbabwe and Rhodesia will both be used in the early part of this story as is most appropriate—until it is better, for the story-telling, to refer to the country by its earlier name, Rhodesia. White-ruled, colonial, and "rebel" Rhodesia was at that time engaged in a bitter guerrilla bush war with what the world now refers to as African freedom fighters. We Rhodesians justifiably called them terrorists. It is crucial to understand that a state of war existed in the country because that fact is an integral and vital part of Shadrek's story.

I have no wish to enter into any kind of political or moral debate regarding the rights and the wrongs of the conflict; suffice it to say that the state of war at the time was a fact. I was then a white Rhodesian in the prime of my life who fought for his country. I felt that the cause of the Rhodesians was honest and just, and I carried out my military duties willingly and with great enthusiasm. That, too, is pertinent to Shadrek's story.

What is more important at this point is that I delve into the background of the tale so that you, the reader, will come to appreciate that part of the Gonarezhou's history that shaped our thinking at the time. It will also allow you to enter Shadrek's world with greater understanding and empathy, and to share in his great passion—hunting the majestic elephant bulls of the Gonarezhou.

The Gonarezhou National Park is two thousand square miles in extent, and it is located in the southeast corner of Zimbabwe. The game reserve's eastern boundary runs along the international border with Mozambique, and its southern boundary, on the Nuanetsi River, is some fifty miles north of the great, green, greasy Limpopo River made famous by Rudyard Kipling. The Limpopo is Zimbabwe's international border with South Africa. The northern boundary of South Africa's Kruger National Park lies on the southern bank of the Limpopo, too, abutting that country's international boundaries with Mozambique and Zimbabwe.

At the point where Zimbabwe, South Africa, and Mozambique meet, the much smaller South African Pafuri River joins the Limpopo. The wedge of South African territory sandwiched between the two rivers was once known as Crook's Corner, because of all the reprobates and scallywags, thieves, and murderers who there skipped across the borders of one or another of the three countries to avoid capture by the authorities.

Crook's Corner was an active reality for some three or four decades following the Anglo-Boer War.

Crook's Corner was made famous by T. V. Bulpin in his book *The Ivory Trail*. That book relates the story of a white South African, Bvekenya Barnard, who, as a result of the book, became southern Africa's most infamous and yet most celebrated old-time elephant poacher. The name Bvekenya—"the one who swaggers as he walks"—was given to Cecil Barnard by the Shangaan people with whom he lived and hunted in the Gonarezhou region for the better part of twenty years.

Bulpin's *Ivory Trail* was well received. It even became a prescribed textbook in South African schools. Had the author told the real story of Bvekenya Barnard, however, the Verwoerdian apartheid government in South Africa would most likely have had the book banned. The author never revealed, for example, that Barnard kept three separate ménages in his Rhodesian territory. Each village was complete with a native Shangaan wife, half-caste children, cattle, sheep, and goats, and his various families plowed their fields and cultivated their crops in exactly the same manner as did all their native neighbours. In truth, during the period that Bvekenya Barnard lived in Rhodesia, he "went native."

I know all this because, as I mentioned earlier, I lived in the Gonarezhou for several years and because the Gonarezhou was the heart of Bvekenya Barnard country. Furthermore, one of my Shangaan staff, Senior Game Scout Machavani (Mack for short), had for a time been Bvekenya's chief gunbearer. I never trusted Mack on an elephant hunt after he once ran away with my rifle when an elephant cow unexpectedly attacked us. Nevertheless, I listened to what he had to say about Bvekenya, and I soaked up many a Bvekenya story from him. And they weren't all about hunting!

I also met three of Bvekenya's half-caste children—two sons and a daughter—when they were well into middle age. All of them displayed the high-yellow complexion common to most people of mixed blood. As a result of those meetings I was able to verify what Mack had told me—that Bvekenya Barnard had had three Shangaan wives whom he kept in different villages in and around present-day Gonarezhou. From Bvekenya's two sons I ascertained that he had some eight or nine legitimate children. Several bastards, too, resulted from his short-term liaisons with other Shangaan women. Not even his children were prepared to hazard a guess at the total number of his illegitimate offspring.

These facts are important to the story of Shadrek, who was, in my estimation, not only Zimbabwe's most notorious elephant poacher but probably also the greatest black elephant poacher on the continent of Africa. In his time, Shadrek was bigger in legendary stature among the local black peoples of the Gonarezhou region than was the great Bvekenya Barnard himself. The difference between the two lay in the fact that Bulpin lionized the white man in *The Ivory Trail*, whereas Shadrek had no such publicity.

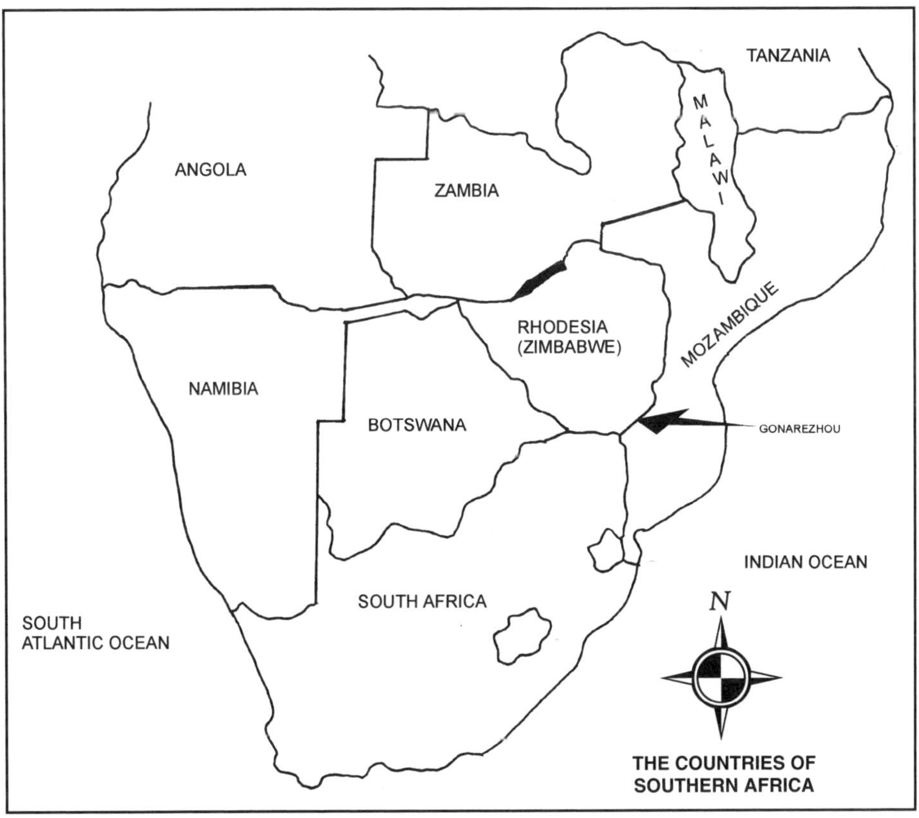

When I first heard about Shadrek, I was told he was the son of one of Bvekenya's illegitimate children. At the time—reluctantly—I thought it was fitting for one of Barnard's grandsons to have been the elephant poacher who wrought so much havoc among the elephant bulls of the Gonarezhou in the 1960s and 1970s. Nevertheless, much later, when I met Shadrek and was able to piece together the many different facets of his story, I discovered that the facts were much more fascinating than the legend.

Shadrek, in fact, was every bit as dashing and daring in his elephant poaching exploits as the infamous Bvekenya Barnard had been in his day, and perhaps more so. Furthermore, an infinitely bigger and much more organized law enforcement agency was ranged against Shadrek than had ever faced his notorious predecessor. Yet he was never caught.

In October 1968, as a game warden in the Rhodesian Department of National Parks and Wildlife Management, I was posted to Mabalauta to take command of the Gonarezhou Game Reserve. At the time of my arrival, the control of the tsetse fly in the area, by the combined means of selective game elimination and the spraying of insecticides, had almost ceased. All I did for the antitsetse campaign in my day was to occasionally shoot an elephant bull fence-breaker and destroy the odd nyala antelope that had strayed into the tsetse corridors. The game reserve at the time had been divided into three parts by means of seven-foot-high, all-steel, game-proof fences.

Mabalauta, on the southern Nuanetsi River, was the game reserve's headquarters. It was on the edge of the only sector that had never suffered from tsetse-fly infestation. The Lundi sector, headquartered at Chipinda Pools, had been recently sprayed with DDT to eliminate the fly.

The Rhodesian Tsetse Department was at that time negotiating with the Portuguese to eradicate the fly inside adjacent Mozambique. Shortly after my arrival, therefore, the Rhodesians began spraying DDT on huge blocks of bush inside Portuguese territory. Thereafter, the department rapidly pushed the fly farther and farther from the Rhodesian border toward the sea. Between the Lundi and Mabalauta sectors of the

Gonarezhou, in what was called the Guluene-Chefu Tsetse Corridor, all the ordinary game animals had been eliminated by shooting. This corridor, too, was isolated by game fencing.

There was also a five-mile-wide fenced corridor along the northern and western boundaries of the game reserve within which all game animals had been shot out and no domestic stock was allowed. The purpose of this animal-free corridor was twofold. Firstly, it was to stop the spread of the tsetse fly westward. Secondly, it was to reduce the chance of foot-and-mouth disease spreading from the sanctuary's Cape buffalo, a natural carrier of the disease, to the native people's domestic herds.

During my sojourn in the Gonarezhou the old bush-pole game fence that ran along the international boundary with Mozambique was replaced with two parallel, all-steel game fences set a mile and a half apart. These seven-foot-high steel fences, with their railway line straining posts concreted into the ground and their many strands of high-tensile oval steel wire, were immensely strong. Bull elephants periodically broke through the fences, but the herds of elephant cows and other game animals were unable to make any impression on the structures. For all intents and purposes, therefore, these fences were truly "game proof."

This meant the elephants of the Lundi became fenced in during my period of service in the Gonarezhou—except for the gap along the game reserve's Sabi River boundary. The human habitation in Chief Mahenya's country across the river, however, was sufficiently dense to compel the cow herds not to venture there. Elephant cows avoid human habitation like the plague so as not to expose their calves to danger. When human populations exceed about forty people per square mile, the cow herds will not go anywhere near them.

Although elephant bulls continued to use Mahenya's country as a feeding area during the rains, and to raid Mahenya's crops, we never ever found any cow herds in the area. So Mahenya's country was just as effective a barrier to elephant migration as were the steel fences that surrounded the game reserve on all the other boundaries.

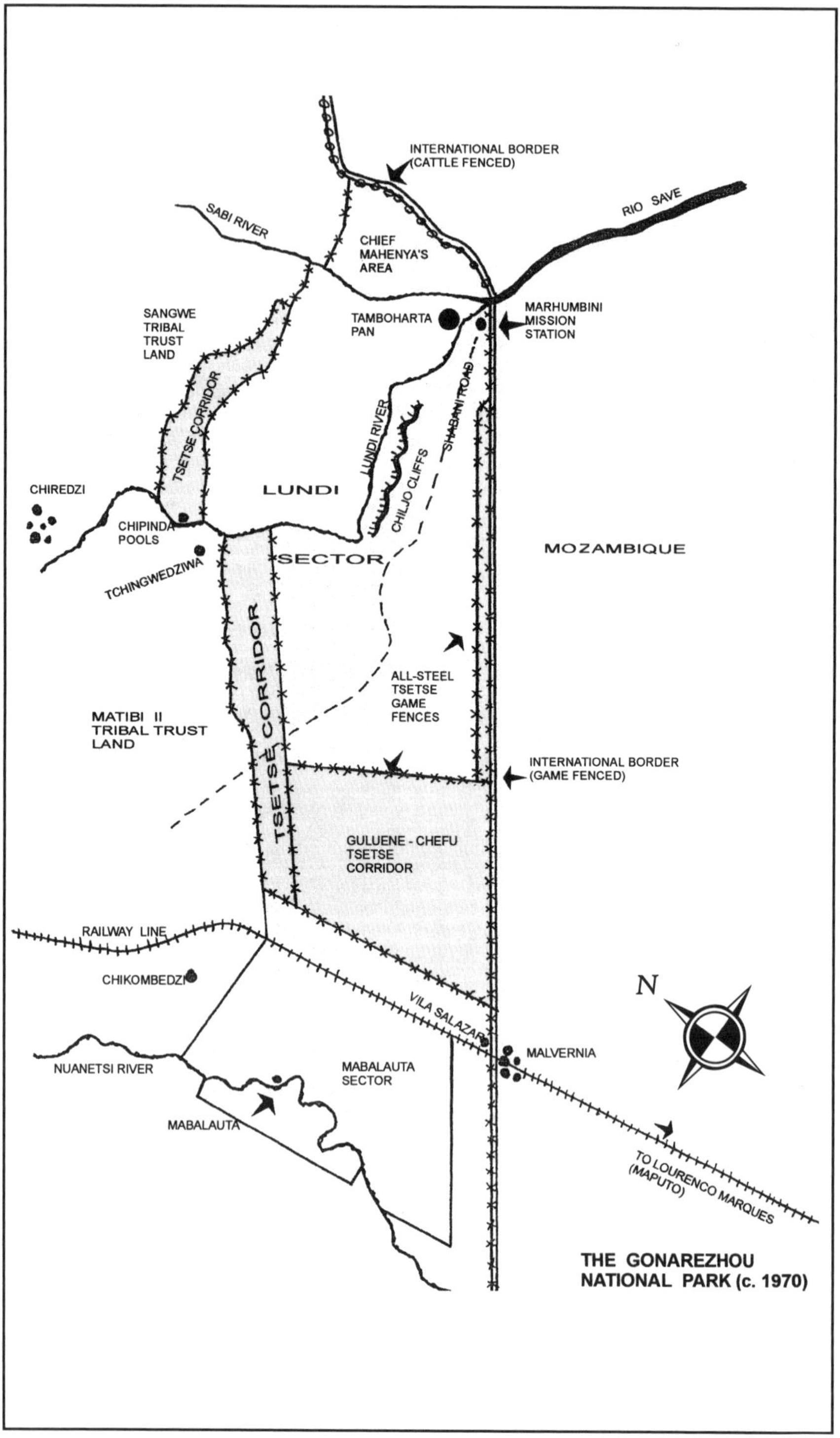

THE GONAREZHOU NATIONAL PARK (c. 1970)

One of the tragedies of the anti-tsetse-fly programme, in my opinion, was that my predecessor made every effort to save the elephants that lived in the Guluene-Chefu from being killed. In this regard, early in the dry season of 1967, the surface waters in the natural pans of the corridor were pumped dry and the resident elephants were forced to migrate to either the Nuanetsi River in the south or the Lundi River in the north. When the elephants had moved, game fences were erected behind them.

The movement of these animals created huge concentrations of elephants on both rivers, far more than the available vegetation could support. The "saving" of the Guluene-Chefu elephants, therefore, resulted in terrible and irreparable damage to the sensitive riverine forest habitats on both the Nuanetsi and Lundi Rivers. In my opinion, the game reserve as a whole would have been much better off had the Guluene-Chefu elephants been killed in the tsetse corridor. Whatever the merits or demerits of the Guluene-Chefu elephant management decision, when I arrived in the Gonarezhou in 1968, both the Lundi and the Mabalauta sectors were crawling with elephants. I had never seen so many together in my entire life.

Probably as a result of the congestion, they were very aggressive. At no other time have I encountered elephants that so deliberately and so repeatedly charged people without any provocation. Some old cows began their attacks at the very first intimation of a human presence and they truly meant business. I shot many of those out of hand because they were a menace to our budding tourism development.

Shadrek, therefore, had no difficulty in finding elephants to shoot. His principal problem was in locating the biggest of the big bulls and avoiding being flattened by the old matriarchs he encountered in the process. The existence of sporadic game-scout patrols in his area of operations was of far less consequence by comparison.

This is not the place to discuss the justification for culling excessive populations of elephants in Africa's national park game reserves. Suffice it to say, we reduced the Gonarezhou's elephant population by 2,500 in

1971 and 1972. Approximately half of these were taken off the Mabalauta sector and the other half from the Lundi.

One might then well ask: What possible harm could Shadrek have done to the Gonarezhou's elephants by removing one or two bulls every now and then? This is a good question when viewed against the reality that the park authorities were busy exterminating many thousands of the big pachyderms for legitimate management purposes.

The answer is twofold. First of all, Shadrek was highly selective. He normally concentrated his attentions on the elephant bulls with the biggest and best ivory, and these were the very animals we were trying to preserve. These bulls carried the genes that would produce new generations of big bulls with heavy ivory, and we avoided killing them at all costs. They were also valuable from a tourism standpoint. Secondly, what Shadrek was doing was illegal. By the time I arrived in the Gonarezhou, he was already a hero among the local people and therefore an important and dangerous role model.

Whereas the local black people saw Shadrek as something of a dashing icon, they considered the game rangers as their enemy. In a nutshell, they hated our guts. This was because we arrested them for poaching the wild animals of the Gonarezhou and we threw them into jail for any transgression committed within the boundaries of the game reserve.

If there had been half-a-dozen more Shadreks, our elephant-protection duties would have been impossible. In fact, that is exactly what happened during the 1980s after Robert Mugabe came to power in Zimbabwe. In that decade, not only were large numbers of elephant killed in the Gonarezhou by many different poachers—using AK-47 assault rifles—so was every single one of the game reserve's black rhino.

The history of the Gonarezhou's black rhino is tragic. The last naturally occurring black rhino was shot near Nyamtongwe in 1934. In the early 1970s, I was one of the principals in the capture team that reintroduced eighty-one black rhino into the Gonarezhou. For fifteen years those animals prospered—and probably tripled their numbers. Then poachers wiped them out in the late 1980s.

So there were several reasons to capture Shadrek and stop his poaching, but we never did. It was only a quirk of fate that finally brought his nefarious activities to an end in the late 1970s. Regrettably, I played a pivotal role in his downfall. But by then, he had had a good run for his money.

You might ask: Why should I regret being the cause of Shadrek's downfall? Well, that is a major part of what this story is all about.

During my service in the Gonarezhou, I had several officers in both sectors of the game reserve. All were geared toward halting Shadrek's poaching. The only ones who are pertinent to this story and whom I will mention, however, are Senior Game Ranger John Osborne at Chipinda Pools and Game Ranger Charles Mackie, who was John's assistant. John Osborne was my overall second-in-command.

I was brutally introduced to the existence of Shadrek, and gained firsthand experience of his poaching activities, on my very first visit to Chipinda Pools in the dying days of October 1968.

Chapter 2

Ten days after arriving at Mabalauta, I visited Chipinda Pools for the first time. I was by then familiar with my new duties as the game warden-in-charge of the Gonarezhou. My family was reasonably settled in our new home, a concrete prefabricated house set amidst a beautiful riverine forest strip on the banks of a wide twist of golden sand that was the Nuanetsi River. There was always very little water in the Nuanetsi during the dry season.

I proceeded to Chipinda Pools, eighty miles north of Mabalauta, along a rough gravel road through the Matibi II Tribal Trust Land west of the game reserve's boundary. I could have used the sandy track that ran through the Guluene-Chefu Tsetse Corridor, but that route took three times as long. The purpose of my journey on this occasion was to meet with John Osborne.

John was to introduce me to the lower Lundi River area, which, I had been told, was the real heart of this great game reserve. My exploration of the wild interior, I reasoned, would have to wait. Senior Game Scout Machavani guided me on this excursion, and my Msili Bushman tracker, Ben, truly my right hand, came along for the ride. I went nowhere without Ben.

That night I stayed with John and his wife, Jill, in their lovely home on the north bank of the Lundi River. Jill was an accomplished artist, and many of her oil landscapes adorned the walls. Her specialty was painting the beautifully ugly giant baobab tree.

Theirs was a very old pioneer house that had been built right on the edge of the river overlooking a four-hundred-yard-wide reedbed of dense phragmites. The house was surrounded by huge and shady riverine trees, in stark contrast to the rest of the riverine forest along the river. Opposite the station and all along the dry Tshingwedziwa stream on the far bank, every one of the giant forest trees had been ringed and killed by the tsetse department. The reason? To remove the shady environment that was essential for the survival of the dreaded tsetse fly. All along the bank opposite the house, bleak skeletons of once huge trees bore testimony to the rape of the land carried out in the name of progress. I was disgusted.

There were channels of running water within the reedbeds and many hidden pools in which hippo grunted and hee-hawed all night long. And in the distance, I could hear the rumble of water cascading over the Chiribira Falls and dropping one hundred feet directly into the first of the long gorges that ran through the rugged Chihunja Hills.

That first afternoon, John showed me the station environs and we visited, a little downstream from the house, the string of very large pools from which the area drew its name. These are located in a rocky region of the river just above the waterfall itself. The main pool held a huge herd of hippo, and they lay higgledy-piggledy, one on top of the other, on the sandbar midstream. Wherever we looked we saw the heads of large and small crocodiles eying the world from their watery domain.

I was pleased to see that here, on the north bank of the pools, the forest trees were still intact. Under them, John had constructed an attractive camping ground for the few tourists who were now beginning to visit the game reserve.

I later learnt that John had had a war of words—which nearly came to blows—with the tsetse department staff, who had wanted to cut down *all* the riverine trees at Chipinda Pools. Indeed, an immense interdepartmental incident had erupted over the issue, but John had won the day. Today, those riverine trees that survived the wave of destruction at Chipinda are monuments to his tenacity. I began then to understand that I was fortunate to have a unique man as my second-in-command.

John was a big man, not only in stature but in his mentality, too, and the Lundi sector of the Gonarezhou was his greatest love. It was with great pride that he drove me the next morning over the incredibly rough Chihunja Hills track down to the lower Lundi.

Access to the lower Lundi was clearly a major problem. The road was barely a track, with many serious obstacles such as broken boulders and rocky streambeds. Even in a four-wheel-drive Land Rover, it was not easy to negotiate. It took us over an hour to traverse the ten-mile route—and this at the height of the dry season. I could just imagine what it was like during the rains!

There was another track south of the river that ran round the Sibonja Hills, but it was a greater distance and took just as long to negotiate. The Sibonjas were really just a continuation of the Chihunjas on the other side of the Lundi.

During the six-month-long rainy season, when the Lundi was swollen, John had to leave a government Land Rover on the far bank of the river across from his house in order to have vehicular access to that area. To reach the Land Rover he had to cross the river by boat. Very often, however, the vehicle tracks throughout the game reserve were a quagmire during the rains and not usable by a vehicle at all.

Administration of the lower Lundi area—which I discovered that day really was the true heart of the Gonarezhou—was fraught with many difficulties. In fact, during the rains, the only antipoaching work that we could consistently carry out east of Chipinda Pools had to be conducted on foot. And there were only ten game scouts at Chipinda to patrol the one-thousand-square-mile Lundi sector.

All these circumstances, of course, provided Shadrek with many golden opportunities, and I was to learn that he took advantage of every one. However, Shadrek was the last thing on my mind as we descended the broken southeastern Chihunja hillside that morning and ran out onto the lower Lundi's wide, flat flood plain. At that stage, I had never even heard of him.

While coming down the southern slopes of the Chihunja Hills, I had my first view of the Chilojo Cliffs, and it took my breath away. They towered six hundred feet above the river's south bank and ran for five miles, in a convoluted fashion, parallel to the Lundi's wide meanders. The lower two-thirds of the feature comprised the talus slope, most of which, in the upstream section, tumbled down right into the river. Farther downstream, the river turned away from the cliffs, leaving a wide swath of alluvial flood plain bedecked with giant evergreen trees.

The cliffs themselves were vertical and fully two hundred feet high, comprising many differently coloured layers of sandstone. There were lateral seams of red, then ochre, then yellow, and the colours were repeated again and again down the cliff face. The cliffs were magnificent, especially when caught in the rays of the early morning sun. The river was wide down here in the lower reaches, and its flow across the broad stretches of golden sand was shallow and languid. A great deal of the water flowed under the sand. Both banks of the river here were clothed in huge trees.

Thank goodness, I thought, *the tsetse department has not cut down the forest trees in this part of the Gonarezhou.*

"It would have been more than any of their lives were worth," John said almost sardonically when I voiced my thoughts. "All they did down here was to spray the country from one end to the other with DDT, and that was bad enough. But it did the trick. There are now no tsetse on the lower Lundi."

We drove easily across the flat flood plain amidst the tall trees, passing many a pool in which hippo disported plentifully. We had left early that morning without breakfast, but there was a box in the back of the vehicle that Jill had packed for us the night before. Soon John drove off the road and stopped at a very large pool, which contained the biggest herd of hippo I have ever seen. Nyahungwe was the pool's name—Fish Eagle Pool.

"One hundred and seven was the last count," John said, answering my question before it had been asked. "We count the hippo from the air every October when the river is at its driest."

He extracted two fishing rods from his vehicle, and soon we were pulling in two-pound black bream one after the other. We had breakfast on the edge of the pool—fillets of fresh fried bream, fried eggs and bacon, and fresh bread that Jill had baked herself. We had our coffee while lounging in our metal camp chairs and watching the hippo and crocodiles. Towering above us on the opposite bank were the magnificent Chilojo Cliffs.

"*Chilojo* means 'the knife sharpener,'" John explained. "In the old days the Shangaans and the Mhlengwes used to travel here from miles around to collect bits of sandstone, which they took home for sharpening their knives."

As we chatted, Ben and Hlupo, John's Shangaan tracker, cleaned the dirty dishes and greasy pans at the river's edge, using river sand as their scouring agent. Both trackers were dressed in raggedy and nondescript mufti, their special expertise hidden away within their souls.

Mack, dressed in a smartly ironed khaki uniform, sat on the riverbank some distance away from us all. As the most senior scout in the game reserve—and someone who considered himself one cut above everybody else because he had once been Bvekenya's gunbearer—he remained aloof from the trackers. It would have been *infra dig* for Mack to partake in such menial chores as cleaning the dishes when there were trackers available to do the job.

The location, the situation, the atmosphere, the company were all terrific. It was idyllic. I felt happy and content. This was the life that kept my spirit alive. And I envied John Osborne for living in this paradise.

By the time we finished our coffee, the trackers had repacked the Land Rover. We were soon on our way again, traveling downstream on the north-bank track. Half an hour later we entered the Sabi-Lundi flood plain, which John advised me was seven miles across at its widest point. Here, about five miles upstream from the confluence of the two rivers, there was an extensive forest of giant riverine trees interspersed with vast thickets of short *mlala* palms, their huge, hand-shaped fronds reaching to the ground. Bigger palms emerged at periodic intervals.

Then we entered a jungle of giant trees with lianas as thick as a man's thigh trailing from the canopies. It was reminiscent of something out of a Tarzan movie. The treetops were bedecked with flowers. There were the red bottlebrush bristles of the lianas, the yellow of the huge *mtondo* trees, and festoons of huge wine-coloured trumpets hanging from the branches of the sausage trees.

Beneath the sausage trees, herds of impala walked about in a desultory fashion until one of the huge wine-coloured flower cups fell to the ground. Then they all rushed toward the trumpet, and the winner would snatch up the flower and run off to eat it. In some of the trees baboons reached down to pull the flowers off for themselves, dislodging many others in the process. And beneath waited the impala.

The treetops were a cacophony of birdcalls. Parrots, glossy starlings, barbets, and the colourful purple-crested louries were abundant everywhere. Here we encountered elephant for the first time that day, and there were buffalo aplenty, too. This was a real paradise.

Throughout the morning, we had encountered very little game. Besides the ubiquitous hippo, we had seen no big-game animals at all. We had come across the odd kudu and waterbuck, and seen a reedbuck or two and one group of zebra, but the land had been strikingly devoid of game.

The tracks, however, told the real story. On the ground all along the river was a myriad of hoofprints, which told me that the wildlife of the Lundi came down to drink only in the late afternoon and at night. The animals did not live on the riverbanks at the height of the dry season, for much earlier in the year they had stripped the land near the river of all edible vegetation. Now they came to the river only to drink, returning to their distant grazing grounds to feed.

The Sabi-Lundi flood plain is one of the richest and most concentrated game-feeding areas in the reserve. In its middle is a huge expanse of open ground called Tamboharta pan. It is over a mile long and three-quarters of a mile wide when full of water, and many hippo live here during the rains. At the time of our visit, however, it was just a vacant stretch of dried-out mud in which the lungfish lay in their cocoons of slime, waiting for the rains. The mud flat was surrounded by fever trees and giant *Acacia albidas*. The *albidas* are called winterthorns because they are clothed in a blanket of dark green leaves in the winter months and are naked in summer. During the summer rainy period they often stand three feet deep in water.

The Sabi-Lundi junction is the richest ecological region of the Gonarezhou, and we saw a huge variety of game in a very short time. Impala and warthog were everywhere, as were nyala and bushbuck. Surprisingly, I saw an oribi, a species I hadn't seen since my teenage years on our family farm in the Karoi area in the far north of the country. John told me that the tiny Livingstone suni lived here, too, but we never saw one. We did see baboons and vervet monkeys aplenty—and waterbuck and kudu and Burchell zebra and duiker and steenbok. I was amazed to find so many of the smaller antelope species in one area, which makes the Gonarezhou ecologically unique.

The junction of the two biggest rivers south of the Rhodesian watershed is an impressive expanse of golden sand and green phragmites. At its widest—from the south bank of the Lundi River to the eastern bank of the Sabi River—it is two miles across. Amidst the reeds, we could see the backs of many elephant bulls. They were busy breaking off succulent young shoots and stuffing huge quantities into their cavernous mouths.

We crossed the Lundi just above the junction and drove up the hill on the south bank to the then-derelict mission station of Marhumbini. Here we could look down over the junction area from on high. There were eighty-two big elephant bulls in the reedbeds. They were very easy to count from this elevation.

Across the Sabi River we could see the first of the village settlements of Chief Mahenya's people. Theirs was a two-mile-wide strip of primitive subsistence agriculture sandwiched between the Sabi and the Mozambique border. The people were largely left to their own devices by the government because, just as the lower Lundi in the Gonarezhou was cut off from civilization during the rains, so was Mahenya's country. During the next ten years, I would come to know Mahenya's country very well indeed—from a number of different perspectives.

John pointed out to me what he called Sabi Island. The local natives, he said, called it Mwachimeni. Three miles long and nearly a mile wide, it was covered in dense riverine forest. Unfortunately, the island is on Chief Mahenya's side of the main Sabi River, which meant the game reserve had no claim to this prize piece of wildlife real estate.

Jill had prepared lunchtime sandwiches for us, and we ate these while sitting on the broken-down walls of the old mission house. We completed our meal with some hot tea that our trackers had brewed. Then we walked to the eastern side of the Marhumbini hill and looked down over the great Rio Save. It meandered sluggishly through the vast, flat Portuguese territory that lay on the other side of the rickety old bush-pole game fence below us that then demarcated the border between Rhodesia and Mozambique.

John explained to me the history of the mission station and how he had been instrumental in having it removed from the game reserve. When the people were gone, he said, he had quickly demolished the structures and removed what building materials he could use. He had done this to make sure the missionaries did not slip back to resurrect their place of worship and restart their "mischief."

He had left no stone unturned to remove the Mhlengwe and Shangaan squatters from the game reserve, too. Most had originally come from the Portuguese territory, he told me, and they had settled on the banks of the Lundi only to claim superficial Rhodesian residency. This status had qualified them to work at the Shabani Mines in central Rhodesia—recruitment that had once taken place at the mission station.

In thinking about all the problems such a setup would have created in a developing game reserve—especially considering our access problems to the lower Lundi—I realized that John had done a fine job indeed. *Yes,* I thought, *he had been a very busy man.* This told me all I needed to know about John Osborne's commitment and dedication to the game reserve. For the second time in two days I experienced a surge of inner contentment knowing that this man was my second-in-command.

We journeyed across the wedge of the Marhumbini flood plain and climbed the sandy hills above and behind the cliffs. We traveled on what the Shangaans called the Shabani Road—because it was on this road that the recruits had been transported to the mines.

We were traveling back toward Chipinga now, and John wanted to show me Fishans, the small but significant flood plain at the junction of the Nyamasikana River and the Lundi. This stretch of flat alluvium filled the five-mile-wide gap between the eastern edge of the Sibonja Hills and the western beginning of the Chilojo Cliffs. But first John had a treat for me. He deviated onto a sandy track that led to the crest of the cliffs high above Nyahungwe Pool.

The view from the cliff top was breathtaking. To the north were the hazy blue southern slopes of the broken Chihunja Hills. Below us meandered the great Lundi with its fringe of riverine forest, its wide stretches of bright yellow sand, and its big pools, home to the many hundreds of hippo that the game reserve supported. We could see the junction area from here, too, and the open expanse of Tamboharta. And beyond that, was Mahenya's country.

A few elephants had begun wandering down out of the hills, moving desultorily. One or two already stood out on the narrow strip of open flood plain at various places along the river. All were bulls. There was a herd of buffalo in the scrubby ironwood thickets on the slope immediately below us. And I could see hippo in all the pools along the river.

I was ecstatic. *This is my game reserve,* I thought proudly. And I wallowed in the knowledge that for the next several years I was going to be permitted to live and work in this Garden of Eden.

"Can I borrow your binoculars, Ron?" John was looking intently at something down near Nyahungwe. I lifted the glasses from around my neck and handed them to him. He focused the lenses and looked down toward the river pool.

"What do you see, John?"

"A bloody elephant. A *dead* bloody elephant," he said, the glasses at his eyes. "Here, have a look." He handed the binoculars back to me.

"That's Nyahungwe Pool down there—the big long one." He pointed with his finger. "We had breakfast on the far bank this morning—at the upper end. Can you see where we had breakfast?"

I looked. "Got it."

"Now look on the flat alluvium behind, slightly to the right. There's a big *albida*. . . ."

"Got it. I see the animal. It's a big one, hey?"

"Damn. I'll bet that's bloody Shadrek."

"Shadrek?"

"Come. We'll have to go back there and see what's killed it. On the way, I'll tell you about Shadrek."

We returned toward Marhumbini but doubled back under the cliffs long before we got anywhere near the old mission, following a rough track to a tsetse camp called Lisodo. The black tsetse department employee stationed there came out to greet us. Incongruously, a rough bush-pole barrier across the road here still "controlled" vehicular traffic in the once-tsetse-infested area. And we had to sign a register. The idea was laughable because sometimes no vehicles at all passed this way for months. This man's principal job, however, was to look after the "test" herd of cattle that the tsetse department kept here.

John told me there was another test herd at the northern end of Tamboharta pan on the Sabi River, and another in the sandveld region above and behind the cliffs. The cattle in these herds were periodically tested to see if their blood carried trypanosomes—the organism that causes the tsetse-borne *ngana* sickness in domestic stock. The presence of a single trypanosome in a cow's blood meant that a tsetse fly had bitten the beast. That, of course, told the tsetse department that there were still tsetse in the area. That discovery would trigger a renewed spraying of DDT to remove the offending remnant flies from the area.

"There's a dead elephant at Nyahungwe," John told the tsetse department cattle guard. "You didn't perhaps hear a gunshot?"

"*Haikona*," the man said, shaking his head. He had heard no gunshot.

I was soon to learn that these cattle guards never heard or saw anything that might involve them in any kind of extra work or bring them into conflict with the local people. Later I discovered, too, that many of them were Shadrek's casual friends and would do nothing to bring about his arrest. Although they were ideally placed to function as extra eyes and ears in the field for the Department of National Parks and Wildlife Management, they were absolutely useless. In fact, they were part of our problem.

At Lisodo we crossed on the river sands to the north bank of the Lundi and raced back along the track to Nyahungwe. John drove as fast as he could without risking our necks. Indeed, he drove like someone possessed. And all along the way he told me the story about a coloured man called Shadrek, who up till that point in time had poached over a hundred elephant bulls in the Lundi sector of the Gonarezhou alone.

Shadrek, John said, was reputed to be the grandson of the infamous Bvekenya Barnard. That was the only part of John's tale to which I could directly relate, for I possessed Bulpin's *Ivory Trail* and had read the book several times. The idea that Shadrek had so brazenly killed another big elephant bull right under John's nose was clearly too much for the game ranger's pride. His agitation was palpable.

We reached Nyahungwe in what must have been record time, and John immediately moved off the track to our breakfast spot earlier in the day. Not fifty yards away, right out in the open, lay the fresh carcass of a truly enormous elephant bull. We left the vehicle and walked through the rough gully that lay between our breakfast site and the elephant.

The animal lay on its side. There was a bullet hole in the lower-middle part of its body, into which I pushed a thin reed. The bullet had clearly raked forward. This fact, together with the drying, frothy pink blood all around the carcass, told us that the bullet had hit the bottom sections of the lungs. The bullet had entered low enough to suggest that it had also probably ripped through the upper heart arteries—a fine body shot by anybody's standards.

The tusks were huge, at least eighty pounds a side.

"*Landa moova*," I instructed Ben. He handed me my .458 magnum rifle, which he had been carrying all day long, and set off backtracking the route taken by the dying elephant in its flight.

"*Hamba!*" John instructed Hlupo, gesturing that he should follow Ben. Mack moved off on his own volition to join the trackers. Tracking was something the proud old scout still knew how to do.

"It's only a couple of hours old," I said to John, mostly to make conversation, for I was sure he could read the sign with equal ease. "And even a blind man could follow this spoor," I said, gesturing to the copious gore the animal had spilled.

"Bastard!" John exclaimed as if to himself. "As sure as hell it's Shadrek."

Within a few minutes, the trackers found the place where the elephant had been standing when it had been shot. It was on the edge of the woodland about three hundred yards away. We cast about looking

for an empty cartridge case but found nothing. We did, however, find the poacher's spoor. But as good as my Bushman tracker was at his job, Ben was unable to find out how the poacher had vacated the scene.

"He walked off stepping on all the rocks," Ben said to me with conviction. I did not doubt him. He was highly experienced at tracking poachers and had tracked many a terrorist with me in the Zambezi Valley, too. He was used to tracking men under a variety of conditions.

"Keep looking," I said to Ben.

"The cheeky bastard!" John said with venom. "As sure as hell it's Shadrek." He had repeated those words many times since leaving the cliff top. He was clearly fuming inside. "This makes his score 121—and that's only the ones we know about."

The trackers cast about in ever-increasing circles, searching for the outgoing spoor. But there were just too many rocks about. Ben pointed out to me the man's incoming tracks, which were as clear as daylight, but the poacher seemed to have evaporated into thin air the moment he had shot the elephant. *Ben is right,* I thought, after assessing the tracks myself. After shooting the elephant, the poacher had walked off on all the rocks he could find. There was absolutely nothing to follow.

The sun was falling fast by the time we called a halt to the search. It was a futile exercise.

"It's Shadrek," John said with finality. "I'm sure it's Shadrek."

"He's got a bloody cheek," I said, now angry myself. "Shooting a jumbo right on the main track in the area!"

"Oh, he's got a cheek, all right," John said. "A bloody great cheek. But one day he'll make a mistake."

"But why'd he leave without cutting out the tusks?"

"I'll bet my bottom dollar he had banked on the jumbo running back up into the hills. Then he could have chopped out the ivory at his leisure and we'd probably never have known that he had killed another elephant." John looked at the carcass and at the open plain that surrounded it. "It was just too risky for him to chop out the ivory here in the open and in broad daylight."

"You know, John," I offered, "I think he saw our tire tracks and realized that we were round and about. He probably thought we might be coming back from the junction area on the same road. That would have scared him off."

"You're probably right. So he cut and ran." John shook his head angrily. "The bastard," he said for the umpteenth time.

"So what're we going to do about the ivory ourselves, John? Do we chop the tusks out right away or leave them until the morning? It's getting late."

John thought for a while. But he was not thinking about the ivory. He was still thinking about what the poacher had done and what he was probably doing right at that moment.

"*Ja,*" John said finally, nodding his head slowly. "He probably chickened out when the jumbo dropped dead out here in the open. I think he's legging it back to Mahenya's right at this moment. He's cheeky, but he doesn't take chances. That is why we haven't caught him yet."

"And what are we going to do about the ivory?" I persisted.

John nodded again as he thought about the poacher, then turned his attention to my question. He looked at his watch and considered the time. Finally, shaking his head, he said: "There's no chance we can cut out the tusks before dark, so we'll go back to Chipinda. I'll send Hlupo down with a gang of boys in the morning."

The next day I traveled back home to Mabalauta, and that evening I radioed John to thank him and Jill for their kind hospitality during my short visit. The news he gave stunned me.

Hlupo had risen early that morning and, in the station's Land Rover, had guided a small gang of labourers back to the elephant. On their arrival at the crack of dawn, they found that the tusks had already been removed. One man's tracks were everywhere about the carcass.

Hlupo worked out that one man alone could not have carried away both the tusks, so he and the boys had searched high and low, believing that at least one of the tusks had been secreted away not far from the carcass. They found nothing. A blanket of new elephant tracks, made by animals that had come down to drink during the night, had all but obliterated the man's footprints—except for those right next to the carcass.

Then the tracker followed the poacher's outgoing spoor away from the carcass. The farther he got from Nyahungwe Pool, the fewer elephant tracks there were and the clearer the poacher's footprints became.

The man had been carrying only one tusk. He had rested often, putting the tusk down, and the imprint of the ivory was clear in the dust. The tracking was easy because the poacher had followed the vehicle track down to Tamboharta and his footprints were obvious, placed as they were on top of our own Land Rover's fresh tire marks. The man had clearly felt there was no point in trying to hide his tracks. His priority had been to vacate the game reserve as fast as he could, so he had taken the easiest and quickest route to Mahenya's. And that route for most of the way was along the open road. Where the man had crossed the wide Sabi River, the tracker lost the spoor—he could find no exit footprints in the sands on the other side. And the Mozambique border at that point was only a few miles away.

Yes, I thought, *from what little I have heard of our friend Shadrek, it must have been he who killed the elephant. Who else would have been so bold as to come back and remove the tusks after we had left?* It was then that I realized that Shadrek must have been hidden somewhere nearby, watching us all the while, when we had returned to Nyahungwe.

This experience gave me some measure of the man. Surprisingly, it also instilled in me a great deal of respect for him—as much as I disapproved of Shadrek's poaching, I could not help but admire his calm temerity.

Chapter 3

I spent three and a half years at Mabalauta. All that while John Osborne remained the senior game ranger-in-charge of the Lundi sector, and throughout that period Shadrek's score mounted. It was not for lack of trying that John failed to catch him. The hunt for Shadrek must have been the most frustrating experience of John Osborne's life.

For a couple of years during that period John had a game ranger working for him named Charles Mackie. Charles was a quiet-spoken but nonetheless dynamic young man who became John's instrument in his attempts to catch Shadrek. But Charles had many other kinds of antipoaching work to do, too. One of his tasks was to stop the fish poaching in the Lundi that took place out of Mahenya's.

Ever since gill nets were introduced to the Rhodesian scene—which occurred after Lake Kariba filled to capacity in 1963 and a major commercial fishing industry developed there—the black people of the country have continuously raped Rhodesia's rivers. Immediately following the Kariba's filling, enterprising poachers acquired or manufactured gill nets and stretched them across all the big pools in all the major river systems throughout the country. The result was a catastrophic collapse of fish populations everywhere.

The Gonarezhou did not escape attention, especially from the remote African communities at Mahenya's. The people there used to sneak into the game reserve at night to string their nets, risking attack by lion and hyena and gambling with the odds of being turned into pancakes by the Gonarezhou's notoriously cheeky elephant cows.

Considering the length and width of the Lundi River, it was not an easy task to find gillnets—especially in some of the pools hidden in the river's extensive reedbeds. When the nets were surface-mounted with floats, and when a patrol happened to walk past the pool in which they had been set, they were not difficult to locate—but they were seldom surface-mounted.

Most of the time the poachers bottom-hung their nets. This entailed fastening stone weights onto the bottom edges and attaching reed floats along the top. The ends of a net were fixed to living reeds on opposite sides of a pool, and the weights carried the net wall to the bottom. The floats along the top kept the nets vertical in the water. Nets that were bottom-hung were doubly difficult to detect.

Whatever their system, however, the Mahenya fish poachers would set their nets very early in the morning or very late in the evening, then retire to a hidden camp nearby to wait out that day's, or the following day's, hot daylight hours. They would return the next night or the night thereafter—or very early in the morning—to lift the nets. Once you had found a set net, therefore, all you had to do to catch the poacher was lie in wait for him to return—and be patient.

After a fish's gill covers become caught in the meshes of a net, it is unable to escape. It remains attached until the poachers haul their nets out of the water and harvest the fish. Many of the nets, however, become twisted into massive tangles by crocodiles that catch their noses in the mesh. This not only ruins the nets but it also often results in drowning the crocodiles. Sometimes hippo will drag nets through the reedbeds and tear them to shreds. And sometimes a crocodile makes a meal out of a poacher or a hippo bites a man in two.

Even with these ever-present risks, still the people of Mahenya's persisted in their fish poaching. When you add that problem to their poaching of elephants and other wild animals in the game reserve, it is no wonder that a bitter war of attrition developed between Mahenya's people and the game rangers of the Gonarezhou.

One must not forget that John Osborne had only ten black game scouts and one white game ranger to combat poaching in his 1,000-

square-mile Lundi sector. That may sound like a small army to some people, but when you take into account the multifaceted circumstances of our antipoaching work and the lack of vehicular access to the lower Lundi River during the rains, it becomes apparent that our capabilities were hopelessly inadequate.

It was not common, but it happened frequently enough to be a hazard, that poachers put up such severe resistance that our scouts and rangers were sometimes killed or seriously injured in the process of trying to make an arrest. We have had our staff—both black and white—knifed, axed, shot dead, and beaten over the head with clubs. One poor fellow was beaten unconscious and left for dead, lying face down in the red-hot coals of a poacher's campfire.

We could, therefore, never happily send scouts out on patrol in units of fewer than four men, and they were always armed with .303 SMLE ex-army World War II rifles. Necessity demanded that we sometimes send out three-man or even two-man patrols, but we always felt the smaller patrols were a risk. We believed we had no right to put the lives of our game-scout staff in jeopardy.

Having just ten game scouts available for patrol duties—and given normal downtime due to injuries, illnesses, and leave commitments—meant that you could not put more than two patrols into the field at any one time. And they could not remain in the field indefinitely. The normal duration of a patrol was ten to fourteen days, after which the scouts would have to return to Chipinda to rest and reequip for the next patrol. They also needed a break from the bush to be with their families.

As all of us did, John tried to make the on-patrol periods overlap so that there was always at least one group of scouts in the field all the time. However, that was not always possible. Very often, and frequently for extended periods, no game scouts were on patrol at all, for one reason or another.

For example, if the scouts made an arrest, they then became involved in preparing for the court hearing. This took them out of the field for periods up to a week or even ten days. Court prep entailed working with

John at his Chipinda office, recording typed statements and labeling the court exhibits. It meant working with the police prosecutor in Chiredzi to prepare the official court dockets. The court case itself took up at least one day in Chiredzi, and all the scouts on the patrol had to appear as witnesses. Then there was the time taken in transporting the staff and the exhibits from one place to another. All in all, one court case took at least a week out of the game scouts' monthly timetable.

Furthermore, Shadrek was just one of many poacher problems on the Lundi. Besides the fish poachers, there were those who set steel-cable snares along game trails. Others set fire to the bush and hunted warthog and other small game with dogs over the exposed burnt areas. And there were honey hunters, too. Our antipoaching potential, therefore, was not just hopelessly inadequate; it was pathetic. Nevertheless, everyone did his best.

Shadrek, of course, quickly worked out all the circumstances of our antipoaching efforts and made it his business to find out all our weak links. That is what set him apart from all the other poachers we had to deal with—that and, of course, the number of big elephant bulls he was killing.

Administering the Gonarezhou was difficult for another reason: It was absolutely essential to the game reserve's long-term survival that we develop a symbiotic relationship with our tribal neighbours. The more we carried out our antipoaching work, however, the larger the wedge we drove between the local people and ourselves. It was a vicious circle that just got tighter and tighter the more we worked to eliminate poaching.

The idea that we could get the local people on our side seemed but a pipe dream—until the National Parks and Wildlife Act was promulgated in 1975. After that year we slowly developed a system whereby Mahenya's people were legally able to benefit from the sustainable harvest of the wildlife that drifted out of the Gonarezhou onto their land. In this regard the elephant became the financial flagship of the program—with big bulls being sold to the hunting safari industry. By the middle 1980s, Sabi Island had become a major source of elephant bulls, and those few

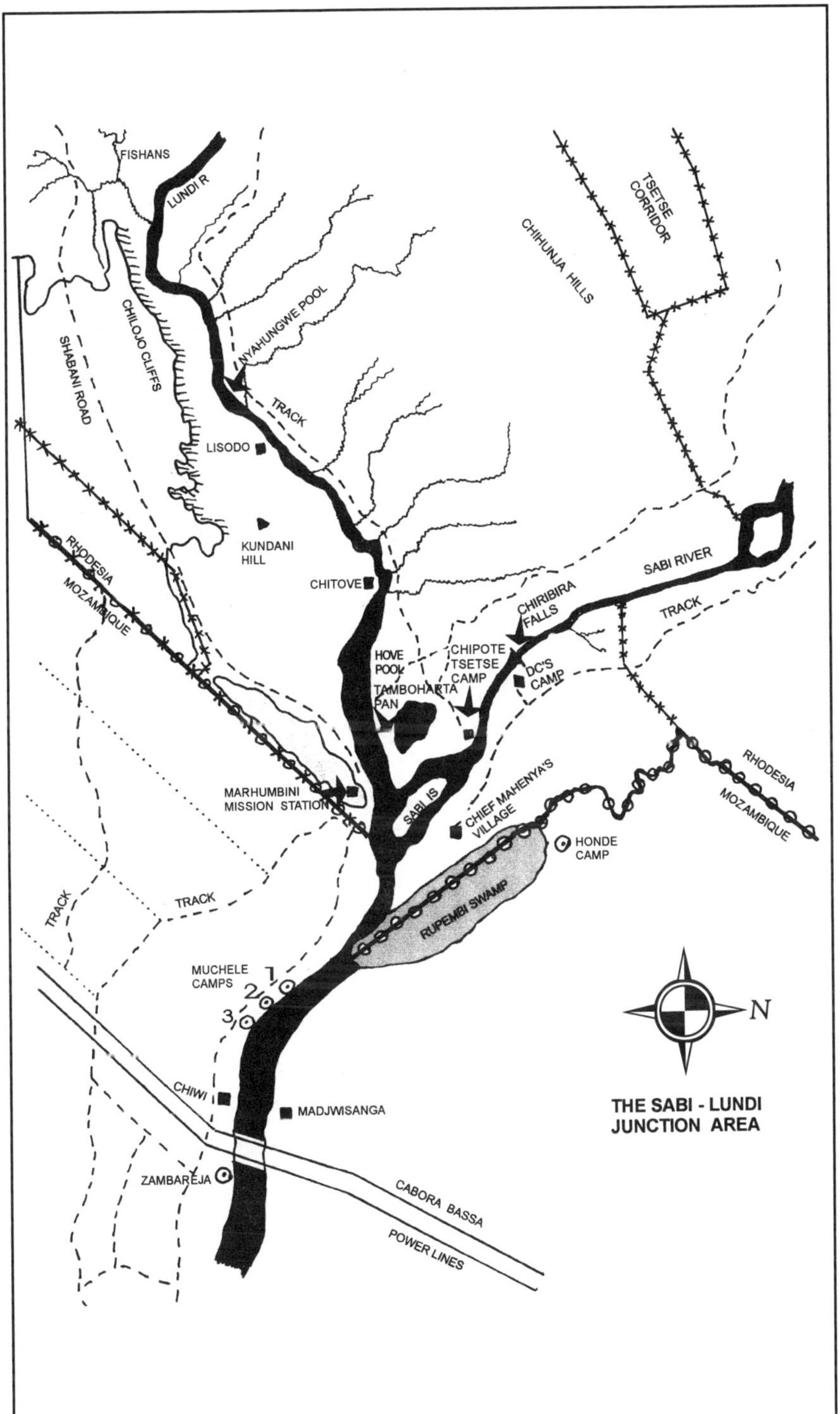
FISHANS
LUNDI R
CHILOJO CLIFFS
SHABANI ROAD
NYAHUNGWE POOL
TRACK
LISODO
KUNDANI HILL
CHITOVE
RHODESIA
MOZAMBIQUE
TSETSE CORRIDOR
CHIHUNJA HILLS
SABI RIVER
TRACK
CHIRIBIRA FALLS
HOVE POOL
CHIPOTE TSETSE CAMP
DC'S CAMP
TAMBOHARTA PAN
MARHUMBINI MISSION STATION
SABI IS
CHIEF MAHENYA'S VILLAGE
HONDE CAMP
RHODESIA
MOZAMBIQUE
RUPEMBI SWAMP
TRACK
TRACK
MUCHELE CAMPS
1
2
3
N
CHIWI
MADJWISANGA
ZAMBAREJA
CABORA BASSA
POWER LINES
THE SABI - LUNDI JUNCTION AREA

that were shot were replenished from the large, renewable bull herds of Tamboharta and the forests of the Sabi-Lundi junction.

When this program was initiated, Chief Mahenya's people, as a community, received the equivalent, in Zimbabwe dollars, of U.S. $5,000 for every elephant shot by licensed safari hunter, and they received a quota of some five big trophy bulls a year. These elephants brought in more money than Mahenya's people had ever dreamt about. The installation of this harvesting scheme, however, was conditional upon a halt in the poaching by Mahenya's people. Chief Mahenya was told that for every elephant found poached by his people, his quota would be reduced by one elephant bull. The threat worked. After they received their first cheque, poaching out of Mahenya's stopped overnight. *All* poaching!

Then followed a remarkable and wonderful transformation. Several of the families that lived on Sabi Island for years were coerced by the local community into moving off the island, thus making it more attractive to the elephants and buffaloes that crossed the river from the Gonarezhou. Thereafter, Sabi Island and many of the dense thickets farther away from the river were reserved by the people for their new and legal hunting enterprise. The person to whom all credit for this innovative idea should go is Dr. Graham Child, director of the Department of National Parks and Wildlife Management.

During the 1960s and throughout the heavy war years of the 1970s, however, this solution to our poaching problem was still developing in the minds of our national park directorate. In the meantime, we had to continue our antipoaching efforts with all the energy and enthusiasm we could muster, for the pressure from the local people in those years was intense. Had we let up for a second, especially during the 1970s, we would have been overwhelmed and there would have been no elephant bulls for Mahenya's people to harvest in the 1980s and beyond.

So it was during the dry season of 1969 that Game Ranger Charles Mackie, accompanied by four black game scouts, lay in ambush over some gillnets they had discovered in a quiet pool of the Lundi a mile or two above the junction. They had been resting quietly on the riverbank all night, taking turns sleeping, hoping that the fish poachers would turn up by dawn. At five o'clock, just as dawn was breaking, they heard a gunshot. It was difficult to determine exactly from which direction the shot had come. Charles thought it had come from somewhere near Tamboharta pan, the closest edge of which lay about a mile behind them. Thinking that perhaps Shadrek was on the move in the area, Charles decided to abandon his long vigil over the gillnets. He and the scouts moved inland toward Tamboharta, combing the forest and *mlala* thickets in search of the poacher's spoor.

At nine o'clock Charles called a halt. They had found no tracks, so they sat down in the shade of a big mahogany tree to confer about what to do next. While they were talking, another shot rang out. Again it was too far away to determine a location—except that they all agreed it seemed to have come from beyond Tamboharta. The higher ground north of Tamboharta is gravelly and very hard, and the forest trees give way to open mopane veld. Picking up human tracks on such terrain is well nigh impossible.

They searched high and low, and the sun beat down on them mercilessly as midday approached. All the time they were hoping to hear another shot to better determine where to look for the poacher's tracks. But no shot was heard. Midday came and went, and their thirst grew unbearable. They had left all their equipment, including waterbags, secreted in the reeds near their last night's ambush position. The sun was very hot. So they headed back to the river, now over five miles away, to slake their thirst.

They approached the river through a dense *mlala* thicket and moved down to the water's edge along a dusty hippo trail. Nobody had come to lift the nets in their absence, so they resumed the vigil they had abandoned early that morning.

A hippo is so fat that its footprints, unlike the spoor of other animals, do not follow one behind the other when the animal walks. Instead, the back feet and the front feet, shuffling in unison on either side of its body, create two parallel sets of grooves in the ground that are reminiscent of railroad tracks. With the soil here being bone dry and powdery—it being the height of the dry season—the footprints of Charles's party were clearly evident in the soft dust on top of the hippo's tracks.

The men drank their fill, then lay down to rest in the shade just below the low river embankment. It had been a long, hard, and hot morning, and they were all very tired. Three of the scouts were lying hidden away under the bank, some distance to one side of the hippo path. Charles and Game Scout Tivani rested close to each other on the other side of the path under a large knobby-thorn tree. The tree was leafless but in full bloom. Charles lay on his back, alternately contemplating the thousands of cream catkin flowers above his head and dozing fitfully. Tivani was sitting, his back against the tree trunk. He was sleepy, too, but on guard. He was holding Charles's .458 magnum in his hands.

Suddenly both Charles and Tivani were shocked into full wakefulness. Both had heard the same sound but did not know what it was. The sound came again. Something, or someone, was pushing through the brittle palm fronds on the riverbank above and behind them.

They bounced to their feet, and Charles took his weapon from Tivani. He was just about to jack a round into the breech when a slim, shortish black man appeared out of the *mlalas* above them. He had a firearm in his hands and a bag was slung over his shoulder. He stopped dead in his tracks and looked down at the fresh human spoor on the hippo path that led down to the river. The heavy treads in the dust, left by the army boots worn by the scouts, told him all he needed to know.

Charles cursed under his breath. They had all been careless in leaving clear tracks on the hippo path. He himself had been careless by lying in ambush with an unloaded weapon. Now he was in a crunch. If he loaded his weapon now, the man would hear the noise of the action and disappear back into the *mlalas* just as quickly as he had emerged from them. So Charles stood for several seconds examining the poacher, his mind awhirl, as he tried to decide what to do.

Under those circumstances, seconds seem like long, long minutes. As the man began to look around, Charles realized that he was going to lose the initiative. And at that moment he had the initiative, for the poacher was in full view and had not seen him.

Charles had to do something—and quickly. So, raising his empty rifle to his shoulder, he stepped out from behind the thin screen of reeds that had been hiding him, his weapon trained on the poacher.

"*Mira wena!*" (Stand still, you!) Charles shouted.

The man turned his head and froze, realizing the danger he was in. His eyes focused on the white man as Charles started to move quickly toward him. No more than thirty feet separated the two men.

The game scouts under the bank bounced to their feet and watched the drama unfold. The poacher's eyes flicked to his right to take in the game scouts rising. He also saw Tivani emerge from the reeds behind Charles. Then he refocused his attention on the much more menacing white man. Negotiating the hippo path up the bank, Charles momentarily took the rifle butt from his shoulder and looked down to check his footing. The second he did that, he lost control of the situation. Seizing his opportunity, the poacher instantly lifted his own weapon and aimed it at Charles's chest. Charles saw the poacher's movement, and an icy coldness swept his being. He could do nothing to defend himself since his weapon was empty. Probably because Charles was in such imminent danger of being killed, everything the poacher did seemed to occur in slow motion.

In raising the weapon to his shoulder the man had also hauled back the ancient hammer on his firearm. Charles realized immediately that it was an old Tower musket. Old as the primitive muzzleloader may have been, however, if it still worked, it was just as lethal as his modern .458 magnum.

Charles made a dive for the riverbank as the man brought the weapon to bear. He was too late—he knew he was too late. Then he heard a loud clunk as the hammer hit the weapon's empty primer-nipple. There was no big bang, no cloud of blue-white smoke, no sickening impact of a heavy lead slug hitting his chest. And Charles understood that he was not about to die after all.

The poacher had called his bluff. He, too, had been carrying an unloaded weapon, and his cheeky deception had gained for him all the advantage he needed to make good his escape. Even as he was falling, Charles heard the poacher chuckle—a derisive and defiant sound that infuriated the game ranger instantly. He looked up angrily and saw the insolent sneer on the man's face before he turned and disappeared into the *mlala* thicket at his back.

Charles hit the ground hard. He rolled and worked the bolt of his rifle feverishly and saw the shiny brass cartridge enter the breech just before he closed the bolt. Then he was on his feet again and running up the hippo path.

The poacher had disappeared, but the still-moving mlala fronds betrayed the route he had taken. Charles fired into the waving fronds. One . . . two . . . three . . . four rounds. Then he reloaded from the cartridge belt about his waist and ran into the thicket, hoping to find the poacher's body. He found nothing.

In those days we game rangers did not shoot poachers. That era in the country's history did not come about until after Robert Mugabe took over

the reins of government in 1980. Despite my total disapproval of Mugabe's racist and totalitarian rule, I strongly approve of his policy of killing poachers who are bent on destroying the country's wildlife resource. I do not look upon wildlife as a sacred cow—as some nature-lovers do—but as a wild product of the land that can and should be used sustainably as an integral part of mankind's life-support system. And I believe that any government in the world is justified in protecting its life-support systems from those who would destroy them—even to the extent of killing the perpetrators. So, in this regard, I give Robert Mugabe full marks.

Charles's shock at his own near demise and his anger at the man's departing mockery provoked his firing after the fleeing poacher. It had not been premeditated, but it had also not been entirely automatic and instinctive. A great deal of rancour had been involved, too. His blood had been up.

It is difficult to say what the furor would have been had he killed the poacher, but we did not let it bother us. It had not happened. After receiving Charles's written report, I handled the whole incident in low profile, and any repercussions there might have been fizzled out before they even started.

The scouts followed the poacher's spoor from the riverbank and discovered there had been a party of four others behind the man who had carried the muzzleloader. Among the *mlala* fronds they found an assortment of abandoned cloth bundles—mainly old clothes—and knives and axes. All of this *katoonda* the scouts gathered together and hid among the palms.

They followed the spoor of the running poachers, and it led them directly to the Sabi River on the opposite side of the flood plain. There it disappeared into the water. Charles and the scouts waded across and relocated the tracks on the other side. At this point the Sabi was half a mile wide, so the poachers were lucky not to have been discovered by the game scouts midstream in broad daylight. The tracks dispersed inside Mahenya's country, mixing with the multiple tracks left by the local community, and the scouts lost them.

The next day, the scouts backtracked the poachers along their incoming route from the place of the confrontation. About a mile away, well hidden among the *mlala* palms and high forest trees, they discovered the poachers' camp and the butchered remains of a large waterbuck bull. There were also bush-racks on which the poachers had split and smoked a large quantity of fish.

This find confirmed that these were the fish poachers for whom Charles and his men had lain in wait the whole night long before the encounter. Now, they knew, the man with the gun would never come back. It had been an opportunity lost.

After concluding his investigation of the incident, Charles drove his Land Rover to the edge of the Sabi above Tamboharta, to the tsetse department camp at Chipote where the test herd of cattle was kept. There he crossed the shallow water at the dry-season ford. John kept a rowboat here for use when the river was too high to cross with a vehicle, but it was not necessary on this occasion.

Inquiries among the people of Mahenya's gave Charles no clues to the identity of the poachers—except for one. The people confirmed that the man with the muzzleloader had been Shadrek. Shadrek apparently had boasted to all and sundry about having had an armed confrontation with a Gonarezhou antipoaching patrol. During the fracas, he told the people, he had shot one of the white game rangers.

Game Scout Tivani visited an old relative in the area who informed him of the location of Shadrek's home at Mahenya's. He learned, too, that Shadrek had another home in Mozambique at a place called Madjwisanga. This was a major breakthrough, for up until that time, nobody had ever volunteered any information that might have compromised the celebrated poacher.

Charles and the scouts made a surprise call on Shadrek's Mahenya village. He was, of course, nowhere in sight. But his wife, Tabita, and their four-year-old son were present.

The scouts ransacked every hut in the village in an effort to find incriminating evidence. They found nothing that would implicate Shadrek in any poaching felony, but in the process they infuriated Tabita. She was not surprised, though, because the search of a suspect's village was common practice. It was hated but expected behaviour from an antipoaching patrol.

Tabita just smiled when Charles—through Tivani, who acted as interpreter—questioned her about her husband. Not surprisingly, he got nothing out of her. She neither confirmed nor denied that Shadrek was Bvekenya's grandson, and she gave nothing else away.

Charles later told me that from what he'd seen of him, he did not think that Shadrek was a coloured—but, if he was the grandson of Bvekenya, I reasoned he would have been only one-quarter European anyway. Charles examined Shadrek's young son and, still pursuing the idea that Shadrek was Bvekenya's grandson, made a note in his written report that the child was "very light in colour."

This incident was Shadrek's second encounter with the game scouts of the Gonarezhou. The first one I shall write about in a later chapter. On this occasion the poacher had been fortunate not to be arrested. He had also been very lucky that one of the four bullets Charles had fired in his direction had not found its mark.

Every elephant Shadrek killed, and every clash that he had with officialdom, gave us additional information about the man. This particular incident had many bonuses. Charles Mackie had had a good look at Shadrek. He had discovered his home at Mahenya's and had also been told the name of Shadrek's second home in Mozambique. These were all significant pieces of the puzzle.

We knew now, too, that Shadrek sometimes indulged in a bit of meat hunting and fish poaching—and that he was a great braggart. This less-than-endearing quality brought him down a peg or two in my estimation at the time. There was really no need for the man to boast so much or to exaggerate his nefarious activities, for he was, in truth and in fact, every bit the biggest rogue and reprobate in the region—with or without the stories he told about himself.

Chapter 4

Charles Mackie's close encounter with Shadrek fired his enthusiasm. It had been such a close call for Shadrek that Charles decided he was going to be the man who arrested the notorious poacher. Thereafter he left no stone unturned in his endeavours to apprehend our elusive quarry. And John Osborne stoked his ardour from behind.

I don't mean to imply that John himself did not participate in the hunt for Shadrek. Far from it. He was just as active and as zealous as was Charles Mackie, but this did not stop John from egging on his young protégé. At the same time, everybody understood that the hunt for Shadrek was no contest. Everyone helped everyone else. It was a joint effort to achieve a common objective.

Living at Mabalauta, a hundred miles from all the action, I was largely a passive supporter. In our own area, we had one or two incidents of elephant poaching, perpetrated by hunters from Mozambique. We automatically attributed all these killings to Shadrek, even though there was never any real proof he was responsible. Much later I learnt that the Mabalauta elephant kills had nothing at all to do with Shadrek. But because we thought they were all his doing, they often led us off on the wrong tack.

After Charles's confrontation with Shadrek, our war against him intensified. The incident was enough to give impetus to our efforts. It was as though we all suddenly realized that Shadrek was human. He did make mistakes. He was not invincible. Nevertheless, Shadrek did not let up on his killing of the big bulls of the Lundi, brazenly operating very close to Chipinda Pools.

Our scouts paid regular visits to Shadrek's home at Mahenya's. This pressure, we believed, forced him to move his family permanently into Mozambique, to Madjwisanga on the Rio Save, a good day's hike from the border. That must have inconvenienced Shadrek, for we understood that Tabita's family all lived at Mahenya's. Shadrek had many family connections in Mozambique—or so we were told. This is the sum total of the information we ever obtained about Shadrek from local sources. In fact, it really came from only one source—Game Scout Tivani's old uncle who lived at Mahenya's.

Charles spent more and more time in the field looking for an opportunity to nail Shadrek. He spent an inordinate amount of time patrolling the Sabi-Lundi junction area, patiently listening for a rifle shot that would betray Shadrek's whereabouts. One day his industry paid off, but not in the manner he had anticipated.

Charles was patrolling with four game scouts south of the Lundi. He parked his Land Rover under a tree on the Lisodo track and set off on foot toward Kundani, a small conical hill halfway between the eastern end of the Chilojo Cliffs and Marhumbini. It is a focal feature in a landscape that is otherwise just an undulating sea of mopane scrub.

The soils around Kundani are very gravelly and tracking is not easy, but Charles came across the track of a bicycle leading away from the hillock. Next to the wheel marks were the footprints of one man—and the man and the bicycle were headed toward the Mozambique border. Charles smelled the scent of Shadrek. The tracks were reasonably fresh, so he followed them.

At the game fence on the border, Charles found what he was looking for—evidence that the man had been carrying elephant tusks on his bicycle. In order to negotiate the fence, the man had removed the two tusks he had roped on either side of his cycle and slipped them under the bottom strand of the fence. The marks of the ivories were clear in the soft sandveld soil.

The man had then carried his bicycle over the seven-foot-high game fence—the strands were too tight to push the cycle through the structure.

On the other side, he reloaded his cycle with the tusks and set off again into Mozambique.

Charles did not hesitate. He sent one of the scouts back to pick up his Land Rover and instructed him to return to this place on the fence, where Charles would meet him.

The scout went off back toward Kundani. Charles and the three remaining scouts climbed over the fence and proceeded to follow the poacher's tracks into Mozambique. Having ascertained that the spoor was angling northeastward toward the Rio Save, Charles returned to the fence line with Game Scout Tivani to await the return of his Land Rover. The two other scouts continued on the spoor.

Across the border fence—between the Rio Save in the north and the Malvernia-to-Lourenço Marques railway line in the south—the Rhodesian Tsetse Department had bulldozed wide parallel lines, five miles apart, through the flat sandveld woodland of Mozambique. Between the strips they had cut tracks every five miles that were just big enough for their vehicles to negotiate. Then they had systematically sprayed each block with DDT to rid the land of the dreaded tsetse fly.

A thousand black labourers, equipped with backpack tanks filled with DDT, did the work. They were lined up ten yards apart along the edge of a five-mile block, and, on a given command, they marched through the block, spraying all the tree trunks and thicket stems and every fallen log and antbear hole with the insecticide. At the other side, their canisters were recharged with DDT. They were realigned farther along the cut line, and they marched into the next section of the strip to repeat the process. And thus, the bushveld had been systematically attacked, block by block, from the Rhodesian border eastward into Mozambique toward the Indian Ocean.

At the time of Charles's sojourn into Mozambique, the spraying operation was going on some thirty miles from the border, so the bush was silent and undisturbed by human intrusions. But the cut lines still scarred the countryside, and the vegetation was still stained white from the persistent insecticide. The whole area still exuded the faint but all-pervading stench of DDT.

In this endeavour, the Portuguese contributed nothing—except their permission. The cost and effort were borne by the Rhodesians. But the Rhodesian Veterinary Department was well satisfied because each year the fly was driven farther and farther from the Rhodesian border toward the sea.

The cut lines served as roads for those who wanted to enter the flat bushland of the region. Visitors included the Rhodesian Tsetse Department staff, who traveled through the area to the continually moving locations of their spraying operations, now far away to the east.

Charles knew all about the tsetse department's operations inside Mozambique, so he had instructed the two scouts who had remained on the tracks to follow the cycle spoor until it crossed the next bulldozed cut line. There they were to wait for Charles, who said he would drive along the track in his Land Rover to meet them.

The spooring was easy through the sandveld scrub, and the trackers ate up the miles quickly. At no time did the man they were following attempt to ride the cycle. All he did was push it through the sandy soils. He was using the vehicle merely as a means of transport for the heavy ivory.

It took nearly two hours for the Land Rover to arrive at the point where Charles and Tivani were waiting. This did not faze Charles in the least, because exercising patience was an integral part of a game ranger's life. Nothing ever happened quickly in the African bush.

When the Land Rover arrived, Charles drove south for ten miles until he came to the tsetse department's Border-B camp on the fence line. This was the department's kickoff point into Mozambique. From the fence gate, the main road ran in a straight southeasterly line for some seventy miles, deep into Mozambique. Every five miles, on either side of this road, began the parallel, bulldozed cut lines that segmented the bush and facilitated the spraying operations.

Driving down the tsetse department road inside Mozambique was a novelty for Charles Mackie, but he was undaunted by the fact that what he was doing was totally illegal. He had no jurisdiction at all in

Mozambique. Indeed, he had no authority even to cross the fence line through the gate. His mind was focused on catching Shadrek.

He took the first cut line that ran northeastward off the road—it was exactly five miles from the border fence—and began traveling toward the Rio Save. The cut lines were wide open, but the vehicular tracks along them were rough in comparison to the main route he had just left behind. The journey was now much slower, but the track took him closer and closer to the big river that he knew lay to the north.

Charles found his two scouts lounging in the shade of a full-leafed pod mahogany tree next to the track. They had been waiting patiently for him for some hours. They had penetrated fully ten miles, diagonally, through the first of the parallel blocks. As Charles stopped and leaned out the Land Rover window, one of his men pointed to the ground beneath him. The cycle tracks were clear in the sand.

"He seems to have traveled down the cut line from here on," the scout told Charles. "Maybe I should sit on the front mudguard and track him while we're traveling?"

"Good idea," Charles said.

So they all traveled in the Land Rover down the cut line, one scout sitting on the front fender and hanging onto the spare wheel bolted to the vehicle's hood, his concentration focused on the ground ahead. As the land began to descend into the Rio Save valley, a fairly well-used vehicle track ran across the cut line, heading more to the east than the north. At this point the cycle tracks left the cut line and followed that road. Presently they emerged onto the high, flat southern bank of the Rio Save.

For the next several miles the cycle spoor never left the vehicle track. Then, abruptly, the narrow tire marks were gone. Charles reversed the vehicle until the scout on the front found where the cycle had turned onto a well-beaten footpath down to the river.

Charles left one scout on the Land Rover and took the three others with him down to where the cycle tracks disappeared into the wide Rio Save. In front of them lay a shallow pedestrian ford below a vertical bank. The banks on either side, however, were far too steep for any kind of vehicular use.

They found an old black man sitting on the edge of the path with his feet in the water. He looked up at Charles and the scouts without any kind of curiosity or concern and greeted them politely, asking if they were tsetse department officials and if they had had a good day.

Realizing their advantage at being taken for a tsetse department patrol, Charles immediately instructed his scouts to remove their green epaulet tabs. The tabs were inscribed with a gold insignia with the words "Parks & Wildlife." He did the same himself. It was doubtful, however, if the old man could read or if he gave any thought at all to the green shoulder tabs they all wore.

Charles had not thought his actions through to the point of considering a cover for his presence in Mozambique. Now a solution to his problem had unexpectedly been handed to him—all at the same time.

Tivani sat down with the old man and asked him a number of questions about the local area. Madjwisanga, it transpired, was just across the river on the north bank. The old man pointed diagonally downstream to thatched villages that they could see about two miles away across the golden sands.

"There is a vehicle crossing a couple of miles downstream from here at a small settlement called Chiwi," the old man said. "Directly opposite Chiwi, on the north bank, there is a small store. That is the Madjwisanga store. It is owned and run by a Portuguese man called Kamali Jhivana."

Charles thanked the old man for his time and trouble, and he and the scouts returned to the Land Rover. They drove on to the Chiwi settlement and, without any formalities, drove past the huts, where people stood about watching them. They followed the now-tortuous track religiously. Eventually it led them to the sandy drift the old man had told them about, and they crossed to the north bank of the Save.

Charles drew up in front of the store and went inside to confront the Portuguese owner. Tivani translated Charles's questions in the Shangaan language, which the man understood much better than Charles or Tivani understood Portuguese.

"Is this Madjwisanga?" Tivani asked.

"Yes," the Portuguese man said, nodding his head sagely.

"Do you know a man called Shadrek?" was the next question.

"What do you want to know about Shadrek for?" The Portuguese avoided the question by asking one of his own. Then he asked another: "Why are you asking questions about Shadrek?"

"I want to buy some ivory off him." Charles's statement, in English, was a stroke of genius. The storekeeper's antagonism miraculously vanished. The stern and worried look that had come over Jhivana's face disappeared. He relaxed visibly. Charles realized then that he at least understood English.

"You Rhodesia?" Jhivana asked, pointing to Charles and then to Tivani. His eyes were now bright and friendly. "You Tsetse?"

Charles looked at Tivani and nodded to confirm the man's understanding of their identities—incorrect though that assumption was.

"Yes," Tivani confirmed in Shangaan. "We are Rhodesian Tsetse Department officials."

"Ha-oohhh," the Portuguese storekeeper exclaimed, very happy now. "So you want buy ivory from Shadrek?" He spoke directly to Charles now, in broken English. So he could speak a bit of English, too!

"Yes," Charles nodded patiently. He spoke to the store owner in English now: "Where can we find Shadrek? He told us that he lives at Madjwisanga."

"You know Shadrek?" The man asked, surprised.

"Yes," Charles confirmed. "We met him yesterday. He was carrying two tusks on his bicycle. He said we should come to Madjwisanga if we wanted to buy ivory off him. He told me that Kamali Jhivana at Madjwisanga store would tell me where he lives.

"Hah!" The storekeeper nodded his head. "That is Shadrek." He then looked at Charles and beamed: "Me Kamali Jhivana."

Charles extended his hand and said, "Me Charles." His hand was taken and shaken enthusiastically by the Portuguese.

"Charohls," Jhivana repeated the name. "Charohls."

"So . . . where can we find Shadrek?" Charles persisted. He was getting tired of all the social niceties, but it was plain the Portuguese was hungry for European company.

"Oh!" Jhivana said as if in surprise—seemingly sorry that he had not been more cooperative. "Shadrek . . . he live down this road." The Portuguese was a big, fat man. He waddled out to the front of his store and pointed down the track that ran away to the west, back toward the Rhodesian border. "His village is first one on right—'bout one mile."

"OK, guys," Charles said when he returned to the Land Rover. "We are about to arrest Shadrek." He turned then to Tivani and said: "Tell them what we've just learned."

Tivani rattled off his story in Shangaan. It brought instant smiles to the faces of the three scouts.

"OK. Now listen. I want you all to lie down flat in the back of the Land Rover," Charles instructed. "Don't let anyone see you until we get to Shadrek's village. Then I want you to get out as quickly as you can and place yourselves all about his huts. We don't want Shadrek to escape this time."

Charles, with Tivani at his side in the cab, traveled fast down the track toward Shadrek's village. On the way, they passed several black people walking in both directions down the road. Unbeknownst to Charles—because he didn't recognize him—one of those people was Shadrek, en route to the store.

The Land Rover with the Rhodesian number plates had passed right next to Shadrek as he walked along the road. He had seen Charles and Tivani sitting in the front of the vehicle but had not recognized them. He had not seen any of the game scouts lying flat in the back of the vehicle. Like the old man on the riverbank and the Portuguese store owner, Shadrek had automatically assumed they were Rhodesian Tsetse Department officials. So he thought nothing of their passage along the road, believing they were en route to Mahenya's, and he had continued his journey to the store.

Shadrek's village was like all the others in the area. The walls of the several huts in the menage were made of poles and mud, and the roofs were thatched. There was a low brush scherm around the cleanly swept courtyard.

Upon the group's arrival at the village, Tabita emerged from the kitchen hut and, recognizing Charles from their previous encounter, immediately harangued him in Shangaan. She was furious at seeing the white man again, especially in her Mozambican home. Charles, of course, was delighted to see Tabita because her presence confirmed that he had arrived at the correct village.

But Shadrek was not at home.

Charles, through Tivani, tried to question Tabita but got nothing out of her. Instead, she stood and glowered at him and the game scouts, treating them to looks of hatred and insolence. And she showered insults all over them.

The scouts then set about searching the huts, just as they had done to Shadrek's other home at Mahenya's. Inside the kitchen hut they discovered a bicycle and two large elephant tusks to which still-damp connective tissue was adhering. There was no firearm of any kind and nothing else of interest except for one thing—a photograph of three young black men. The man in the middle was down on one knee. He held a small transistor radio in his raised left hand. All three were posing dramatically in an exaggerated manner—poses that only boastful young African males can strike. They were clearly showing off to the camera.

Charles examined the photograph but did not recognize any of the three as being the man he had recently confronted on the Lundi. Tivani questioned Tabita in Shangaan about the photograph, but she remained uncooperative and hostile.

Meanwhile more and more local villagers began gathering about Shadrek's huts, and Tabita berated them furiously until their mood turned belligerent. More and more people began drifting in from the surrounding area, converging on the disturbance. Some were running hard. The gathering of the clan made Charles apprehensive. So he decided, as a prudent person in such circumstances should do, that discretion is the better part of valour.

Accepting the fact that he had missed Shadrek once again, he abruptly called off the search and had the two elephant tusks quickly loaded onto his Land Rover. He placed the photograph in the breast pocket of his bush shirt, and, without further ceremony, they vacated the village in a hurry. Fortunately the angry crowd gave way before the Land Rover's bumper.

In retrospect, Charles was lucky to get off so lightly. Deep inside Portuguese territory, without legal protection, he would not have had a leg to stand on had the people attacked him. And the people here were openly hostile. They were clearly on Shadrek's side and prepared to defend him and his family no matter what. It was fortunate that Charles recognized the growing belligerence of the crowd early enough and drove out when he did. Had only one or two key villagers arrived on the scene before he departed—for example, particular friends of Shadrek's—he might never have left Madjwisanga alive.

None of us in the Gonarezhou was sorry that Charles had carried out this raid because we were all sure that he had come back with a picture of our nemesis. The only problem was that we did not know which of the three men in the picture was Shadrek. Charles thought that the man on his knee in the middle was the one, but he was not sure.

As always, my main job was to pour oil on troubled waters. The *chefe de posto* at Espungabera lodged an official complaint, and the Chiredzi police made the necessary approaches to me, but we all denied the incident outright.

Charles Mackie received a pat on the back with one hand and a slap on the bottom with the other. He was instructed, and he promised, never to repeat what he had done. But he had got his prize, and we were all well pleased!

We were very soon left in no doubt that Shadrek was furious with us because there followed a string of elephant killings the likes of which we had not before experienced. And each one was more brazen than the last. It seemed that Shadrek was inviting us to attempt his arrest. That meant he was now probably very dangerous. Despite his extravagant hunting during this brief period, however, he did not let down his defenses one iota.

It was Shadrek's blitz, in fact, that triggered my appeal to the Rhodesian government to solicit Portuguese assistance in bringing Shadrek to book. This resulted in the police Special Branch at Chiredzi arranging with the *chefe de posto* at Espungabera to apprehend Shadrek in his Mozambican home. We even gave the Portuguese a six-figure map reference and a sketch plan pinpointing the location of Shadrek's village. But as I explained earlier, this effort came to naught.

Finally, when the ball came back into our own court, we realized that we would have to play the game out by ourselves. Nobody on the Mozambican side could, or wanted to, assist us.

This state of affairs vindicated, in our own minds at least, Charles Mackie's raid on Shadrek's Mozambican home. Charles's little sojourn across the border, besides representing a serious harassment of our quarry and revealing the location of his home in Mozambique, had provided us with a very important piece of the puzzle—a photograph of Shadrek. All we now had to do was find out which of the three was our man.

Game Scout Tivani made a special visit to his uncle at Mahenya's, but he, too, was unable to identify Shadrek in the photograph. Indeed, he had never seen Shadrek, although he knew all about him. None of the other people at Mahenya's was prepared to assist us.

The Rhodesian administrative provinces were subdivided in such a manner that, strangely, Mahenya's country fell under the jurisdiction of our game ranger at Melsetter, two hundred miles to the north. Governments work in weird and wonderful ways! It so happened, however, that Glen Tatham, the game ranger based at Melsetter at the time, was a very fine African linguist. I decided to take advantage of Glen's language skills and sent a copy of the photograph to him with a request that he visit Mahenya's to ascertain which of the three men in the picture was Shadrek. I gave him a six-figure map reference pinpointing Shadrek's Mahenya home—although at that stage reports seemed to suggest that he had left Mahenya's permanently. I recommended that Glen visit the area not in uniform but in civilian clothes—to minimize the possibility of a hostile reception.

Glen was unable to assist us until January 1971, when he had to visit Mahenya's to investigate the death of a native killed by an elephant. Shadrek and four accomplices had apparently entered the junction flood plain with the object of shooting elephants in the Gonarezhou. They had split up, and one of them had been killed by an elephant he had wounded with a muzzleloader. Glen visited the area with a policeman to investigate the man's death. He went in uniform and was accompanied by Game Ranger Graham Hall.

During this visit Glen tried to find out which of the three men in the photograph was Shadrek. He visited Shadrek's old home and, surprisingly, found Tabita in residence together with one of Shadrek's sons, a lad about seven years of age. He engaged the little boy in conversation in his own language and thus gained his confidence. Suddenly, without any warning, Glen showed him the picture of the three men. "Which one is your Daddy?" Glen asked innocently—and without hesitation, the boy pointed to the man in the middle, the one on his knees holding the radio.

So Charles's hunch had been right. Now we knew for sure what Shadrek looked like.

Glen did very well on that trip. Besides positively identifying Shadrek, he recovered eight elephant tusks and a .375 magnum rifle from Shadrek's Mahenya home. The tusks were hidden under a bed in one of the living huts, and he found the rifle secreted inside the thatch of the kitchen hut. He confiscated all the tusks and the rifle.

Although we had not yet captured Shadrek, we all hoped that now that he had lost his rifle, his elephant poaching days would come to an end.

Chapter 5

Between 1969 and 1971, I co-led the team that captured eighty-one black rhino in the far north of Rhodesia and introduced them to the Gonarezhou, some six hundred miles to the south. In 1972, I led the culling team that removed the first batch of 2,500 elephants—some from Mabalauta and some from the Lundi sector—in a belatedly approved population-reduction programme. This culling alleviated the heavy feeding burden that the game reserve's habitats had been forced to endure for far too long.

At Mabalauta I built a new office complex and a camping ground for tourists complete with ablution block, and a small tourist rest camp with chalets. I also installed three new water holes away from the Nuanetsi to help spread the elephant feeding pressure. Water for these ponds traveled through many miles of very expensive pipeline, via a pump on the river's edge. Finally, we completed an extensive game-viewing road complex for our slowly developing tourist trade.

On the lower Lundi, John Osborne completed two ablution blocks and opened up two new tourist camping grounds. He also reared two baby black rhino and looked after a herd of some sixty elephant calves that we had "rescued" from the cull. These elephants were sold to zoos and parks all over the world.

So neither John and his staff at Chipinda Pools nor I and my staff at Mabalauta were idle during those years. We all did many things besides trying to arrest Shadrek. But the rosy view of my world as an idyllic place was soon to be shattered.

To say that I was shocked when John Osborne resigned would be the understatement of the century. And when I learned that he was going to work for a lowveld businessman, I was even more perplexed. He was leaving the department to run the game section on a private cattle ranch!

To me John Osborne was the epitome of everything a dedicated game ranger should be. To me, the Department of National Parks and Wildlife Management was not just an organization that provided me with a job. It was my religion. Anyone who voluntarily chose to leave the department, therefore, was no different from a priest who abandoned his faith.

News of John's imminent departure left me stunned.

Nevertheless, after three and a half very happy and productive years at Mabalauta, I found myself negotiating with the department for a transfer to Chipinda Pools. The black rhino had always been a very special animal to me, and, at that stage, I had captured and translocated more of these prehistoric beasts than anyone else in the country—than anyone else in Africa—than anyone else in the world! Since we had just introduced these animals to the Chihunja Hills, I wanted to follow up the success of the translocation exercise by continuing my research on the new population we had established. But it was with mixed feelings that my family and I moved to Chipinda Pools and occupied John's and Jill's old house on the banks of the Lundi.

No sooner had I transferred than we were back into culling, removing the last of 2,500 elephants that had to be taken off. I then shot 160 hippo from the overpopulated Lundi, and we installed ten bore-holed water supplies in the upper catchment of the Nyamasikana behind the cliffs. Finally, we introduced some eighty Lichtenstein hartebeest into the Chihunjas to bolster the remnant endemic population. They came from the faraway Gorongoza game reserve in Mozambique.

While all this was going on I also completed a major game-viewing road network on the south bank of the lower Lundi, in the Nyamasikana catchment above Fishans, to serve our growing tourism trade in this section of the reserve. The Gonarezhou was slowly coming of age!

Arresting Shadrek, however, remained a major priority that we were never allowed to forget—because game-scout patrols invariably came back with stories of new elephant carcasses found in the field.

Strangely, Shadrek's loss of his .375 magnum to Glen Tatham seemed not to have affected his ability to kill elephants in any way at all. It made us all wonder where he was getting his rifles and ammunition. We had no answer to that question.

Shortly after my transfer to Chipinda, Shadrek had another narrow escape. Early one morning I transported a patrol of four game scouts to the Sabi-Lundi junction. There they were to begin a routine antipoaching patrol on a route that would bring them back to Chipinda Pools on foot some ten days later. As we entered the flood plain I noticed a kettle of vultures circling low over a wide stretch of coarse grassland near Tamboharta.

I stopped the Land Rover and, after instructing the scouts to follow, walked about a mile to where I thought I would find the dead animal that was attracting the scavengers. I rarely ignored circling vultures, for they often introduced me to interesting things. Sometimes it was a lion kill. Sometimes it was an animal that had died of a disease that we should know about. And sometimes it provided evidence of poaching.

I was not unduly surprised, therefore, to hear the sounds of chopping as I drew closer. The thud of heavy blades clunking onto bone told me that we had surprised a gang of poachers at their work. Silently I deployed the scouts in a big arc, and we approached the axmen cautiously through the tall grass.

As we closed the net I saw two black men busy chopping out the tusks of an elephant that we later discovered had been shot earlier in the day. Naturally, I thought that at last Shadrek had made a mistake. At last we would have him in custody.

The men did not see us approaching, and we took them completely by surprise. And when they realized that we were armed and had them surrounded, they did not try to run away. They merely put down their axes and leant against the carcass, waiting for us to approach.

We questioned the men regarding the elephant's shooting, and they both readily admitted that Shadrek had done the killing. In fact, they told us that Shadrek had left the dead elephant not half an hour before we had arrived on the scene—to go and shoot another one.

Why they were so open about Shadrek's involvement, I have no idea. Perhaps it was just an act of bravado. The fact remains they were now quite happy to tell me that it was Shadrek who had shot the elephant. They also advised us that Shadrek had gone off with two other men and that they did not expect him to come back to this carcass. He had instructed them to cut out the tusks and carry them back to his village in Mozambique.

I showed both men the photograph we had of Shadrek—which I always carried with me in the field. They smiled and shook their heads. No, they said, none of the three men in the photograph was Shadrek.

Their mischievous smirks told me they were lying about the photograph. They were lying also, I thought, about Shadrek's not coming

back to the dead elephant. At subsequent interrogations, however, neither of them changed his story about Shadrek's not being in the photograph. That fact cast doubt on Glen Tatham's confirmation of Shadrek as the man on one knee. But, maybe, I thought, these men were just trying to protect him.

Nevertheless, I instructed the scouts to begin their patrol by lying in ambush around the elephant carcass. I then returned to Chipinda with the two handcuffed captives in the back of the Land Rover. My tracker, Ben, stood guard over them all the way.

Shadrek did not come back to the elephant carcass.

The names of my captives were John Chauke and Josiah Chiranzwa. These names were known to me; they had been recorded several times in the now-bulging file John Osborne had kept on Shadrek. Indeed, we had reason to believe that these two men were among Shadrek's staunchest supporters and most regular assistants.

Because we had recovered no rifle and could not prove that they had been responsible for the elephant's death—and because in court they refused to divulge Shadrek's culpability in the killing—the magistrate was obliged to accept in part the prisoners' version of what had happened.

They had been walking through the game reserve, they said, en route to Chipinda Pools to seek work when, lo and behold, they had come across a dead elephant. Believing that if they recovered the ivory and gave it to the game warden-in-charge at Chipinda it would stand them in better stead, they had begun chopping out the tusks. Not long after that, we had come along to catch them red-handed. But they insisted they had not been poaching. After all, they said, they had made no attempt to run away. They also had had no firearm, so how could they possibly be blamed for the elephant's death?

The magistrate had heard this kind of tale many times before, but he could convict only on the evidence presented, and we had no poaching case that we could prove. Instead, we were obliged to charge them only with illegally entering the game reserve and with trying to steal ivory from a dead elephant. They were both sentenced to six months in jail.

I spent two years at Chipinga Pools reveling in what must surely have been the wildest and most beautiful part of Rhodesia at that time. Then the time came for me to leave. On reflection I was well pleased with my performance and my accomplishments. They had been very busy years. And I had the satisfaction of knowing before I left that the following year the Gonarezhou was going to become a national park. During the period of my service it had been only an undeclared game reserve.

As always when I was transferred from longstanding postings, I was sad to leave. But I was being groomed for greater things. The department had me earmarked for promotion to provincial game warden, and I was required to leave the Gonarezhou early in 1974.

I spent the next year supervising the erection of buildings at Mushandike (near Fort Victoria, now Masvingo) for the environmental education school that had been established there. The project cost several million dollars, and while the building was in progress I was involved in formulating the school's environmental education curriculum and in teaching the environmental courses that we conducted there weekly. My pupils were eleven- and twelve-year-old children.

Mushandike was a very different experience for me, and, though I enjoyed it, it was the one posting in my career that I was not really all that sad to leave. Behind me, the administration of the Gonarezhou continued under the direction of another game warden, to whom I had to hand over the task of trying to apprehend Shadrek. Not catching Shadrek had been my biggest failure.

Chapter 6

My promotion to provincial game warden was finally approved in December 1974. I was desperately hoping for the provincial warden's post at Hwange National Park, the biggest and most prestigious game reserve in the country, but that was not to be—at least not for another seven years.

My post was provincial game warden-in-charge of the Mashonaland South province. This was the largest of all the provinces, but it did not include any big-game territory except Mahenya's—Melsetter fell under my command. This posting was strange since my forte was the capture and hunting of big-game animals and the administration and management of big-game sanctuaries. Still I was happy with the promotion. It was a step in the direction I wanted to go—Hwange. But it had one serious drawback: I was required to live in the city of Salisbury (now Harare).

I arrived in Salisbury in January of 1975 and purchased a home in the eastern suburb of Mandara. Very soon I became entangled with some of my old cronies who flew and hunted falcons for a hobby. In a short while I was in their midst hunting wild ducks with peregrines, and, surprisingly, I settled into a very comfortable niche in the city. I missed the bush very much, but falconry became my substitution.

While I had been happily engaged in my various backwater pursuits in the Gonarezhou and at Mushandike, momentous things had been happening in the country. In 1972 a new phase of the liberation war had erupted with a vengeance in the northeast, and by the middle of 1975 the terrorists were achieving unexpected and considerable success.

I had been engaged in the war effort since my days in Binga, nearly ten years before. In those days I was the senior game ranger-in-charge of the district and was called upon, informally at first, to assist the army when the first infiltrating terrorists crossed Lake Kariba from Zambia. It had been the security force's honest intention not to include civilians in the conflict, and the police, the army, and the air force had all established specialist forces to deal with the insurgents. But that good intention was not to be.

The first group of armed terrorists who crossed the lake did so under a full moon during the dry season of 1966. When they hit the Rhodesian shore, in the dead of night, they set off on a forced march for Bulawayo, three hundred miles to the southeast.

These men were Matabele guerrillas belonging to ZIPRA—the Zimbabwe People's Revolutionary Army. They were heavily armed and had been trained by the Russians, who had taught them that superior firepower was the factor that won battles. Coming from Zulu stock, the Matabeles are also very proud men who are prepared to stand up and fight. Their intention was not to seek a confrontation but to slip quietly into the country and head for hidden bases in their home territory, Matabeleland. There they had an underground organization that would hide and feed them while they carried out their nefarious work of sabotage and the murder of soft-target whites. Their objectives were to make the country ungovernable by the white regime of Ian Smith and to demoralize the white community. Once they had defeated the white Rhodesians, it was their intention to establish an all-black government in the land that they intended to call Zimbabwe.

To get to the first of the Matabele villages, however, the guerrillas had to traverse a hundred miles of the rugged and hostile Zambezi Valley. That territory was heavily populated by Ba Tonka people near the lake and on the upper Zambezi River, and they had no love for the Matabele.

Once the ZIPRA fighters had passed through the populated rim near the lake, they entered a vast area of undisturbed country characterized by broken, rocky ridges and heavy bush. If they got into that wild country undetected, they were home free because thereafter there was little chance of their being seen and reported.

Burdened with heavy packs of arms and ammunition, they traveled mostly in the moonlight so that their chances of being compromised were minimal. What they could not hide, however, were the tracks they left behind. They could not hide them, that is, from my Bushmen trackers, Ben and Mbuyotsi.

Shortly after each party landed, their tracks were discovered and reported by the Ba Tonka, and the security forces gave chase. The fact that the Ba Tonka were given substantial rewards for this service helped in getting the local people to report the terrorists' spoor.

When the very first ZIPRA gang crossed the lake that very hot October in 1966, the spoor was taken up by the police-dog section; the trained Alsatians followed the scent unerringly until about ten o'clock in the morning. By that time the mercury had already risen to well over 100 degrees Fahrenheit in the shade. The sun beat down mercilessly on everyone's back and heated the ground to roasting point, burning off the scent. Soon the dogs were whimpering and seeking shade because they were unable to stand on the baking-hot ground. Their handlers had to carry them back to base.

By midday the shade temperature had risen to 120 degrees and there was absolutely no scent left, even on the visible tracks. It was then, in desperation, that the army commander asked my Bushmen trackers and me to follow the spoor.

In those days my trackers and I were hunting elephant and buffalo in the Sebungwe Tsetse Fly Corridor practically every day, or catching black rhino to restock Hwange National Park, so it was an easy matter to transfer our big-game hunting skills to the task of tracking the terrorists. What is more, we were used to tracking in the heat of the day, so the job was admirably suited to our skills. That day, toward evening, I had my first contact with armed terrorists. It was a new and unnerving experience to have our quarry firing machine guns at us. On that day I drew my first blood of the war.

Tracking the ZIPRA terrorists became a regular duty, and my trackers and I became constant visitors to the army camp that had been set up in the Binga government outpost where I lived. Our modus operandi required me to stick to a prearranged timetable wherever I was working in the district. The location of my overnight camps and the details of my weekly work programmes were lodged with the military, enabling them to locate me quickly when our services were urgently needed. Whenever there was a "crossing" of the lake, my trackers and I—wherever we might be—would be whisked away by helicopter and dropped directly onto the terrorists' tracks within an hour or so of their being located.

I was, in those days, not issued an automatic or self-loading military weapon. Instead, I carried my .458 magnum elephant rifle. My trackers went unarmed. I used the heavy 500-grain bullets to kill terrorists

whenever I had a clear target. Our contacts, however, were normally very messy, running affairs in dense bush—the terrorists running, we giving chase. There were few good, clear targets.

We were instructed to "go to ground" once the action started and let the four-man soldier units that accompanied us, called protection sticks, do all the fighting. It never worked out that way, however, because we were often up against twenty or more terrorists. I normally found myself in the thick of the battle with my big cannon. Under those conditions, every weapon helped.

It was, however, truly not our job to fight. It was our job to find the terrorists and report their position by radio. More troops then flew in by helicopter to reinforce our protection unit, and the guerrillas were pinned down by circling helicopters. At the time, those aircraft were armed only with twin Browning .303-calibre machine guns of World War II vintage.

The ZIPRA war, as I came to call it, lasted until the dry season of 1968, when the ZIPRA high command in Zambia's capital, Lusaka, halted further infiltrations. Their lack of success and the heavy loss of their trained men were just too much to bear. During those three long years, only one group of ZIPRA fighters managed to slip through the Binga district undetected. Except for that one group—so the district commissioner told me later—we accounted for every member of every party that crossed the lake—killed, captured, or wounded. This success was attributable in no small measure to our tracking duties with the army.

We were not the only game-department staff tracking terrorists in those days. Other game rangers were performing similar military tracking duties and achieving equal success in other parts of the country.

The collapse of the ZIPRA war effort coincided with my transfer to Mabalauta. There followed a hiatus in the war that lasted until December 1972. Throughout that period the Rhodesian security forces remained alert all along the country's borders with Zambia in the north and northwest. The border with Portuguese Mozambique in the east and southeast, by contrast, remained totally unaffected by the ZIPRA war.

My transfer out of the war zone was a huge relief for my family and me. No longer did I lie in bed at night thinking how lucky my trackers and I had been to survive the last ambush we had walked into—or the one before that—and wondering when our luck would run out. I gave my wife no details of what we got up to when tracking the terrorists, and she never heard of the many ambushes we walked into. She was astute enough, however, to understand that I spoke little of my war experiences so that she would not worry—and she never asked. But she did worry, and the constant strain at Binga had worked on all our nerves.

At Mabalauta it was great to go to sleep at night without worrying about whether or not the doors were locked. No longer did we become instantly alert when one of the dogs growled—we knew it was only responding to a leopard's grunt outside in the garden, or the scratching of a honey badger in the dustbin. The threat of being attacked in our home at night was completely absent throughout my service in the Gonarezhou.

Still, the threat of renewed hostilities simmered. Even so, after 1968 the Rhodesians largely believed that the war was over because ZIPRA had been truly mauled and thrashed. So it was with surprise and alarm that we all learned of the attack on Whistlefield Farm in the Centenary area just before Christmas in 1972. That attack was carried out by the Mashona guerrillas of ZANLA, the Zimbabwe African National Liberation Army, operating out of Mozambique.

In those days the Portuguese were fighting a guerrilla army in Mozambique called FRELIMO—"Freddy" to the Rhodesians. Until the beginning of the 1970s, however, this war had waged north of the Zambezi. Then FRELIMO crossed the Zambezi and established bases in the Tete province, which abutted the Mozambique border in northeast Rhodesia. After the Whistlefield attack it became clear that FRELIMO had for some time been assisting ZANLA to establish itself in northeastern Rhodesia.

Following the Whistlefield attack, the well-oiled Rhodesian security machine swung into action, but this time the Rhodesians found themselves up against a very different kind of adversary. The ZANLA fighters had been trained by the Chinese and taught never to confront our well-armed and well-organized security forces. Their tactics were to hit a soft target and run away—to live and fight another day.

Theirs was a war of attrition aimed at wearing away at the economy and spirit of the white Rhodesians—like water dripping on a stone. They had no immediate timetable; they were prepared to fight indefinitely. They were also able to "swim among the people," as the Chinese communist leader Mao Tse-tung was wont to say, because they had thoroughly prepared the local populace to support their cause long before that first attack took place.

Throughout 1973 skirmishes with ZANLA took place in the northeast. Over the next several months the war zone became even

wider, as the guerrillas consolidated their positions and expanded their areas of influence. Success bred success and encouraged the local people to succour the ZANLA cause even more.

Then, in 1974, catastrophe struck the Rhodesians. The Portuguese in Mozambique suddenly and unexpectedly abdicated. They withdrew from the country and returned to Portugal almost overnight, handing Mozambique to FRELIMO on a plate. This opened up the whole of the Mozambican/Rhodesian border to the ZANLA guerrillas, and they gradually established new bases inside Mozambique, close to the Rhodesian border, right down to the Limpopo River. That brought the Gonarezhou into the war zone.

The ZANLA successes encouraged ZIPRA to renew its own war efforts out of Zambia, and by 1975 the Rhodesians were fighting the war all along the borders with both Zambia and Mozambique. Only the South African and Botswana borders remained clear of terrorist infiltration. This conflict was very different from what we had encountered in the Zambezi Valley in the 1960s.

National park trackers were called upon in even greater numbers to assist the military, so the department formed what it called the National Parks Volunteer Tracker Combat Unit, or VTCU. Naturally I volunteered my services. This time we were given proper military training and were issued NATO FN 7.62mm military self-loading rifles, camouflage uniforms, and other necessary military equipment.

My Bushman tracker, Ben, was trained and equipped in exactly the same manner as I. My other tracker, Mbuyotsi, did not accompany me to Salisbury and was never involved with the 1970s bush war to the extent that Ben and I were. The VTCU became not just a passive tracking unit but a disciplined fighting force of highly experienced big-game hunters and African trackers that the terrorists soon found were not a pushover. We were truly a fighting force to be reckoned with.

A tracker unit consisted of four men—one senior white game warden, one junior white game ranger, and two black trackers. Four men composed a helicopter "stick"—the maximum number of fully equipped soldiers that an air force Allouette III helicopter could carry. Each tracker unit was normally accompanied on its allocated tasks by one "protection stick" of four soldiers. Each time we were deployed, therefore, two helicopters were required to take the eight of us to the site of our operations.

The rules of the game were that the tracker combat leader commanded the task force and the protection stick did what we asked of them. But as soon as we sighted terrorists or we came under fire, the roles were reversed. In every punch-up, however, the tracker units participated with the protection stick as a full fighting unit.

The tracker teams did not perform routine patrolling as did the other soldiers in the army. Instead, we remained in what were called the Joint Operational Command Headquarters—JOC-HQs, for short—where we were in constant readiness to react to developments. Whenever there was a murder or an attack on a farmhouse, or when a vehicle was blown up by a land mine or ambushed, or when terrorists were merely sighted, we deployed and took up the terrorists' tracks. We were constantly in hot pursuit of terrorists. And when we were on their tracks, our JOCs remained on constant radio alert, ready to come to our assistance at a moment's notice.

The longest that I personally was engaged in a single tracking duty was five days. We slept on the tracks and followed them the next day, then slept on the tracks again, and so on. The tracking was difficult and slow, but we persevered. On the afternoon of the fifth day we came under heavy fire. We radioed JOC and requested support from what was called the Fire Force, an elite group of helicopter-borne troops specially trained to react to such a situation.

Five helicopters arrived. Some were armed with twin .303 Browning machine guns, others with 20mm cannons firing high-explosive shells. From the air the Fire Force commander discovered that we had walked onto the edge of a very large and well-hidden terrorist base, so he immediately called in both paratroopers and ground troops to assist.

When the troops arrived, we trackers fell back, our work well done, and we left the professionals to do their job. The air force bombed and strafed the ZANLA guerrillas, softening them up for the ground push that was to follow. At the end of the day there were fifty-one dead terrorists, and many more had been captured. The base was utterly destroyed. We lost one man, and two were wounded.

That was the nature of the work carried out by the National Parks VTCU. Soon the VTCU was fighting with other military units all over the country. Our main job remained the tracking of terrorists. Because we were always "at the point" when tracking, we were the first to walk into terrorist ambushes, which the guerrillas would set on their back trails. Our casualties mounted. Many friends and colleagues were killed or wounded. Sometimes their vehicles were blown up by land mines. All our game reserves became war zones.

The war was running hot by 1975. Thereafter the local populace grew tired of the conflict, for they were always caught in the middle. Slowly the black people living in the most vicious areas of the war zone began to inform the security forces about terrorist whereabouts and movements. This resulted in major battles during which many terrorists were killed or captured.

Taken aback by the turncoating of their onetime staunch supporters, ZANLA reacted by cruelly and publicly torturing, then killing, what they called "sellouts." This created real terror among the people. The ZANLA "freedom fighters" had become terrorists in the true sense of the word—of their own people! They were prepared to do *anything* to keep the people on their side—including the use of horrific terror tactics—for without the support of the people, they knew they could not win the war.

At the height of the war, most white Rhodesians were required to fight in the army for six weeks and then allowed to return to their civilian jobs for the next six weeks, a regimen that went on without end. Members of the VTCU, however, tracked for the army for only three weeks, then spent nine weeks at home. That was because we were at the point nearly every day—following spoor, walking into ambushes, coming under fire—and by the end of three weeks our nerves were sticking out like porcupine quills. We also served in a military capacity back on our field stations, helping the police and the air force. We were also always available for extra tracking duties in and around our places of normal work.

All this began happening just before I left Chipinda Pools. By the time I was promoted and transferred to Salisbury, the whole syndrome had been set in motion. The one advantage I had above most of my colleagues was that my family was now living in the biggest city in the country, so they were reasonably safe from terrorist attack.

Those living on stations such as Mabalauta and Chipinda Pools were not so lucky. They had to protect themselves and their families from attacks at night by surrounding their houses with electrified security fences. They were also constantly conscious of the fact that they might be blown up by a land mine on the gravel roads and tracks on which they had to travel all the time.

Compared to the freedom I had enjoyed on my own field stations throughout my career up to that point, the conditions under which my colleagues now had to live and work were chalk and cheese. Their situation was tantamount to living in a dangerous prison where the good guys were behind bars and the bad guys outside.

All my life I have had a problem with my ankles, resulting from an old pole-vaulting accident when I was at school. Both ankles are susceptible to twists and sprains, and periodically one or the other suffers a torn tendon that makes walking great distances a real problem. This interfered with my tracking duties from time to time, and when it happened, I was seconded to the Rhodesian Intelligence Corps. I was then obliged to spend six weeks in the army and six weeks out—like all the other civilians who fought in the war. Fortunately, one six-week tour of sedentary duty with the RIC was normally enough to see my damaged ankle right.

On one of these stints with the RIC, I started a process that ended up with me renewing my personal interest in Shadrek. The rainy season of 1977–78 was very wet. The roads were impassable everywhere, and many parts of the country were cut off from civilization for months on end. Mahenya's was one of these areas, and the terrorists living in camps in nearby Mozambique had almost established Mahenya's as a free zone for themselves. Certainly, there had been no civil administration or security force presence at Mahenya's since the rains began in November. In early March 1978, when the crops were starting to ripen, Chief Mahenya began complaining bitterly about elephants in his crops and the fact that the government was doing nothing to help him.

Via a runner, word got back to the district commissioner at Chipinga that Chief Mahenya was unhappy. Chipinga is a small town high up in the eastern-district mountains where the local government is centered. It is a much bigger town than Melsetter, an hour's drive away.

It was not the chief's unhappiness that worried the DC, it was the information he had also received from the runner that ZANLA terrorists were openly present at the chief's kraal. This prompted the DC to call upon the local army commander, Col. Peter Brown.

The principal military camp in that eastern sector was on the outskirts of Chipinga, alongside the Chipinga airfield, and it so happened that I was doing a stint with the RIC in this JOC-HQ at the time. Peter Brown knew I was in camp, and when the DC asked for his assistance he summoned me to his office. He was alone when I arrived.

"How'd you like to go and shoot a couple of jumbo?" he asked as I entered his office. He gestured to a chair, and I sat down.

"Where and why?" I asked immediately. I was not about to go killing elephants for Peter Brown no matter what his military rank.

"At Mahenya's. It's a hearts-and-minds exercise."

"A what?"

It was the first time I had ever heard the term, although we practiced the concept in many different ways ourselves. One way was to allow the people who lived on our borders to collect meat from elephants that we culled in our game reserves—in the pious hope that we would thereby gain their confidence and support.

"A hearts-and-minds exercise," the colonel repeated, smiling. "Chief Mahenya has complained to the DC that elephants are raiding his crops and that the government is doing nothing about it. We also know that the gooks are walking about freely down there—even in Mahenya's own village."

I raised my eyebrows in surprise. *Terrorists at Mahenya's!* I wondered why Shadrek had not helped the old chief with his elephant problem. It was my first thought about Shadrek in a long time.

"I'd like you to go down there and knock off a couple of jumbo to keep the old boy happy. Maybe it will help to convince him that the Rhodesian government isn't so bad after all."

"I don't have a suitable rifle," I said.

The NATO 7.62mm rifle was now my department's standard weapon for culling elephant. I had killed many a big bull with that tiny bullet. But I knew that crop-raiders would probably lead me into the densest bush, which was *very* thick in many parts of Mahenya's country, and would be doubly thick at this time of the year, near to the end of the rains. Following big bulls into such cover with only a small-calibre military rifle in my hands would be asking for trouble.

"The DC is prepared to lend you his .375 magnum. Is that big enough?"

"Sure."

"And he says you can use his camp at Mahenya's."

I smiled at that. And I thought about the last time I had visited the DC's so-called "camp" at Mahenya's. It brought back many memories of my days in the Gonarezhou.

We then began discussing the details of my proposed task. That conversation set the scene for the greatest and most unusual adventure of my entire military career.

Chapter 7

Col. Peter Brown issued me two Unimog four-wheel-drive lorries (known in the army as 2x5s) and sixteen white soldiers to assist in my "hearts-and-minds" task at Mahenya's. On the surface, mine was a simple task, but we had to be aware of other realities. For example, Mahenya's was a very narrow strip of land sandwiched between the flooding Sabi River and the Mozambique border. Military intelligence told us that a number of terrorist bases were somewhere inside Mozambique not far from Mahenya's, and ZANLA groups were openly visiting Mahenya's in broad daylight. So the sixteen fighting men who accompanied me were very necessary under the circumstances. There was the added reality that the roads were almost impassable. We were soon to discover just how impassable!

All went well until we began to traverse the broken hill country that effectively isolates Mahenya's from the rest of the country. These hills, an extension of the Chihunjas on the eastern side of the Sabi River, were a quagmire. Fortunately the Unimogs had a combination of sixteen forward gears and four reverse gears. I had thought these vehicles to be unboggable, but we would soon discover otherwise.

We were high up in hills, following the twin tracks that served as a road, when the leading Unimog sank to its axles. The surface seemed firm enough, but the cumbersome machine just wallowed onto its belly without warning.

We all climbed out to examine the problem. Strangely, we found that the soil surface was firm, so much so that our feet hardly made an impression. On closer examination, however, we discovered that eighteen inches beneath the surface the soil was virtually liquid, a runny muck that resembled semolina pudding.

Using our multiple gears and a steel cable attached to the winch on the rear vehicle, we extracted the bogged truck from the mud—backward. Now what to do? Mahenya's village was still thirty miles away, and on the road in front of us was the deep mud puddle we had just created.

We successfully negotiated both vehicles over the rocks to one side of the road and returned to the track some distance higher up. Then we were on our way again. But half a mile farther on the front vehicle went down again, just as deep. The soils of the hills were simply supersaturated with rain. We tried the same technique to extract it, but this time the rear vehicle broke through the surface crust and sank into the mire too. Now we were in a pickle.

We tried everything in the book, but nothing worked. Both vehicles dug themselves deeper into the mud. In fact, the front vehicle went down so deep we were unable to open the doors of the cab, the bottom parts of which were normally four feet off the ground.

We were now in a real predicament. Just two miles to the east lay Mozambique, where untold numbers of terrorists were wandering around. Not too far in front of us lay Mahenya's, where we had been told ZANLA had a holiday camp inside Rhodesia. And here we were high up in the hills, thoroughly bogged down, with no practical means of extracting ourselves.

Although I was responsible for the elephant-killing exercise, my friend and RIC colleague, Lieutenant Don Boyd, was in command of the operation as a whole. Don and I conferred. The first thing we had to do was radio back to Chipinga, a couple of hundred miles to the north, to report our situation. We knew that the colonel was hard-pressed with other, more important and more immediate problems and that he would be unlikely to send us any help, but we had to advise him. Our presumptions proved to be on target: We were on our own.

"We'll have to dig ourselves out," I said to Don with a sigh. I could see that we were in for some heavy slogging over the next many hours.

Fortunately, we had come prepared with shovels and axes. I had insisted these be brought along for just such a contingency.

"OK, guys," Don said authoritatively. "Let's move it. The quicker we get started, the sooner we will finish." There was some grumbling at first, but soon everyone was mucking in to get the job done as quickly as possible.

Don deployed two men with machine guns to guard both our front and rear. He placed them in hidden positions with good fields of fire a hundred yards or so away, one behind us on the track, the other in front of us. A third man he located on high ground to the east. The rest of us formulated and rejected plans, one after another, to extract the vehicles from the mud.

The four-wheel-drive gears were useless. The winches were useless. All we could do was to jack the vehicles up, one wheel at a time, and place logs under the wheels. Some of the lads dug out the mud from the side of, and then from under, the right front wheel of the lead vehicle. Others began chopping down small trees that, fortunately, were abundant all around. Indeed, we were surrounded by a virtual forest of small trees.

We rammed the first logs under the wheel, then placed a shorter, thicker log crosswise on top of those. Then we inserted the truck's hydraulic jack between the axle and the crosswise log and began working the lever. The lorry didn't budge. Instead, the logs were all forced deeper and deeper into the mire.

We extracted the jack and inserted several more logs on top of the first ones. We replaced the jack and pumped again. Again the logs were pushed deeper into the mud. Another team began working on the left front wheel, using the hydraulic jack from the second vehicle. They experienced exactly the same syndrome. It was soul-destroying work that sapped the spirit, but all we could do was persevere.

Eventually the bottom logs must have hit bedrock because, inch by inch, we began to raise the vehicle. When the front wheels were standing firmly on their bed of logs, I called a halt. We all sat down to a late lunch, eaten cold and raw from our army "rat packs." We washed the food down with some hot and heavily sugared tea. We were exhausted, but our spirits were buoyed by seeing some light at the end of the tunnel.

Don changed the three guards, and our fresh hands, in unsoiled camouflage fatigues, were soon up to their eyes in mud like the rest of us. Before attempting any kind of miracle extraction, I insisted that we prepare a corduroy of logs across the suspect ground in front of the vehicle. Technically, I was second-in-command of the operation, but since I had more experience in such work, Don left me to supervise the task.

Finally, with everything prepared, we attached the vehicle's front-mounted winch to a tree trunk some distance along the track in front of us. Then, using the lowest four-wheel-drive gear and the winch, we slowly dragged the vehicle out of the slush. Moving slowly but steadily forward onto the corduroy, the Unimog crept out of its slimy grave. When the back wheels finally emerged from the mud, everyone gave a loud cheer.

I was already moving back to see how badly the second vehicle was bogged down when I heard a chorus of moans from the front. I turned back just in time to see the first vehicle sinking slowly back into the ground. One by one the wheels settled in the mud, rocking gently. The truck looked for all the world like an elderly hippo sedately submerging itself into its wallow.

Don swore under his breath. We looked at each other, and I looked at my watch. It was 4 PM and the sun was sinking toward the western skyline. In three hours it would be dark. "We'll have to stay here the night," I said to Don. "We'd better set up camp before we do anything else." He agreed and gave the necessary orders.

Then, we began again exactly where we had begun hours before: digging out the front wheels of the front Unimog, pressing down new logs with the jack, inserting new logs—and yet more logs—until we had the vehicle's front "feet" on a mat of firm logs once again. By then dusk was descending on the land.

"I think we should leave it until the morning," Don opined. He was not about to remove control of the extraction from me, but he had other things to consider. "We can't possibly get the second truck out before dark now," he said, "even if we get this one out. That means we'll *have* to stay here the night anyway."

I agreed.

Don then set about securing the area and arranged a preliminary roster of guards that gave everyone the opportunity to set up his bivouac. This amounted to nothing more than a tiny, lightweight, plasticized canvas tent sheet. It was just big enough for one man to sleep under and remain dry should it happen to rain during the night. Every soldier was allowed to select his own bivvy site, which scattered the men among the nearby rocks and all around the trucks. Everyone cleaned himself up as best he could and prepared a hot evening meal from his rat pack.

When everybody had eaten, guards were appointed and allocated three-hour time slots for the night. Each man made certain where his guard post was located, what his time slot was, who his relief was, and where he was sleeping during the night. The last thing any soldier wanted was to be awakened unnecessarily by the off-coming guard because the man had not made sure who his relief was or where he was sleeping.

Everyone was exhausted, so despite the damp and the mosquitoes nobody had any difficulty falling asleep. Nevertheless, I awoke every three hours as the guards changed, for I woke the moment I heard movement. It was an internal survival mechanism that lasted for decades after the war was over. I could not just go to sleep and let the world pass by. People who are able to sleep in dangerous situations without being awakened by sounds in the night are those who get themselves murdered in their beds.

During one of these changes of the guard I lay in my sleeping bag and wondered why Shadrek had not volunteered his services to Mahenya. He knew the area intimately, and hunting elephant was his greatest joy. *He must be having a ball in the Gonarezhou now that the war has further curtailed the game rangers' movements out of Chipinda Pools*, I thought. I had no answer to my wondering, so after a while I put it out of my mind and went to sleep.

Come dawn we all crawled out of our sleeping bags, rested but aching from head to toe and experiencing twinges in muscles that we had never known existed. We had a light meal and brewed up some hot, sweet tea. Then we got back to work.

We repeated yesterday's performance. Winching the truck forward with the help of the gears, we managed once again to get it onto the corduroy. Then we drove slowly forward—only to have the old bitch settle back into the mud once again. Resolutely, we began anew. It was my and Don's biggest problem to keep the men's spirits up, for nothing makes a man so despondent as failing time and time again at a repetitive task that takes up so much time and energy.

After the third attempt, we succeeded in getting the vehicle onto drier and firmer ground fifty yards ahead of the huge quagmire we had created. The Unimog looked dejected but happy, dripping gray mud all over the yellow, sandy surface of the track. It was by then nearly midday.

After lunch we began the task of extracting the second vehicle. This one, of course, had an even greater distance to travel through the mud pond than had the first one. Furthermore, it had to travel in the churned-up soup that the first one had left behind. Our method of extraction did not differ. Indeed, we had no alternative—except that we could now use the winch on the first vehicle to help pull the second one forward.

We chopped down yet more trees and used the logs to fill up the holes the first vehicle had left behind. We had learned our lesson well—that we would pay dearly for any lack of preparation in our efforts. Even so, the second vehicle was still bogged down—though for the last time—by the evening of the second day.

Once again we prepared for the night, conscious of the fact that for a day and a half we had been chopping down trees all around our position. The sound of all that chopping could easily have attracted the attention of terrorists, and if they had been able to sneak in and see our predicament they would have had ample time to organize a force to attack us. Indeed, we were sitting ducks! If an attack came, we knew it would be during this second night in our bogged-down position.

We were even more tired that second night, but also acutely aware of the possibility of attack. Don organized the guards on one-hour shifts to make sure they remained on maximum alert. Everyone had a restless night.

I don't think I slept at all. I merely dozed deeply between each changing of the guard.

We were lucky. No attack came. The gooks must not have heard us. At dawn we crawled out of our sleeping bags feeling even more jaded than on the previous morning. Nevertheless, we could not dally. By nine o'clock we had both vehicles, repacked with our kit, standing on the hard ground beyond the mud puddle.

I looked back at where we had spent the last two days. When that first vehicle went down into the mud, we had been surrounded by a forest of small trees. Now, for a hundred yards around the mud puddle, no small trees were left standing. Instead, a sea of branches and limp green leaves lay among the rocks. And on the track itself, the ends of the logs we had used to extract the vehicles stuck out of the mud like a long line of jumbled swizzle sticks.

We would have to negotiate that same mud puddle on our way out. I shuddered at the thought and immediately banished it from my mind. Then I realized that we might yet encounter another mud puddle on our way to Mahenya's—and maybe a third, or God forbid, a fourth.

I switched off the scene behind us and concentrated on the reality of the here and now. Oddly enough, I gave no thought at all to the terrorist presence in the area. At that point in time another mud puddle up ahead was of far more concern to me. *What will be will be*, I thought and turned the ignition key.

We were lucky. We encountered no more mud puddles, and an hour later we drove into the district commissioner's patrol camp at Chiribira Falls on the Sabi.

The Mhlengwe people had given exactly the same name to the Sabi River waterfall as they had given to the waterfall below Chipinda Pools on the Lundi. Chiribira means "the place where the water boils." Both waterfalls marked the places where the rivers fell off the higher Rhodesian plateau into the true lowveld of Mozambique.

I stopped the vehicle at the back door of the DC's "camp" and climbed down from the cab. The second vehicle drew up behind me, and Don immediately sent half-a-dozen soldiers out to secure the area. Then he joined me as we looked over the building.

"Some camp," he said succinctly. He called over two of his men and directed them to clear the building, too. We had long ago learned the folly of not checking for booby traps and antipersonnel mines before entering structures that had been unoccupied for a long time.

These DC field bases were not "camps" at all but proper little houses with asbestos roofs, steel-framed windows, and lockable doors. From my previous visits to this one, I knew that it had a large sitting room-cum-dining room, a veranda, and two bedrooms. The bathroom had both a bath and a shower, as well as a wash basin and a flush toilet. There was a kitchen complete with sink, a paraffin (kerosene) fridge with a deep-freeze compartment, and a gas-burning stove. All the windows and the veranda had copper-gauze screening to keep out the mosquitoes, and the two doors leading to the outside— one on the veranda and one in the kitchen—had been equipped with a gauze-screened outer door. There was even a *bundu* wood-burning boiler behind the kitchen to supply hot water. A pump had been located at the river's edge to send water to an overhead metal tank behind the house. There was also a large, round, brick reservoir next to the outside kitchen corner that collected rainwater from the roof.

The cottage had once been properly furnished with both lounge and veranda chairs. There had been a dining room suite with six chairs, and three beds in each bedroom. Linens and blankets and pillows, enough for the six beds in winter, had been kept in one of the two built-in cupboards in the bedrooms. The kitchen had everything a family of six would need on a month's holiday. Finally, a permanent camp attendant had looked after the property even when it was not in use, which was most of the time.

Since I had last visited the DC's Mahenya camp, it had been security-fenced and the bush had been cleared for a hundred yards all around the perimeter to provide a good field of fire in case of attack. A double security gate at the entrance gave both our large vehicles access to the protected area inside the fence. A sandbagged guard post now commanded the rise at the back of the kitchen. No stone had been left unturned to render the building secure.

All this security effort, however, had been to no avail. Terrorists had recently hit the camp when it was empty. This is something, I thought with some rancour, that *Mahenya's runner had* not *told the DC*. Most of the windows had been smashed with fire from Chinese-supplied AK-47s and RPD light machine guns. The walls were pockmarked with myriad bullet holes. Mortar shells had penetrated the roof and exploded inside the house, demolishing many of the internal walls and blowing fragments of the asbestos sheeting all over the open places about the ruin. There were four large holes in the outer walls made by RPG rockets.

It was probable that the terrorists had first stripped the cottage of everything they could move and use and press-ganged some of the local people to carry these prizes back to their bases across the border. Knowing the black man as I do, I was sure, too, that Mahenya's people had then themselves raided what was left of the cottage, scavenging whatever they could use. All the doors and steel window frames had been removed, for example, and I felt sure these would shortly be built into local Mhlengwe structures.

The DC's camp was just a shell. Nevertheless, it had been built to resist attack, the walls still provided considerable cover, there was a good open field of fire all around, and the security fence gave us an additional level of safety. Though ruined and bombed out, it still represented the most secure position we had in which to make our base for the next several days.

We made ourselves as comfortable as we could, using our bivvy sheets and the shattered wooden beams of the roof to create rough but waterproof shelters inside the rooms. There was still rainwater in the round brick tank behind the kitchen. It was clear and sweet. That was a major asset.

Someone blocked up a ruptured pipe in the *bundu* boiler by ramming a wooden peg into the open pipe end. That made it serviceable once again. We had to carry rainwater in buckets to fill the drum and carry in firewood from the veld nearby to fuel the fire, but at least it provided the men with some hot water with which to wash away the mud of the three previous days. The following day we decided to reserve our limited supply of rainwater for cooking and drinking purposes only.

We spent that first day organizing our base, and that evening Don and I sat on camp chairs on the blitzed veranda and watched the sun go down. We had brought some cases of beer with us and rationed the men to one bottle a night, and we sat sipping our own allocation in the twilight.

The lower Sabi gorge was stretched out beneath us. We could see the far edge of the waterfall round a bend in the river on our right. Everything around us was richly green from that season's heavy rains, and the roar of the Sabi in flood tumbling over the high waterfall was stupendous.

"The DC sure knows how to rough it," I said to Don wryly.

He smiled and nodded. He clearly didn't want conversation to spoil the tranquillity of the evening. I agreed. So we sat there in silence and let the night descend around us.

Chapter 8

The next morning we assigned four men to guard our base camp and left with them one of our two MAG machine guns. Then Don and I and twelve fully armed soldiers, traveling in one vehicle, visited Chief Mahenya's village. Knowing there was a ZANLA presence in the area, we had no idea what our reception would be like, so we took no chances.

There was nothing pretentious about the chief's home—it was like all the others in the area. It included pole-and-mud thatched huts around which roamed herds of chickens and goats and some mangy, half-starved dogs.

Nearby stood the only brick buildings in the entire area—a short row of primitive classrooms and a small one-room store. This was the Mahenya "business centre."

We found Mahenya, as I had usually found him, slouched in a filthy deck chair still seven sheets to the wind from last night's binge—and, I suspected, from an early morning indulgence in marijuana. I noticed several large dagga plants growing alongside his chicken coop.

I had met Mahenya many times when I was the game warden-in-charge of the Gonarezhou, but he did not recognize me now, either because he was still under the influence or because I was one of a bunch of soldiers all dressed in Rhodesian military camouflage. It had, after all, been at least five years since I had seen him last.

I opened the discussion by saying, "*Sabona*, Chief." The greeting implied: "Good morning, Chief. I acknowledge you." I squatted down in front of him so that our eyes could meet on the level. It helped that I understood and could speak the chief's language.

"*Sabona, Baba*," he replied cautiously. *Well, he's courteous enough*, I thought. *That's a good start*. Nevertheless, he eyed the outfacing guards that Don had placed around his kraal with apprehensive and suspicious eyes. All the soldiers had their weapons trained on the surrounding bush.

"The DC has sent us down here to help you with your elephant problem," I told the old man. He immediately beamed and visibly relaxed.

"*Hah!*" he exclaimed, shaking his head. "We have had lots of troubles with elephants. Lots of troubles."

"Well, soon you will have lots of elephant meat to compensate you for your troubles, Chief," I replied. "We will be here for the next ten days—lots of time to shoot lots of elephants for you."

"Ten days to shoot elephants! That will be good, Baba," he said, smiling at me for the first time. "That will be very good."

Despite his more relaxed disposition, Mahenya made no move to sit up from his supine position, and there was an insolence about his manner that annoyed me. He had always been an arrogant son of a bitch, but today he was more disdainfully provocative than normal. It was almost as though he wanted us to understand he had the upper hand in this encounter, and I wondered if it was because he knew he had ZANLA's support nearby. At the same time, there was a nervousness about the man that was disconcerting.

I knew we would have to be on our guard. If they did not already know it, the ZANLA commanders in the camps across the border would soon learn of our presence at Mahenya's. We would have to be prepared for all manner of surprises. There was a good chance they would launch an attack on our base camp at night, along with the possibility of our being ambushed on our various journeys around the area in search of elephant. And, God forbid, there was the chance we could be blown up by a land mine.

"Chief," I said purposefully, "I hear that you have ZANLA friends in the area." I eyed the old man speculatively and tried to assess his reaction.

"ZANLA?" He sat up suddenly in his chair.

That did the trick, I thought. The name had really made him sit up and take notice. A smirk twitched on my lips.

"ZANLA? What is this ZANLA?" Mahenya feigned annoyance at being fed such a sudden conundrum.

"*Magandanga, mdala*" (Terrorists, old man), I said pointedly. There was no point in beating around the bush. "The *vakomana*." (The boys from the bush, which is what the ZANLA cadres liked to call themselves.)

"*Haaiee!*" exclaimed the old chief, feigning annoyance with me and bewilderment at my question. "I know of no *magandangas.* I know of no *vakomana*. What are these strange things?"

He was lying through his teeth, but there was no point in arguing with him. I sighed. I had my answer: The rumours we had heard were all true. ZANLA were indeed present at Mahenya's. I couldn't say that I was surprised. The old chief had always been a bit of a rebel.

"Listen, Chief," I said. "We have not come here to fight with ZANLA. Do you understand that? We have come to help you with the elephants that are raiding your crops."

I looked at the old man intently. He would not meet my eyes.

"But I want you to understand one thing," I continued, trying to put as much steel as possible into my voice. "If ZANLA try to harm us in any way, not only will we stop killing your problem elephants, we will arrest you and take you to Chipinga."

"*Hau!*" Now the old man was really taking note.

"And at Chipinga the soldiers and the police Special Branch will want to hear from you all about the ZANLA *magandangas* that we know are operating in your area. And they will want to know why you have not reported them."

"What are these ZANLA *magandangas*?" he muttered under his breath. "I tell you I know of no things like ZANLA or *magandangas.*"

"OK, I'll believe you," I said in English. *Though thousands wouldn't,* I said to myself under my breath. I smiled at the old chief. He was so transparent. "Do you understand what I have told you?" I added. "Do you understand what will happen if we are attacked by ZANLA?"

"*Haaaiie.* I tell you, *Baba*, I do not know of this ZANLA thing," he insisted.

I had conveyed my message, and the old chief had understood it. Of that I was quite sure. My threat might just save us from an attack. I also knew that ZANLA would want fresh meat from the elephants we were about to kill. Maybe that would be a greater incentive for them to leave us alone—at least for the time being. Once ZANLA's pantries were replenished, however, I felt sure they would try to take us out. We were just too good a target to ignore—a small contingent of Rhodesian soldiers far out on a limb and clearly without any immediate logistical support. It would be imprudent for us to overstay our welcome.

Ten days, I had told the chief. We would be here for ten days killing elephants for him. ZANLA would learn of this programme. Ten days would give the terrorist commanders a relaxed time frame in which to recover meat from the dead elephants and to plan their attack on us. So we would probably have a week's grace before any kind of ZANLA mischief occurred.

"All right," I said, putting aside further discussion about ZANLA. "Now, can you give us a guide to show us where the elephants raided the crops last night?"

"*Haaiee, Nkosi*," Mahenya said. He still would not meet my eyes. He sat and looked at the ground, shaking his head.

Nkosi? Big Chief? So now I'm the Big Chief! I have come up in the world! I smiled again at the man's simplicity.

"I know of no ZANLA," the old chief lamented pitiably.

At that point I felt sorry for him. Like all the other tribal leaders in Rhodesia, he was caught between a rock and a very hard place. All the traditional leaders were very exposed and at the mercy of the terrorists, yet we white Rhodesians were constantly putting pressure on them to nail their colours to our mast.

"OK, Chief," I said, rising from my haunches."What about a guide—preferably someone who can track, too?" I missed Ben. I couldn't remember when I had last hunted elephant or anything else without my faithful tracker at my side.

The chief called out to one of his daughters. She had been standing nearby with other members of the family, listening to our conversation.

After she came over and knelt down in front of her father, he said "Take these soldiers to Jake. Tell him that he must help the soldiers find the elephants that have been eating our crops." The young woman rose to her feet and looked at me shyly, waiting. The chief said to me, "She will take you to a man who can help you. He is not very far away."

I nodded. "*Siabongha, mdala*" (Thank you, old man), I said. The conversation was over.

Don summoned me with an inclination of his head. I went over to him, and unobtrusively he opened his hand, shielding the action from the old Mhlengwe chief. I looked down and saw that he had a handful of empty AK-47 cartridge cases. They were a dull, coppery colour and I recognized them immediately as being of Chinese origin. I had seen tens of thousands of these over the last few years. They were ZANLA cartridges, all right.

"The whole place is thick with them," Don told me. "And many of them are fresh as a daisy." He sniffed at one of the cases. "ZANLA must be giving the chief regular exhibitions of its firepower." It was all the proof we needed.

Don selected four soldiers as a protection stick and instructed them to accompany us on the hunt. The others were tasked to remain with the vehicle at the chief's kraal, there to await radio instructions from us later in the day. Then we set off with the chief's daughter to find Jake.

Jake, the tracker-guide Mahenya had given us, was useless. He led us to fresh spoor in the nearby lands, but his tracking abilities were zero. I quickly relegated him to the rank of water carrier. He took over the two full waterbags that two of the soldiers had been carrying. I assumed the tracking duties myself.

In fact, the tracking was very easy. The ground was damp, the vegetation was lush, and the elephants had traveled in a leisurely fashion during the night. Following them from the crops they had raided was a cinch. Long before midday, we came upon our quarry. The two bulls were standing silently in a shallow, grassed depression on the Sabi flood plain. In the background I could hear the silky hiss of the swollen river as it boiled its way toward the sea.

The animals were stuffing huge quantities of succulent green Panicum grass into their great maws. Periodically they growled at each other as they swished through the tall grass. It was a deep, rich, and companionable noise that came from deep down in the elephants' throats. Old-time hunters had erroneously called this sound of communication a tummy rumble.

Don had borrowed a .375 magnum from a mutual friend in Chipinga, John Henry. John was an animal health inspector employed by the Department of Veterinary Services. I had known him from back in my days as a baby game ranger in Hwange National Park. The night before we left for Mahenya's we had had dinner with John, his lovely wife, Wendy, and their two young daughters. A month later he was ambushed and shot to death in his vehicle by ZANLA terrorists. The attack had taken place one evening when John had gone to pay the black staff on his farm, just outside Chipinga. It was pure chance that on that day Wendy and the two girls had chosen not to accompany him. He was one of many of my friends and relatives who died at the cowardly hands of ZANLA during the Rhodesian bush war.

I had coached Don on how to shoot an elephant in the brain, and where the vital organs were in the animal's huge body. From all accounts Don was a reasonably good small-game hunter. But he had never shot an elephant before. It was our plan that he would not shoot an elephant today, either, for his position at my side was merely as a backup—which I really didn't need. Still, it made Don feel good to be part of the hunt, and it was useful to have a second weapon on hand. Little did we know it, but Don was about to face his moment of truth.

The two elephants were meandering about the open woodland without a care in the world. The breeze was in our favour, so our approach was fairly direct. I instructed the four soldiers we had brought along to stay a hundred yards back. I did not want an army crashing through the bush at my side during that final stalk.

I told Jake to come along with us. I wanted Mahenya's man to be in on the kill—close enough that he could "feel" it so that he would report back to the chief regarding our hunting skills. It was another small tactic to keep ZANLA off our backs for just a little longer. The closer we got to the elephants, however, the more visibly distressed Jake became. I smiled wickedly to myself. *He'll spin a good yarn when he gets back to the old chief,* I thought.

Don was nervous, too. I could see the fear in his wide-open and wild-looking eyes. Nevertheless, he stuck stoically to my left side.

At thirty yards one of the elephants heard the sound of our progress through the thick, waist-high grass. It threw up its head and turned to face us. A loud swoosh of air left its trunk. It stretched its ears out wide and it peered down its trunk in our direction. Swinging its head from side to side, it canvassed the bush all around our position for sight or further sound of our presence. The three of us froze in our tracks.

The second elephant now turned to face us. It, too, spread out its ears and swung its head about, trying to detect what had alarmed its companion. The second elephant's trunk lifted high as it probed the air for a betraying scent.

They had not seen or smelt us. But that first elephant had definitely heard our approach. However, it didn't know what we were, so if we stood perfectly still the animal would likely soon tire of its vigil and move off quietly. There were lots of other game animals about, and the noise the elephant heard could easily have been made by a kudu or a buffalo—or anything else for that matter. I knew the old bull would be working out all these possibilities itself.

We were within a comfortable shooting range, although I would have liked to have both elephants ten yards closer. As it was, I had two very open targets standing right in front of me. They were both facing us, however, and with their heads now thrown high, they offered us brain shots—but at an angle of penetration that would require the bullet to plow through five feet of heavy bone and tough, sinewy muscle to reach its target. I was very conscious of the fact that I had only a .375 magnum

in my hands. The .375 magnum calibre is perfectly adequate for elephant under most hunting conditions, but the bullet is light compared with that of my .458 magnum and has nowhere near the knockdown power.

Under the circumstances, waiting for the animals to turn sideways was definitely the prudent thing to do. A side shot into the brain was a piece of cake at this range.

I had been in this kind of situation a hundred times before and knew that I would just have to wait. Sooner or later they would have to either drop their heads or turn sideways. Either way, they would then offer me much more presentable brain targets.

But I had not taken into account the wavering nerves of my two companions, both quite unfamiliar with being so close to huge and very wild elephants. To them the elephants' behaviour appeared belligerent and threatening.

Jake's nerve broke first. With a loud, whimpering cry he took to his heels and raced off. The elephants reacted immediately. Hearing the thrashing in the grass and the loud human voice, both bulls dropped their heads and instantly gave chase. There was no trumpeting and no threatening ear-spreading, so I knew they really meant business. I was angry at Jake but not flustered. Indeed, I felt completely in control. I didn't have time even to think about what might be going through Don's head at that moment. I needed to concentrate all my faculties on solving the problem at hand.

The elephants erupted toward us, gathering speed. Then, as I knew they would, they saw Don and me standing resolutely in the sea of green grass like two brown-clad monoliths. They hesitated for a moment, then turned their attention to us. Having located and identified their adversaries, the elephants came on in a full-blown charge.

I held my fire. I wanted them to drop their heads and expose their brains before I pulled the trigger. A charging elephant is the easiest elephant in the world to kill provided the hunter waits for the animal to drop its head. Then the penetration needed to reach the brain is only some two feet.

When the lead bull dropped its head in the last phase of its attack, I put a bullet through its forehead and into its brain. I reloaded and had another bullet into the second bull's brain before the first one had properly hit the ground. Both animals rolled over and began kicking their legs in the air. The soggy sound of their hip joints articulating—a sound familiar to me—told me that both bulls were very dead.

I reloaded the magazine of my weapon, taking rounds from the cartridge belt about my waist, and turned, grinning, toward my companion. "Two down," I said to Don happily. "At least two more to go."

"One apiece," Don said happily as we moved toward the still jostling animals.

I was perplexed. "One apiece?"

"*Ja*," he said emphatically. "The first one goes to me, the second one to you."

I laughed. "Bulls---, Don," I said. "I shot them both."

"Negative," he replied in army jargon. "I definitely shot the first one." He looked at me queerly. There was a question mark written all over his face.

This is a bizarre conversation, I thought. *I had definitely shot both animals. What the hell is Don up to?*

The problem was solved when we reached the first bull. There were two bullet holes in its forehead just half an inch apart. Don and I must have squeezed off our triggers at exactly the same moment, for I had not heard a sound to suggest that Don had fired his weapon, and I had felt no muzzle-blast.

I looked at Don and smiled. "Problem solved," I stated, placing two fingertips at the site of the two punctures. "I must say, Don, for a novice your shooting is tops. I'm impressed. You placed your bullet absolutely perfectly in the brain."

"I had a good teacher," he smiled, slapping an arm about my shoulders.

I was smiling into Don's face when I saw his bravado suddenly desert him. His face blanched, and his jaw dropped precipitously. It was a delayed reaction to the danger he had just averted.

"Wow!" he said, relaxing at last. I could see his body shaking with the suddenly released tension. "I didn't think you were ever going to shoot, Ron." He was breathing heavily. "Sorry, but I couldn't help myself. Either I shot at that moment or I was going to do a Jake on you."

"You OK?" I asked with some concern.

"*Ja.* I'm fine. A bit shaken—but fine. It all happened so fast I wasn't ready for that sudden charge."

I smiled to myself. *Yes,* I thought, *nobody really knows if he's got the* tsibindi *to stand and face an elephant's charge—until his moment of truth arrives.*

Tsibindi in most African languages means "liver"—implying courage—and to be an elephant hunter you just have to have *tsibindi.* Lots of it. Don had done well.

I could hear much whistling and yodeling from the army guys we had left in the bush behind us. They must have known that the hunt was over when they heard the shooting. Now they wanted to come and see the results of our endeavours. I returned their call, using the far-reaching whoop of the spotted hyena. Then I bellowed at them to come forward. Soon the four young white men, bristling with weapons, came traipsing out of the bush behind us.

In their company were two black men, each armed with a knobkerrie, ax, and a knife. They apparently had visited the chief's kraal shortly after we had departed and, seeing the army vehicle with its armed guard, had asked the chief the purpose of the soldiers' visit. Told that we had set off to kill an elephant, the two men took up our tracks and followed us, intent upon being among the first of the villagers to collect some meat.

As the two black men drew closer I recognized them both. They were John Chauke and Josiah Chiranzwa, the two men I had caught and arrested at Tamboharta five or six years previously—the ones Shadrek had left behind to chop out the tusks of an elephant he had shot earlier in the day. They were Shadrek's right and left hands.

Chapter 9

Shadrek's two lieutenants glanced only briefly at Don and me. Their attention was drawn completely to the two carcasses that lay in front of them. I watched them as they set about interpreting the spoor and piecing together the story the various signs told of the animals' last moments. These men were good. They knew exactly what they were doing. I could see that at a glance.

They moved to the front of the bulls and located the bullet holes in the foreheads, now weeping blood and lymph. Glancing back at Don and me, they conversed in low tones. They were talking about what the signs had told them, and I knew we had gained their respect as hunters of elephant.

"I know these two guys," I informed Don quietly. "But they don't seem to recognize me."

"Who are they?" he asked.

"Remember I told you about a poacher in the Gonarezhou?"

"Shadrek, yes." He turned to look over the two black men with greater interest. "Is one of them Shadrek?"

"*Shsssssh,*" I cautioned. "Don't mention Shadrek's name so loudly."

"Sorry," he said, looking contrite and puzzled.

"Neither of them is Shadrek," I continued quietly. "These two guys are his chief sidekicks. Five or six years ago I caught them red-handed chopping out the tusks of one of Shadrek's elephant bulls, and I sent them away for six months."

"These two guys? Six months in jail?"

I nodded.

"Good God," Don exclaimed, looking back at the two men.

"Don't look at them, Don," I said quickly. "Just treat them as you would any other strange black man."

"Are you thinking they may lead you to Shadrek?" Don asked, obviously confused at my sudden secrecy.

"Better still," I said quietly. "I have an idea we can use them, and Shadrek, to get to ZANLA across the border."

"*What?*"

"*Shssssh,*" I cautioned him again. My mind was racing like an express train. We had a golden opportunity here that we just could not ignore. It had struck me like a thunderbolt, but Don wasn't even on the same planet.

Our escort soldiers, also gathered about the carcasses, now began firing questions at us. "Field their questions, Don," I said. "I want to keep a low profile with these two guys—at least until I can sass them out."

"Hang on a minute," Don instructed the men. He turned to me: "What do you have in mind, Ron? Do you want to take these two guys into custody?"

"No!" I said quickly. "It's important that they remain here at Mahenya's. Listen, I'll explain my ideas when we're back in camp tonight. Just don't queer my pitch with these guys right now. I'm going to have to tease out the possibilities with them as we go along. I have a hunch—and it's only a hunch—that we will be able to use these two to get to Shadrek."

"And then?"

"Then we use Shadrek to get to ZANLA. But it'll only work if they don't recognize me."

"OK," Don said skeptically. "So what do you want me to do with *our* men?"

"Call them over and tell them not to compromise me. Tell them they mustn't say a word about my being a national parks game warden."

While Don was talking to the soldiers, the two black men came over and asked me if they could begin cutting meat off the carcasses. I looked them over and smiled in a friendly manner. There was absolutely no recognition in their eyes. All they wanted was some meat.

In the distance I could hear more of Mahenya's people shouting to each other, and I knew the rest of the tribe was about to descend upon us.

"OK," I said, accommodating their wishes, "but first I want the tusks chopped out. Then I want both hearts—one for Chief Mahenya and one for us soldiers."

They nodded and muttered their agreement.

"Do you know how to chop out an elephant's tusks?" I asked—as if I didn't know!

Yes, they said, they knew how to do that. "OK, start cutting. I want the two hearts and the four tusks out before anyone touches any meat—then you can have the meat." That was a fair enough bargain that any tribesman would accept. The two men returned to the carcasses and began stripping the hide from the face of one of the elephants. Soon they would use their small knobkerrie axes to shave off the bone of the socket that secured the top tusk in the elephant's head.

Yes, I thought, *you bastards should know how to chop out jumbo tusks. You've had lots of practice.* Nevertheless, I watched them with interest as they set about their task with precision and expertise.

As the minutes ticked by, more and more of Mahenya's people filtered out through the bush and surrounded the elephants. Don stopped them from cutting any meat from the carcasses. First, he told them, the tusks and hearts had to be removed. Very soon, Josiah and John had an army of helpers.

The tusks came out one by one with a precision that astonished even me. Josiah then cut holes in the hides of both carcasses and sectioned off a plate of ribs directly over the elephants' hearts. His instruments were his little knobkerrie ax and one sharp knife. Then he probed inside the carcasses with the knife and excised the huge hearts one by one, severing the giant blood vessels without even seeing them. He knew *exactly* what he was doing.

Willing and bloody arms were inserted into the jagged holes to haul out the huge organs. Each heart was as big as a man's upper torso, and it took two men to extricate each from its bloody pit. The men laid them down on a bed of green leaves that others had prepared to one side.

Removing the bottom tusks was not so easy. It took time to lift up the heads on crude pole levers, but there were many willing hands, for the people all knew that there would be no meat today until the tusks were out.

About this time, I heard the murmur of the Unimog engine in the distance. Don had summoned the vehicle to the carcasses using our backpack TR 48 radio. I was glad. It would save us a long walk back to Mahenya's village.

Josiah came over to me grinning happily. Despite my having thrust all the public exposure onto Don, Josiah had obviously singled me out as the MMWC—the Main-Man-Wot-Counted. I hoped fervently that this did not mean he had recognized me from days gone by.

"It won't be long now, *baas*," he said, without any kind of subservience. "John and those people," he said, indicating the men working on the last of the lower tusks, "will have that tusk out in no time." He carried a primitive but very sharp knife in his right hand. Both hands were dripping blood up to the elbows. He was clearly very happy.

"Can I start cutting our meat now?" he asked politely.

"Better still," I replied in Chi-Shangaan, "why don't we get some of these guys to cut it for you?"

Josiah raised an eyebrow, smiled, and nodded, clearly thinking that was a very good idea.

A whole squad of Mahenya's people was standing by, waiting to get at the meat once that last tusk was out. I walked over and instructed them to start peeling the heavy hide from the hindquarters of one elephant. The meat from that whole leg, I told them, was for the soldiers who had shot the elephants today and for me. Once the meat was removed and laid to one side, I told them, they could start cutting their own meat. By then, the last tusk would have been chopped out.

"Your meat is on the way," I said to Josiah. "Thank you for your help."

"Aieee . . . Siabongha wena, Nkosi" (Nooooo . . . Thank you, Big Chief). Then he turned to supervise the cutting.

"Don't go," I said quickly. "I want to talk to you." He turned back to face me. There was no arrogance in this man and no obsequiousness either. Despite what I knew of his past, I was beginning to like him.

"What is your name?"

"Josiah," he replied straightforwardly. "Josiah Chiranzwa."

"And your friend?"

"John Chauke."

"Where do you live? Here at Mahenya's?"

"John lives here," he said. "I live in the Sangwe Tribal Trust Land."

"Sangwe! That's about fifty miles away," I said. "What the hell are you doing down at Mahenya's at this time of the year?"

"I have relatives here," Josiah said openly. Then he grinned lasciviously and added, "And there is this girl. . . ."

I laughed. "OK, enough said."

"Listen, Josiah," I said, pulling him off to one side so that not even Don could hear what we were about to say to each other, "I know that you guys have contacts across the border in Mozambique. . . ."

The man's countenance suddenly changed. It was a dangerous question, and I could see him withdrawing into himself. In time of war such a conversation was normally bad news.

"Aiiiieee," he said, shaking his head. The negativity was there even before I had made the man any kind of proposition.

"No-no-no!" I said quickly. "Listen to what *I* have to say before *you* say anything."

Josiah looked at me. All the friendliness that had been in his face before was now gone. Now his eyes were serious—very serious. *Damn*, I thought, *I've blown it.*

"Can you sell ivory across the border?" I asked quietly, seriously, and conspiratorially.

Surprise washed across Josiah's face. *So that's the man's game*, I could see him thinking. He smiled and shook his head.

"*Haaiee . . . Nkosi!*" he said quietly. "There was a time, yes, but not now. When the Portuguese were there, it was possible. But not with FRELIMO."

"Josiah, that's nonsense," I said in a more positive manner. My mind was whirling as I tried to conjure up a plausible story for this man. I wanted him on our side, for I just knew we could get him to lead us to Shadrek. Then, I had a feeling, the sky would be the limit.

"I've done this kind of thing before," I said slowly, thinking all the time. "Up at Mtoko. You know Mtoko?"

"I've heard of it," he said.

"Well, two months ago, at Mtoko, I sold elephant tusks in Mozambique for gold. You know how they put gold dust inside porcupine quills?"

He nodded.

"So I know it can be done," I coaxed him.

He shook his head. "Not now. Not here."

Just then John Chauke came over and joined us. He was a much older man and more reserved than Josiah, but he was clearly curious about our secretive conversation. Josiah introduced his friend to my proposition. Chauke listened and immediately shook his head.

"*Aiiiee!*" That was all he said—but his head shake was emphatic. He turned and walked back to the carcasses.

"Don't you know *anybody* in Mozambique who buys and sells ivory?" I asked, gnawing at the bone.

Josiah looked at me intently. A smile broke upon his face. "Yes," he said, he knew of somebody over the border who dealt in ivory. "But he's not there at the moment," he asserted. "He's gone to Jo'burg. He's working in the mines."

Hah, I thought. *So that's why Shadrek had not helped Mahenya with his elephant problem. He isn't here.*

"When will he be back?"

Josiah shrugged and said, "Who knows? When us Shangaan people go to Johannesburg, we sometimes never come back." I noted that he had referred to Shadrek as a Shangaan. *So he is black!* I tentatively tucked the information away in the back of my mind. *But then again*, I thought, *they may have just ignored his one-quarter white blood.*

"How long has this friend of yours been away?"

Josiah pondered the question. "About a year," he said. Then he volunteered that the man was normally away for a year at a time when he went to Johannesburg.

"So he's about due back?" I suggested.

Josiah nodded.

"OK, then," I continued, "how about you and John Chauke take these tusks." I indicated the four ivories now lying next to the two hearts. I noticed that the pile of meat from that one back leg was growing by the minute. "You can hang onto them until your friend gets back from Johannesburg."

"These tusks?" Josiah asked incredulously.

"Yah!" I said quite positively. "We'll be shooting more elephants here over the next ten days, and the DC has no way of knowing just how many elephants we will have killed before we leave. If we shoot six, we'll tell him we shot only four."

"*Haaaieee!*" Josiah said in disbelief, shaking his head. "The DC has many spies among the people here at Mahenya's. He will get to know how many elephants you have shot. You can't hide that sort of thing from the DC." He looked at me as though I were a fool.

I was stymied. The man had a point. And he clearly was not about to get involved with the theft of the DC's ivory. District commissioners were all-powerful in their areas of jurisdiction, and they could make a man's life not worth living if they had a mind to do so.

"OK," I said slowly, a new plan formulating in my mind. "What if we cross the river and shoot elephant on the other side?"

"In the game reserve? In the Gonarezhou?" Josiah exclaimed. He was clearly doubtful that a white man could have made such a suggestion seriously.

I nodded.

"They've got game rangers in the reserve who will shoot you on sight," he stated emphatically.

"That's nonsense, Josiah," I said and laughed. "We could be in and out with a pile of ivory before they even knew we were anywhere near the place. And remember, I'm a soldier. If they caught me in the game reserve, all I'd have to tell the game rangers is that I was following up some *magandangas.*"

Josiah thought about that idea and nodded. *He* knew what a *magandanga* was! We were back on track.

"But we can't cross the Sabi now," he said, smiling slyly. "The river is a torrent. Nobody will be able to cross it for months."

I grimaced. He was right. And I felt he was somewhat relieved, too.

In retrospect, I understood that my proposition had been thrust upon Josiah too suddenly, too unexpectedly. *Much of what he had said about the DC's being informed about the number of elephants I would shoot was baloney,* I thought, *especially if it were I who reported to the DC how many elephants I had shot.* Josiah, of course, not knowing my connection with national parks, would not understand that!

Josiah would need time to chew on my suggestion that he smuggle ivory into Mozambique, time to properly digest it all, to let the possibilities and the implications gel in his mind. He needed time to make contact with Shadrek when he came home from the mines—and to discuss the prospects with him. This was Africa, and nothing worthwhile is ever accomplished in Africa in a hurry.

Josiah's safety, maybe even his life, would depend upon how he worked out his deliberations. That is how the African black man's mind works: slowly—methodically—carefully! Josiah simply could not make a hasty decision on such an important matter. So my impetuous suggestion had been doomed to failure from the start.

But it was a start . . . and I had precious little time available to set the seeds of an idea in Josiah's mind—an idea that I was going to have to tease out and consolidate over the next several months myself. "What if I were to come back here in six months when the river is down? Would you cross the river with me and shoot elephant in the game reserve then?"

Josiah beamed and nodded. He agreed that it was a possibility. He would certainly join me on a poaching trip into the Gonarezhou in six months' time. And John Chauke? Yes, Josiah confirmed, John Chauke would come with us. He would talk to Chauke about the plan. He would come. It remained then for me to jot down the particulars regarding the whereabouts of Josiah's village in the Sangwe and to make a list of people I could contact to locate him.

We loaded the tusks and hearts onto the Unimog and left the villagers swarming all over the two carcasses. There were now over a hundred of Mahenya's people on the scene, and, strangely, many of them were strong and alert-looking young men. This was abnormal in war-torn Rhodesia, where all the young men were either employed by the security forces or had left the country to train as ZIPRA or ZANLA freedom fighters.

As I drove away, therefore, I knew I had been looking at ZANLA cadres who had just put down their weapons in the nearby bush. Unlike ZIPRA members, who had worn dark green uniforms in the 1960s, ZANLA fought in civilian clothes. If they did not have weapons in their hands, they simply blended with the local populace. These young men had come to collect meat, not to wage war. The sure knowledge of that fact left me with a creepy feeling. Nevertheless, it confirmed my belief that we were safe from attack for the moment.

We shot three more elephant bulls over the next two days. And each morning, by prior arrangement, we met Josiah and John Chauke at Chief Mahenya's village. The two men became our guides and trackers on the hunt each day, which gave us the opportunity to get to know each other better and to cement some kind of relationship.

At the crack of dawn after our fourth night at the DC's battered camp, we departed without prior warning. We had done what we had been asked to do, and it would have been foolhardy to announce our intended departure to the enemy. The road out did not present any real difficulties. We knew now where the bad spots were, and these we circumvented by driving over nearby rocks. The task would have been impossible without the Unimogs.

We left Mahenya's behind us with some relief. Working virtually among ZANLA terrorist forces was an eerie experience. Our expedition had been a calculated risk based on the belief that the terrorists would not harm us before they had recovered enough fresh meat to satisfy their needs. It was also based on the belief that they would fall for our early announcement that we were to be in the area for ten days. By leaving unannounced much earlier, we had preempted their attack on our camp. And, finally, it was based on the belief that ZANLA would plan its attack for nights seven, eight, or nine of our announced ten-day programme. It was a calculated risk that had worked. We came back to Chipinga unscathed and with a great deal of information useful to our military intelligence people.

I personally went back to Chipinga with something else—a plan brewing in my mind. Shadrek—still in faraway Johannesburg, or so I thought—didn't know it, but he was already hitched to my wagon.

Chapter 10

Some might say it was little more than a pious hope that I could bring Shadrek into my net at that time. After all, he had adroitly avoided capture for well over a decade, and now the country's circumstances were drastically changed.

We had been unable to catch Shadrek during the 1960s, when Rhodesia had a well-oiled and highly efficient policing and game-ranging machine in place, and when the Portuguese in Mozambique had stated their preparedness to help us on the other side of the border. Now a full-scale war was raging, the Portuguese had abdicated, and FRELIMO, a hostile regime, held the reins of power across the border. And FRELIMO was helping our enemy, ZANLA, to destroy the white-controlled government of our country.

Anyone might well ask: How on earth did I think it was possible, now, not only to make contact with Shadrek but also to persuade him to work with the Rhodesians against ZANLA?

I believed that a number of conjectural factors were working in favour of my plan. First of all, I believed that FRELIMO would not be so lax as the Portuguese had been about Shadrek's owning an elephant gun—or about his shooting elephants whenever and wherever he felt so disposed. FRELIMO would also most certainly have viewed with great suspicion anyone who wandered across the border into enemy territory to shoot elephants without its approval.

Secondly, I believed that elephant hunting was such a passion with Shadrek that the circumstances under which he presumably had to live now, under FRELIMO's yoke, would be eating away at his very reason for living. Only someone such as I, who had an equal love for elephants and an equal passion for hunting them, could have evaluated Shadrek's soul and come to such a conclusion.

There were other factors, too. As has happened with most African freedom-seeking and freedom-fighting ideologies, FRELIMO began its governance of Mozambique with seemingly altruistic policies based upon communism. This ideal failed in Mozambique, and it has not lasted for long anywhere else in Africa, either, because communism has no place in the African psyche. Nevertheless, during the period of this story, FRELIMO practiced communism with fervour.

I had heard, for example, that although the people were permitted and encouraged to grow their own crops, they were also required to spend a minimum of one day per week cultivating crops for the state, on state-owned farms. I could just imagine Shadrek's heart withering away as he was forced to hoe the weeds from FRELIMO's maize fields. It was no wonder he had recently escaped to work in the gold mines of the Witwatersrand in South Africa.

I wondered how he had swung that one with FRELIMO!

Another major factor was my belief that Shadrek was a dyed-in-the-wool capitalist. He had killed elephants, not just for the love of hunting them but also because he could sell their tusks for money—and money had given him a quality of life that was a cut above that of his neighbours. He had sold ivory to the Portuguese. Rumour had it that he had also sold ivory to the South African helicopter crews who maintained the power lines that took electricity from Mozambique's Cabora Bassa hydroelectric turbines on the Zambezi to South Africa. Now the Portuguese were gone, and FRELIMO had canceled the old Portuguese/South African contracts. South Africa, at that time, was an enemy of Mozambique. The power line helicopters, therefore, were also a thing of the past.

And there was Shadrek's ego to consider. Shadrek had lived among the Ndaus, the Shangaans, and the Mhlengwes of the region all his life. Whether or not he was the grandson of Bvekenya Barnard did not matter.

The most he could possibly be was one-quarter European anyway. In reality, he lived like a native and among the natives, but he was not "just" one of them. Shadrek had a persona that lifted him above mediocrity, and his elephant poaching exploits had made him something of a legend in his own lifetime. For years he had continually and persistently singed the beards of the Rhodesian authorities, and his compatriots had loved him for it. His name had then been on the lips of everyone on both sides of the border. He had been a somebody—a somebody everyone had heard of—a somebody everybody spoke about. Now that FRELIMO and the war had brought his elephant poaching activities to a virtual halt, I felt sure that Shadrek would be fretting as he was slowly and forcibly submerged by the FRELIMO administration into the amorphous mass of Mozambique's populace—in short, forced to become a *nobody*.

At the height of the Rhodesian Bush War, therefore, many factors were limiting Shadrek's old-style elephant hunting activities. But I knew his soul would have remained intact, and that his heart would be crying out for the good old days. I also surmised that he would have no love for FRELIMO, which would have placed many serious constrictions on every facet of his life. I felt sure, therefore, that he was floundering in a rough and hostile sea full of communistic flotsam that he abhorred. Nothing could have been the same for Shadrek in Mozambique after FRELIMO took power.

It would be a gross exaggeration to say that I had considered all these things when I saw John Chauke and Josiah Chiranzwa emerge out of the bush that day at Mahenya's. Nevertheless, I felt that I knew Shadrek and that I knew what made him tick, for in our hearts we were kindred spirits. So when his two top henchmen presented themselves that day, the possibility of some sort of plan immediately began spinning round and round inside my head. At that moment I was overwhelmed by a powerful intuition. Only much later, after I had turned and twisted all the facts and rumours around in my head, was I able to piece together the prospects and the potentials of getting Shadrek to work for the Rhodesian war machine.

My stint with the Rhodesian Intelligence Corps came to an end three weeks after the Mahenya hearts-and-minds exercise, by which time I had a plan pretty well worked out. And the more I thought about the details, the more feasible the whole idea seemed.

It was with considerable confidence, therefore, that I took my plan to the director of my department, Dr. Graham Child, the day after I was demobbed. Graham was a captain in the Rhodesian Intelligence Corps and, of course, knew all about Shadrek. He had little difficulty in seeing the huge potential in the concept that I presented to him.

For some years the Rhodesian security forces (SF) had been paying anonymous informers huge sums of money for information that led to the arrest or killing of terrorists and the recovery of enemy arms. Indeed, notices advertising a sliding scale of rewards appeared in every post office and government building throughout the country. So there was nothing underhanded in what I was proposing. In a nutshell, my idea was to get Shadrek to advise our security forces about the location of ZANLA terrorist bases in the vicinity of the Rio Save inside Mozambique. The security forces knew of the existence of these bases but did not know their whereabouts. And the Rhodesian SF could not attack and wipe them out until we knew exactly where they were.

I felt sure that I could persuade Shadrek to give us the information we needed if we promised him a reward based upon the number of terrorists killed or captured when the SF attacked the ZANLA bases that he located for us. I felt, too, that a major prerequisite of our agreement would be that we grant him amnesty for all his past killings of Gonarezhou elephant bulls.

At that time, the Rhodesian government was paying $5,000 Rhodesian for information that led to the killing or capture of a terrorist sectorial commander or someone of higher rank. One thousand dollars was paid for an ordinary armed cadre. There was a sliding scale of rewards for the recovery of RPD machine guns, RPG rocket launchers, AK-47 assault rifles, land mines, and RPG rockets, grenades, and ammunition. If Shadrek came on board with us, there was the potential for him to earn huge sums of money simply for the information he passed on to us. As I saw it, he would not be required to lift a single finger under combat conditions.

As I recited the potential benefits for both the Rhodesian SF and for Shadrek, I could not help but smile at Graham. "He'll take the bait," I said, grinning inanely. "He'll take it. I know it."

"You've still got to get to him," Graham said sagely. He was always a stickler for detail and practicalities. But in my mind we already had Shadrek in the bag.

"I'll get to him," I asserted. "Just so long as we can go back to Mahenya's and shoot some jumbo bulls in the Gonarezhou. First things first."

"And how many elephants will you need to shoot?" Graham asked, raising his eyebrows quizzically. "I'll need to issue you a permit."

"Graham . . . no! Let's keep it simple. No permits. No quotas. I don't want my hands tied before we even begin."

"You want carte blanche?"

"Yes," I replied emphatically. "I want you to leave all that up to me. I want to feel free enough to make whatever decisions I have to as the circumstances unfold."

He looked at me skeptically. What I was asking was totally irregular. It would put both of us in a spot if my killing of elephants in the Gonarezhou became public knowledge. Acquiring permits and covering our backsides with board approvals was the proper bureaucratic way to handle this situation—but that might compromise the whole operation.

"And I would prefer that you inform nobody in the department and nobody on the board," I said, "about what we'll be trying to achieve. It would be best if this whole operation were carried out in total secrecy."

"Hah! That would be impossible, Ron," Graham asserted. "First of all, I couldn't give you permission even to start *planning* this operation until I got the blessing of Com-Ops." My spirits plummeted. Letting Combined Operations know of my plan would be tantamount to broadcasting it on television—well, not quite, but that was the way I felt about my idea. I felt an emotional ownership over this operation. Shadrek was *mine*!

Graham Child, as CEO of the country's national parks, had direct access to many senior military commanders. This was common knowledge, and I was about to suggest that he use these contacts to obtain a simple clearance for me when he said: "The best I can do is have a chat with General Walls. I know Peter Walls on a personal basis, and we both know that he'll be discreet." It *was* the best that he could do.

Three days later Graham summoned me to his office. He told me to shut the door and take a seat. He smiled at me across his desk. "Peter Walls thinks your idea might just work. He likes it. He's given us the go-ahead, with certain provisos."

"No debate on the matter at Com-Ops?"

"No debate at Com-Ops."

"And what are the provisos?"

"First of all, he agrees with you that we should keep this whole operation low key. Hence, no meetings. No discussions. He, too, is afraid that if too many people know about it there could be a leak, and that might compromise us."

I smiled and bubbled inwardly. I could feel tingles running up and down my spine. The drug was beginning to work. Everything was beginning to fall into place.

"But he insists that you operate under the auspices of one of the specialized arms of the security forces."

"Like who?"

"He wants you to meet with Colonel Ron Reid-Daly, commander of the Selous Scouts. As you know, they operate clandestinely internally and externally, and they are perhaps the best-placed unit to provide you with the backup you'll need."

"I don't like that idea, Graham," I said immediately. "You do know that I have an investigation underway at the moment to try to prove that certain senior officers in the Selous Scouts are involved in elephant poaching?"

The director took a deep breath. "Yes, you mentioned it once before but without any details. Tell me more."

"Well, after the Scouts had unfrozen the Guluene-Chefu last year, Mike Broome, the warden at Mabalauta, discovered half-a-dozen dead elephant bulls in the area, all with their ivory chopped out. The carcasses were fresh. They could only have been killed when the Scouts were operating in the frozen area."

The Selous Scouts regiment of the Rhodesian security forces operated within Rhodesia and externally across the country's borders, fighting as pseudo-terrorists. The unit contained both black and white elements and thus represented the most multiracial group of fighting men in the Rhodesian SF. They dressed like terrorists, they carried terrorist arms, and the white soldiers in the regiment blackened their faces and arms and legs so as to look like ZANLA guerrillas.

Periodically, they "froze" selected parts of the country in which other elements of the security forces were not allowed to operate, and therein they posed as terrorists. They were thus able to make contact with locally resident or incoming terrorist forces, which they promptly annihilated. There were several legitimate reasons why the Scouts "froze" areas. One was obvious—to eliminate the possibility that other units of the SF would mistake them for real terrorists and kill their own people on sight. The Guluene-Chefu Corridor of the Gonarezhou was one such area that the Scouts froze. This meant that not even the local game warden was allowed to venture into the area until it had been unfrozen.

"We have information, too," I told Graham, "that one of the air force helicopter pilots assigned permanently to the Selous Scouts has been ferrying ivory in his chopper directly into the Scouts' fort at Chiredzi."

"That doesn't sound very good."

"There's more," I continued determinedly. "We have information that a Dakota loaded with a large quantity of ivory recently took off from Malipati airstrip south of Mabalauta. We are told that it went to South Africa." I paused to let that idea sink in. "We have reason to believe that most of this ivory came from elephants that had been blown up in the Malipati minefields."

Graham Child looked shocked. "What proof have you to support these allegations?"

"Precious little at this time," I told him regretfully. "Certainly not enough to push for a prosecution. But it seems reasonable to believe that Ron Reid-Daly himself is not ignorant about what is going on. If he doesn't know about it, then he hasn't got the kind of control over his unit that he is reported to have."

"Or it's not going on at all?"

"Some of our information might be considered conjectural or an exaggeration, Graham, but the dead elephants that Mike Broome found in the Guluene-Chefu with their ivory hacked out are a fact."

"What are your other sources?"

"Some information has come from our own game wardens on the ground, who in turn have been told about what is going on by their ground coverage network in the tribal areas. A great deal of it, however, has come from our own game rangers who are part-time members of the Selous Scouts."

"That's bad news," Graham said solemnly. "Still, you are under instructions to report to Major Reid-Daly at the Andre Rabie Barracks next Tuesday at 10 AM. You'll have to tell him what you have to tell him and see if he wants to come on board with Operation Poacher. That, by the way, is the official name for the operation from now on."

Operation Poacher! It's an apt name. I made no comment.

"There's more," I continued. "One of Reid-Daly's right-hand men, Lt. Jack Squires, has a trophy dealer's license, and we have reason to believe he has been using it to launder lion and leopard skins out of the Scouts' training base at Kariba."

"Is there anything else?"

"No. That's the lot. But it's enough, don't you think? And I really find it hard to believe that the colonel doesn't know what is going on. The questions I have asked myself are: If he does know, why hasn't he put a stop to it? And, if he does know and hasn't put a stop to it, is that because he is part of it?"

"Who's handling the case?"

"Willie de Beer."

Game Warden Willie de Beer was my second-in-command in the province, and he operated out of my office in Salisbury. He had served for twenty years as a permanent-force soldier in the Rhodesian Territorial Force, in which unit he'd had the honour of being appointed the regimental sergeant major. Later he achieved officer rank and retired as a captain. Willie knew all the current senior officers in the army personally, having worked with them for many years when they were young soldiers. Now he was applying his knowledge of the military to bring to book some apparent loose cannons in the Selous Scouts regiment.

Some time later, after Operation Poacher was in full swing and after we had accumulated yet more information regarding our suspicions, Willie and I visited Gen. John Hickman at his home in the Borrowdale suburb of Salisbury. Our investigations into the suspected elephant poaching by the Selous Scouts high command had reached stalemate. There was no way we could penetrate the veil of military secrecy that surrounded this famous unit. We needed help from a higher authority, and John Hickman was Willie's choice. Gen. John Hickman was at that time commander of the Rhodesian army and was in a position to further our investigation. He fell under the overall command of Gen. Peter Walls of Combined Operations, but he had very extensive and independent authority that went with his rank and status. And he had the power to institute investigative actions within the military that were out of our reach. Willie, of course, knew John Hickman personally, and it was Willie who set up the meeting.

There were complicating issues, however, that placed General Hickman in a difficult position. The Selous Scouts did not report to either the commander of the Rhodesian army or to Combined Operations headquarters, which latter body represented the army, the air force, the police, and the civil administration. Com-Ops was in overall command of the war effort. Such was the secrecy commanded by the Selous Scouts regiment, however, that Col. Ron Reid-Daly answered only to the prime minister—directly to Ian Smith himself.

This does not imply that the Scouts were a law unto themselves. Nor does it imply that they did not cooperate with the other units of the security forces—they did, at all levels. Indeed, though they were a special and separate entity, they were also an integral part of the security forces, which required that they coordinate most of their activities with appropriate other branches of the SF—especially with Police SB (External) and with Com-Ops. But ultimately, Colonel Reid-Daly did not "take orders" from General Walls, General Hickman, or SB. This placed the Selous Scouts in a unique and powerful position within the Rhodesian SF as a whole. It also put General Hickman's investigation on our behalf on very thin ice.

Our main target was Lt. Jack Squires, who, we knew, was very close to Reid-Daly. We were convinced that this man was guilty of poaching, but we could not lay our hands on the corroborating evidence that we needed to prosecute him. At the same time, we were still not surc of the colonel's own involvement. Whatever the facts of the matter, it was not kosher that any officer in the Selous Scouts should use his position to enrich himself at the expense of the country's wildlife. Even if Reid-Daly was himself not involved but knew what was going on and had done nothing about it, that fact alone was a huge indictment against the colonel and his regiment. In truth, we really did not know what was going on, but we knew that *something* was. It was a scenario to which we just could not turn a blind eye.

Consequently, we asked Gen. John Hickman to put a tap on the telephones of Lt. Jack Squires and the colonel himself. One way or another, we were determined to get to the bottom of the whole sorry mess. In the event, General Hickman tasked his military intelligence department (not the RIC) with the responsibility of tapping the phones and monitoring the conversations that took place. Willie and I had absolutely no access to those taped conversations, most of which contained top-secret military information that had nothing at all to do with what we were trying to find out.

General Hickman assured us, however, that should any incriminating evidence on the poaching issue be forthcoming, we would be advised. In actual fact, that was as far as our investigation ever went, for we heard nothing more from General Hickman about the entire matter. Our investigation came to a sudden full stop the moment we left General Hickman's home that evening.

The telephone taps must have remained in place for some time, however, for later in the year a military intelligence officer, who did not approve of the phone tapping, blew the gaff. He advised Colonel Reid-Daly in confidence that his phone calls were being monitored, and told him why. This caused a huge furor in military circles. In later years Reid-Daly revealed in his own book on the Selous Scouts that military intelligence had extended the investigation beyond our ivory-tracking inquiry to include the possibility that some elements of the Selous Scouts were also involved in transporting terrorist weapons out of the country for private sale overseas.

At an official military function late in 1979, Colonel Reid-Daly accused General Hickman of a breach of security. The insults he threw at the general that evening resulted in Reid-Daly's court-martial for insubordination. He was found guilty and sentenced—*to a reprimand!*

There were many senior officers in the Rhodesian security forces at that time who considered the charge of illegal ivory trafficking too "frivolous," as they called it, to warrant the phone-tapping exercise. They provided mitigating factors in defense of Reid-Daly and the Selous Scouts at the court-martial hearing. They cited all the good work carried out by the Selous Scouts over the years, and they stated emphatically that other, far more serious matters—matters of war—outweighed any of the alleged breaches of conduct by Colonel Reid-Daly or his merry men. Indeed, they said, the very survival of the country was at stake.

I doubt that I will ever get to know the truth of the matter, but I am not repentant about my part in the debacle. Our target had not been Reid-Daly but Jack Squires. We never brought Squires to book. And at the end of the war, Squires left the country. He became involved in various international political intrigues that hit the headlines in later years—including alleged political assassinations in Europe.

The day I walked into the Selous Scouts' barracks at Nkomo to discuss Operation Poacher, the atmosphere was already stigmatized because of my belief that something fishy was going on. Jack Squires met me in the front office. I had met him on several previous occasions in my own office when it had been necessary to clear up errors in his trophy-dealer records. He handled me that morning, I felt, with kid gloves, and that fact did not allay any of my suspicions.

There was no delay. Squires took me straight in to see the great man himself—and shut the door behind us, which meant that he intended to include himself in the discussion. Reid-Daly received me courteously enough, but I felt, or imagined, that there was some reserve in his initial reception.

After the introductions were over, I immediately questioned Squires's continued presence. "With respect, Mr. Daly," I said, "I understood that my discussion with you on this matter is on a 'need-to-know' basis. I have nothing against Mr. Squires, but is it necessary that he be party to our discussion at this time?"

"Jack . . . would you mind?" The colonel thus dismissed his subordinate politely.

"Not at all, sir," Squires said, and left the room promptly.

"Now, what is all this about, Mr. Thomson? General Walls gave me only the briefest outline, so you'll have to fill me in with the details."

So I told the commanding officer of the Selous Scouts all that I could about Operation Poacher. Reid-Daly was very patient, and he listened to me intently right through to the very end of my tale. Then he gave a big sigh. "So what do you want from the Selous Scouts?" he asked.

"I have been informed that I will have to operate under the auspices of an existing military unit that can provide me with the logistical support that I will need," I said simply. "Just exactly what I will need I don't know at this time, but I can let you know just as soon as I start the ball rolling."

"You haven't made contact with this Shadrek fellow yet?"

"No, sir. But I have made contact with his two top lieutenants."

"Why don't we just send some Scouts into Mozambique and bring this Shadrek fellow back for interrogation?"

"I don't think that will work at all, sir," I responded quickly. "If Shadrek is abducted and returns home sometime later, FRELIMO will forever afterward suspect that he had been 'turned' by the Rhodesian SF. That reputation would be as good as his death warrant if ZANLA heard about it."

"True," Reid-Daly nodded sagely. "We know all about that."

"I want him left in situ," I stated openly. "We'll have to entice him over into Rhodesia and *then* "turn" him onto our side."

"And you think you can do that?"

"Yes, sir. I'm already partway there."

The colonel pondered what I had told him. Then he straightened and shook his head. "I think what you have in mind is worth a shot, but the Selous Scouts is not the unit you need for support. We don't really do the sort of thing you are suggesting." He looked me straight in the eye and smiled.

I felt both disappointment and relief. Under the circumstances of my ongoing investigation of the truly charming man who sat across the desk in front of me, I really didn't want to work with the Selous Scouts on this task.

"Can I make a suggestion?" he asked.

"Certainly," I agreed. "I need all the ideas I can lay my hands on."

"What you need, in the first instance, is support from the Police Special Branch. That is, SB Internal. You are aware that there are two arms of SB?"

"One operates internally and the other externally."

"That's right," he nodded. "The external branch operates with us and with the SAS—the Special Air Services. What you want is to work with SB Internal until you succeed in getting Shadrek to agree to your plan. Then, when you are in a position to work with him in Mozambique, you will have to work with SB External. At that point SB may ask that we get involved, but until they do I want the Scouts left out of it."

From what I had heard of the way SB operated, what the colonel said made total sense.

"I'm sorry that I can't work with you on this project," he said in summation. "It sounds like an interesting exercise, but it's not really the sort of thing we Scouts get up to. Tell you what, though—I'll set you up with the right people." He smiled at me encouragingly. "I'll be in touch through your director."

I left Reid-Daly's office that morning in a confused state. He had been an absolute gentleman throughout our long discussion, and I drove back to Salisbury with serious doubts about his involvement in the ivory racket. But I could not ignore the facts, or the multiple rumours from a host of different sources. There was definitely something seedy going on behind the scenes in the Selous Scouts, and it was my duty to uncover it.

Many people have asked me why I did not operate with the Selous Scouts on Operation Poacher rather than with the two police Special Branch units. It is a legitimate question, for I still believe the task was admirably suited to Selous Scouts operations.

Jack Squires, however, knew that Willie de Beer and I were on to him. I would brand him a fool had he not sensed that. Willie and I were continually querying the perpetual irregularities that cropped up in his trophy-dealer's register, which was a private business run ostensibly by his wife. He must have realized that we suspected him, but he carried on regardless. I still have no proof of the culpability of either Squires or Reid-Daly in any of the wrongdoings we were investigating. Reid-Daly has publicly protested his innocence—and he may well be totally innocent. Squires, too, might have been innocent, but at the time of our meeting they were both under heavy suspicion.

Chapter 11

Detective Inspector John Davey, based in the lowveld town of Chiredzi, was appointed my police Special Branch (Internal) controller. I had not met the man, but he sounded a likable sort on the telephone. I gave him all the details concerning my two contacts, Josiah Chiranzwa and John Chauke, and he arranged with Josiah that the two men should meet Don Boyd and me at the district commissioner's Mahenya camp in early May. At that time of the year, the river would still be flowing strongly but would not be in flood. We would be able to cross from Mahenya's into the Gonarezhou.

Davey and I had decided it would be better if we began this exercise with familiar faces and familiar places, and the police out of the programme. So once again, we operated under the auspices of the Rhodesian Intelligence Corps and proceeded to Mahenya's in one Unimog with a protection force of ten soldiers.

The road proved to be no impediment—even those sections where we had bogged down months before. They now looked like tank traps. The mud had dried and hardened, and the protruding logs were fixed tight. Other military traffic and the DC's vehicles, however, had made a deviation to one side of the old mud puddles, so they were easy to circumvent.

Now that access to Mahenya's country was once again possible, the military and the DC's staff had reestablished some control over Chief Mahenya and his people. If ZANLA fighters ever visited the area now, their presence was not as obvious as it had been on our last expedition. In fact, we had been assured there was no ZANLA presence in Mahenya's at all—but I am sure that was not true. Nevertheless, our visit on this occasion was not marked with as much tension as our previous trip.

The DC's camp was unchanged except that a new pump had been installed on the river and there was now water in the high-level tank inside the fenced enclosure. There was also a pile of river sand outside the kitchen door and several large stacks of bricks. Obviously, the DC intended to repair the damage that ZANLA and Mahenya's people had done to his camp.

Josiah and John came to the camp in late afternoon on the day of our arrival, and we immediately arranged to go hunting the following day. We agreed to meet at Chief Mahenya's village in the morning.

The next morning we traveled down to Mahenya's kraal and paid our respects to the chief. We told the old reprobate that we had come to shoot more elephants for him. He was delighted with this idea but lamented the fact that we might have some difficulty since most of the elephants had returned to the Gonarezhou at the cessation of the rains.

"Maybe you'll find some bulls on Sabi Island," he said.

We thanked the old chief for his advice, picked up Josiah and John, and drove to a location just opposite Sabi Island. There the truck dropped us off and returned to the DC's camp.

From here on out we were on our own. Don and I had remained in military camouflage because we were still posing as soldiers, but I had relinquished my military FN rifle in favour of my .458 magnum. I had four rounds in the weapon, one up the spout and three in the magazine, and a cartridge belt around my waist held an additional twenty-five cartridges.

Don had retained his military FN rifle with its magazine of twenty rounds. He also had four spare magazines in chest webbing strapped around his upper torso. We had decided that only one elephant rifle was necessary. Prudence, however, had dictated that we take along at least one military weapon capable of providing some rapid firepower should we be confronted by a ZANLA reception committee. There was no telling whose side Josiah and John were on at that stage, and we had given them advance warning of our arrival, so they could easily have advised ZANLA friends of our intentions.

We could have taken a protection stick of armed soldiers with us, but that might have compromised our purposes, which were to gain Josiah's and John's confidence and to provide them with elephant tusks to take to Shadrek. The ivory was to be our entree to the great elephant poacher himself.

We crossed, barefoot, onto Sabi Island through an ankle-deep stream of murky brown water. After we'd put on our boots again, Josiah led the way through the heavy riverine forest on the island to the banks of the Sabi River beyond. The main stream, between the island and the Gonarezhou, was over half a mile wide at this point and still very swollen. The swirling brown waters drifted like viscous oil toward the Sabi's nearby junction with the Lundi.

I was dismayed. The river was much higher than I had anticipated, and I realized that I should have done my homework better. Maybe we should have waited another month. I had a vision of us having to abandon our task because the river was impassable.

Josiah was unperturbed. As affable as ever, he sat down at the water's edge and began pulling off his shoes again. He laughed at our obvious anxiety. "We can cross here," he said assuredly. "We've done it often. In fact, when we knew for sure you were coming down, John and I crossed here just last week to test the passage—and the river's gone down a bit since then."

"You're sure?"

"Ja." He nodded, laughing. He noted that I had made no attempt to remove my footwear but gazed forlornly at the swollen river.

"Just take off your boots and follow me," Josiah urged. "You won't want to spend the day walking about the game reserve in wet boots."

Once again—as on our previous meeting—I felt drawn to this man. He was open and friendly and clearly had no inhibitions about what we were about to do.

John Chauke, on the other hand, was a totally different character. He was much older than Josiah and reserved and introverted to the point of being unfriendly. Indeed, I had no idea why he'd come along with us at all. He hardly said two words at any one time, and he seemed to suffer us in silence all the while. Only much later did I learn that he was Shadrek's brother-in-law!

Josiah again led the way, carrying one of our waterbags in one hand and his small knobkerrie ax and shoes in the other. He had a large knife in a sheath at his belt. John Chauke, walking at Josiah's side, was similarly equipped. They both set off without batting an eyelid, wading ever deeper into the turbid waters of the great river. Apprehensively, Don and I followed close behind.

The water was winter-cold, and as we waded deeper and deeper, the swirls tugged ever more strongly at our clothing, threatening to wash us downstream. The substrate under our feet, however, was solid sand, giving us a firm footing.

I carried my rifle in my right hand and my cartridge belt and boots in the other. Don did likewise. As the water rose higher and higher, we lifted our loads higher and higher above our heads.

The deepest part of the river was just before the reedbeds on the far side. Here the water rose up to my armpits. Don, much shorter than the rest of us, nearly submerged altogether. At one point, with just his face above the water, he protested that he was about to be swept away. To maintain his position he had settled his hand burdens into the water. His rifle, chest-webbing, and boots were all now thoroughly soaked.

Josiah quickly moved over to his side and took Don's burdens from his hands. Don then used the big black man's heavy body as a stanchion, and the two of them struggled along together. Josiah, both his hands high in the air, remained with Don until they were safely through the deepest section. This experience welded a special bond between the two men.

In the meantime, John Chauke and I looked after ourselves. All the while I thought of the giant crocodiles that I knew frequented the lower reaches of both the Lundi and Sabi Rivers. And I remembered some of the mutilated bodies I had recovered from both waters—human cadavers with arms and legs torn off by the twisting actions of the great saurians as they broke off edible-size body parts to swallow.

I am prepared to face all kinds of danger on land—charging elephant and rhino, man-eating lion, even armed terrorists. However, I have a phobia about crocodiles, hippo in the water, and sharks in the sea. Water is not my element, and I freely admit my special fear of crocodiles.

I do not have enough fingers on one hand to count the number of my personal friends and other acquaintances who have been killed by or lost limbs to crocodiles. And I do not have enough fingers on both hands and toes on both feet to count the number of times I have responded to complaints about natives being taken by crocodiles in Rhodesia's rural areas. Large wild crocodiles, therefore, are not my favourite animal, and as we laboriously crossed the wide Sabi that morning my mind ran rife with the possibility of encountering one of the big reptiles in that muddy brown water.

Josiah had preselected our exit point from the river. It was a well-used hippo path that opened invitingly at the edge of the reedbed. Soon we were stumbling through the reeds in waist-deep water. The heavy mud beneath our feet was pocked with the deep indentations of hippo and elephant footprints. They caused us to stumble and flounder repeatedly as we pushed our way toward the welcome riverbank that lay beyond the high canes—canes that hummed and thrummed as they strained against the current.

The reeds closed around us, forming a canopy above our heads. John Chauke pushed his way forward ahead of me. I struggled on right behind him, and behind me I could hear Don and Josiah splashing into the shallower waters at the riverside entrance to the pathway.

I prayed all the while that we would not disturb a hippo basking on the bank. All we needed at that point was for a frightened hippo to come storming down our narrow channel en route to the safety of the open water behind us.

Fortunately the reedbed was not very wide and we were soon scrambling up the dry riverbank to the safety of the high flatland above. Here we found ourselves surrounded by huge forest trees trailing liana vines. As usual, a cacophony of birdsong beat down at us from the treetops.

We were sopping wet, so we sat and rested on the high bank overlooking the swirling Sabi, letting the worst of the water drain from our bodies and clothes. I knew that before the day was out I would have fist-size welts in my crotch from the chafing of wet clothes on my upper thighs. I cursed myself for not having had the foresight to bring along some Vaseline. I had been in this kind of situation many times before and should have known what was coming.

Don wasted no time in stripping his rifle right down to the last little piston and steel spring. He had a small screw-top plastic cleaning kit fastened to his chest webbing, and its contents had remained dry despite his dousing. He pulled a dry rag through the barrel, thoroughly oiled all the working parts of the mechanism, then put the weapon together again. Finally, he removed every round from the magazines, took out the magazine springs, and blew out the damp from the metal boxes. Within five minutes he was content that his weapon was once again serviceable.

We worked the Sabi-Lundi forests all morning and found precious little evidence of elephant or anything else. That was strange because normally the forests around Tamboharta are alive with big-game animals of all kinds. The grass under the trees, however, was waist-high and lush. That meant the grass elsewhere in the game reserve would be tall and lush, too. Elephant prefer to graze during the wet season, so I surmised they were probably scattered throughout the sanctuary, walking waist-deep all day long in their favourite food.

Sometime after midday we came across an elephant cow herd in which there was a young bull carrying passable ivory. Almost at the point of desperation I shot the animal, but I was very disappointed with the trophies. If I was to impress Shadrek, I would have to present him with much better tusks. But our time was running out.

As we were about to start cutting out the ivory, we heard the splintering sound of a big tree being pushed over in the far distance. After that came the cracking noise of yet another big tree going down. The shot I had fired must have disturbed some big bulls at their siesta, for only big bulls push over big trees. So we abandoned the small elephant we had killed and moved toward familiar sounds that told me a herd of big bull elephants was feeding.

As we drew closer we could hear the crunching sounds of elephants chewing the bark off sticks and ripping small branches from pushed-over trees. There were the swishing sounds of big, rough bodies forcing their way through the forest understory.

I approached very close, but the bush was so thick I couldn't see how many elephants were in the group. At first I thought there were only six or seven, but later, when they took flight, I saw at least twice that number.

When we caught up with them, the elephants were ambling slowly through the forest, stopping here and there to rip a branch from a tree or to fill their bellies with the succulent green grass that grew abundantly everywhere. We had approached from downwind, and the elephants were oblivious to our presence.

These were the big bulls I had been looking for. Their tusks hung thick and long from their lips. All were good-looking animals, carrying the kind of ivory that I needed, so it would matter little which ones I shot.

Two bulls were standing apart, feeding on either side of a small fever tree that one of them had pushed over. Both had good tusks and were in a suitable position for me to dispatch them quickly and easily. At a range of ten yards I downed the first bull with a side-on brain shot. The second bull was swinging away, beginning its escape, when my second bullet caught it behind the ear. It, too, collapsed where it had been standing. The shooting was all over in a matter of five or six seconds.

Then pandemonium broke loose. As always happens when a hunter surprises big elephant bulls, the first shot triggered every animal in the group into instant flight. It was a case of every man for himself as huge pachyderms raced for the horizon.

The noise of their panicky flight was tremendous. Trees were run over and others bulldozed by flat foreheads. Tree trunks splintered, branches snapped, and dead logs were shoved along the ground. Rough hides grated unceremoniously through the heavy undergrowth and rasped against one another. Deep-throated growls everywhere told me that, even in their flight, the elephants were keeping in touch with each other.

Gradually the sounds faded into the distance, and a light haze of dust permeated the area. It is amazing how, even in fairly damp conditions, fleeing elephants always seem to leave dry dust in the air behind them. And as the sounds of the flight grew dim, we became more and more conscious of rhythmic, soggy noises coming from the two dead elephants left behind. Both animals had rolled onto their sides and now were kicking their back legs for the last time before their bodies shut down completely.

Both Josiah and John were greatly impressed by the efficiency and ease with which I had killed the two elephants. They had witnessed this before, but it did no harm to reinforce the experience. It was good for my purpose that they should have a wholesome respect for my abilities because they would pass the message on to Shadrek—a message that would tell him I was someone who could compete with his own prowess. A great deal of showmanship was integral to this exercise, and I had to play the game. What I could not do was tell either of these men that I'd had lots of practice shooting elephant in my job as a national parks game ranger.

Both black men walked about the dead elephants reenacting the entire hunt, for they had kept a safe distance back, with Don, when I had gone in to do the killing. They had been unable to see just how close I had been to the elephants before I had shot them. Now they were able to piece together the details, and they realized the very short range of the shots.

But they were wasting time. Only a few hours of daylight were left, and we had a mammoth task to complete before dark. And we still had the river to cross!

"Josiah," I said, as I helped him loosen a top tusk from its socket, "are you *sure* you have a contact in Mozambique who will buy the tusks off us?" I said "us" because all day long I had been reaffirming the fact that we were all in this enterprise together.

"*Ja*," he said. "I don't know what we'll get for them, but he will take them off our hands."

"I'd prefer gold," I said. "But if he can get his hands on some AK-47s, that will do. There are lots of AKs in Mozambique. FRELIMO use them. So do ZANLA. I'd say that ten AKs would be a fair price for these four tusks."

"Uh-huh," Josiah grunted noncommittally.

"Then we can give the weapons to the Rhodesian police and claim the reward."

"Aha!" Josiah's face lit up with sudden understanding. "Is that why Mr. Davey is involved in all this?"

"What do you mean?"

"Well, it was Mr. Davey who arranged this meeting between us, and I know he is a policeman."

"How do you know that?"

Josiah just looked at me and said with a smile, "We Shangaans know all these things."

He stooped down, put the back of his shoulders under the top tusk, and straightened his legs, lifting. There was the sound of connective tissue tearing. Suddenly the tusk ripped away from its dismantled bony socket.

"But up till now," Josiah said, breathing heavily and looking at me pointedly, "I haven't understood what this is really all about. Now I am beginning to understand."

"It's about making money, Josiah," I said. "And we can make lots of money by selling ivory *and* by selling arms of war to the government." I held the loosened tusk upright while he chopped away the last of the bone and fibres to free the ivory completely.

"And what else?"

Together we carried the tusk away from the carcass and laid it on the ground to one side.

"There is nothing else, Josiah. It's all about making money, and we can all make lots of money if we play our cards right."

"And what will Chauke and me make out of all this?"

"You will both make lots of money, too. I told you we are all in this together."

"How much?"

"I don't know. It all depends on how successful we are in setting up business with your friend in Mozambique."

Josiah grunted and went off to cut a pole with which to lever the elephant's head off the ground. The bottom tusk would take much longer to extract.

As Josiah went about his task, I knew that his mind was silently ticking. It was clear that he had given a great deal of prior thought to today's poaching exercise and that he still had not worked out what it was all about. He was intrigued enough, however, to go along with our plan in order to find out.

I, too, had no idea how my still-vague plans would proceed, or end up. I was playing everything by ear. At that stage I had to. I was simply flying kites—working in what I considered to be a positive direction. I was making things happen and adjusting to the reactions. I had a hunch that we could work something out because I was convinced that Shadrek was unhappy in present-day communist Mozambique, was a heavy capitalist, and had a passion for elephant hunting. Ivory, elephant hunting, and money, therefore, were the keys to my linking up with him. What would happen when Shadrek and I did link up, however, was all in the lap of the gods.

"Is your friend back from South Africa?" I asked Josiah as he hacked away at the bottom socket. I had never asked Josiah what his friend's name was. My instinct told me that question was taboo. I was afraid that asking it would shut down his cooperation. In the meantime we both seemed content to continue discussing Shadrek in this nameless fashion.

I looked over and saw that Don and John were nearly at the same stage as we were, working now on the second elephant's bottom tusk.

"Yes," Josiah said, responding to my question. "He came back about a month ago."

"Does he know what he is doing?"

"Yes," Josiah said, "but it's a pity we didn't get together a few years ago." Josiah avoided my eyes. "I had another friend then who was a very good elephant hunter and used to sell lots of ivory to the Portuguese—and to the people who flew helicopters along the power lines."

So that rumour is true, I thought. *Shadrek had sold ivory to the South Africans.* And Josiah was clearly referring to Shadrek in his statement. But I was suddenly worried. Josiah said he'd had another friend: *Had something happened to Shadrek?*

"So what happened to this other friend of yours?"

"He was killed in a rockfall in the mines," Josiah said matter-of-factly.

My heart dropped six feet. *Shadrek was dead?*

Josiah looked at me surreptitiously. I caught the look and quickly masked my inner feelings. *Dammit. What's he up to? He's testing me!* I thought. I had nearly given myself away. *If Josiah knew the game, he'd make a good poker player,* I thought.

"That *is* a pity," I responded noncommittally. "We need every outlet for ivory that we can get."

As Josiah concentrated on the task at hand, there was blankness in his face. Like the look he had given me earlier, it conveyed a message. I was missing it completely. "Anyway," he said, "this other friend of mine is just as good. But he may take some time to get our business going. It's not so easy to do this kind of thing now that FRELIMO is the government in Mozambique."

There was something in Josiah's words—in his body language—in his eyes. But I failed to grasp its meaning. It was not so much what he had said as how he had said it. I worried away at the problem, like a dog gnawing at a bone.

He's throwing me a curve ball! The thought came through clear as a bell.

Suddenly I knew it: Josiah's two friends were one and the same. They were both Shadrek. *Shadrek was still alive.* At that moment I knew for sure my plan was going to succeed. And I knew, too, that Josiah was the linchpin in the whole exercise.

"Just remember that these four tusks today are just the start. If he can get rid of these four tusks for a good price—or swap them for AK-47s—we can then get down to talking real business with him."

Josiah looked at me in surprise. "You want to talk business with this friend of mine? Face to face?"

"Face to face," I confirmed. Now we were getting hot!

"Huhhh," Josiah retorted, his little chopper continuing to hack away at the bone of the bottom socket. "I don't know if he will agree to that."

"Well, you'll just have to talk him into it, Josiah. As you now understand, we have some police protection in this business, so our chances of getting caught are zero. But for all of us to make money, we'll have to work out our business arrangements very carefully." I was getting used to improvising on our theme, but I'd have to remember what I had said previously. Liars need good memories.

It was dusk by the time the last tusk came free from its socket. We were all exhausted, but we could not dally. We each lifted a tusk to our shoulders. They were heavy—each weighed between sixty and seventy pounds—and the outgoing trip was going to be tough. We set off in the gathering gloom toward the Sabi.

We were forced to rest often and shift the tusks from one shoulder to the other, but we eventually reached the Sabi without mishap. By the time we fetched up on the riverbank, however, we were dead beat and our shoulders were numb. Josiah had guided us, in the dark, back to the selfsame hippo path we had used early that morning. He obviously knew the Gonarezhou's junction area intimately.

We crossed the river in darkness, except for the light cast by the stars. I carried a tusk over one shoulder, holding it secure with one hand. In my other hand I carried my .458 magnum rifle, cartridge belt, and hunting boots. Don could not manage all his accoutrements because of his lesser height, so Josiah carried his FN rifle and chest-webbing. At times, only Don's head showed above the flowing waters, but the weight of the tusk held his feet firmly to the sand. Stoically he soldiered on. Josiah remained on Don's downstream side and offered his large body for the white man to lean against whenever the current proved too strong. Fortunately, it was a steady but gentle current we had to contend with and not a raging torrent.

I was very conscious of the fact that our tusks were freshly cut from an elephant's head and were often awash in the water. There must have been a heavy scent flowing downstream, therefore, telling every crocodile in creation that there was fresh meat up ahead. I was petrified, and every bit of flotsam that touched my body made me jump in anticipation of a crocodile's bite.

The only problem we had was with a curious hippo that kept rising and blowing at us from not more than twenty yards downstream. It followed us across the deeper section of the river, then abandoned its sport when we reached shallower waters.

Nobody was more relieved than I when we fetched up safe and sound on the dry land of Sabi Island. We all sat down and rested and once again waited for the bulk of the water to flow out of our clothes and off our bodies. I took my clothes off and rung them as dry as I could manage. Then I dressed again and put on my boots.

"Let's go," I said, eager now to get the night over with. My inner thighs were indeed raw with chafe welts. I just wanted to get back to camp, have a hot bath, salve my wounds, and crawl into bed on my camp stretcher. I was physically, mentally, and emotionally finished.

Don recovered his FN rifle from Josiah and strapped on his chest-webbing. Then we each picked up a tusk and wearily set off on the last leg of our journey.

"Mahenya's village," I instructed Josiah. "Just go in that direction." But I had no intention of ever reaching Mahenya's village. When we reached the far side of Sabi Island, I dumped the tusk I was carrying on the ground. Don did the same. Our two black companions did likewise, for they, too, were very tired. I looked at my watch. It was 11 PM. Our protection unit back in camp would be wondering where the hell we were.

The stars were bright, and our eyes had become accustomed to the minimal light. "OK," I said, turning to Josiah. I saw a flash of white teeth as he turned and smiled at me out of the darkness. "This is as far as we go. Now you and John can take these tusks to your friend in Mozambique. Tell him there are a lot more where these four came from and that we can set up a business. Tell him I want to speak with him."

"You are really going to leave the tusks with us?"

"Of course. What do you think we are playing at? Why do you think we have gone to all this trouble? I told you that you can have the tusks to take to your friend in Mozambique. I meant it. If we are going to make a lot of money together, Josiah, you and I must learn to trust each other."

John Chauke said nothing. He just stood in the darkness and listened.

"If my friend agrees to meet with you, how can I get in touch with you?" Josiah asked.

"You have met Mr. Davey," I reminded him. "Just go to Mr. Davey at the police station in Chiredzi. He works for the Special Branch there. If you give him a message, he'll get it to me in Salisbury."

We left the two black men there on Sabi Island with the four tusks in the middle of the night. Throughout the day I had sensed Josiah's hesitancy to accept our bona fides. John Chauke had remained what I had come to accept as his normal noncommittal and uncommunicative self. I assigned no importance to his opinions, and he gave none anyway. But when we left Josiah and Chauke in charge of the ivory, at that moment a true trust was born between us. It developed later into a genuine and warm friendship.

As Don and I, tired and sore, trudged the seven long miles back to the DC's camp that night, a comfortable feeling in my gut told me all was on course for our meeting with Shadrek. All was going according to plan.

Chapter 12

The weeks and months dragged on. May became June and then July. There were no new developments since our elephant-poaching expedition to the Gonarezhou with Josiah and John Chauke. John Davey and I kept in contact by telephone, and he kept in touch with Josiah. And it was not just a case of my keeping in touch with my Special Branch controller. He phoned me, too, on a pretty regular basis. Nothing seemed to be happening, and I began to think that nothing would ever come of my grandiose plans.

Early in July the Rhodesian security forces attacked and destroyed a FRELIMO barracks on the Rio Save at a place called Chiwi. The newspapers said the justification for the attack was that FRELIMO had been assisting ZANLA terrorists to infiltrate the Rhodesian lowveld out of Chiwi.

Chiwi was a familiar name to me. It was similar to the native name for the spurwing goose—*chigwi*—which name I used often in discussions with my black staff. The name Chiwi rang a bell for another reason. I remembered that it was at Chiwi that Charles Mackie had crossed from the south to the north bank of the Rio Save when he had raided Shadrek's home at Madjwisanga. So I knew that Shadrek's village was just across the river from the Chiwi barracks. Knowing the pattern of events of a Rhodesian raid into Mozambique, I began to wonder if Shadrek had been a casualty in the raid.

Then, out of the blue, during the last week of August, I received a telephone call from John Davey. It was imperative, he said, that I fly down to Chiredzi on the commercial Air Rhodesia flight as soon as possible.

"Just when do you want me down?" I asked.

"Yesterday," he answered. I could sense the excitement in his voice.

"As soon as that?"

"Ja. And bring along your old smoke pole."

"My elephant rifle?"

"Of course. This time I'm going in with you. From now on you and I will be operating together in the field. The RIC are out of it."

"Don Boyd?"

"No Don Boyd. We're now moving into Phase Two of the operation."

"I'd like to come with my tracker combat unit, John. You know I'm the leader of a tracker combat team?"

"Yes, I know that. But why do you want them with you on this exercise?"

"Well, if I'm to work in you-know-where, I'd like to have them along with me. They are very trustworthy, and we don't know what we'll be walking into."

"Humph." Davey was clearly not convinced. "We still have to discuss just how we are going to operate, Ron. Maybe working with your trackers is not what we will want. Anyway, who are they? How many people are we talking about?"

"Well, there's a young white game ranger called John Fynnes-Clinton and my two African trackers—one's a Bushman from Hwange. That's all. Just the four of us."

"Did you have these trackers with you when you served in the Gonarezhou?"

"Just my Bushman, Ben."

"And was this Bushman perhaps with you on the day that you arrested Josiah and John Chauke in the game reserve? The day you caught them chopping out ivory?"

Damn! John Davey was quite right. Ben had been with me on that day. He had sat over them in the back of the Land Rover all the way back to Chipinda Pools. Because he was a Bushman, they'd remember him the minute they laid eyes on him. My estimation of John Davey as a policeman suddenly soared.

"Yes. Yes! He was with me on that day," I admitted reluctantly.

"OK. So they'd probably recognize him. No black trackers, Ron. We can't risk compromising the operation by including any black guys at this stage. Even if they didn't recognize him, your tracker might just let something of importance slip in passing conversation. Remember, we will all be sitting around the campfire together at night. There's no saying what will pass between them. But you can bring along your white game ranger."

"All right. Accepted. Now, can you tell me what's going on?"

"Not on the phone. This phone is not secure. But I can say that you will be going into familiar territory."

That meant we'd not be going into Mozambique. We'd be going into the Gonarezhou again—back to the junction.

"How long will you need us?" I asked. It was imperative that I know roughly how long I'd be away.

"About a week. Not longer than ten days."

"OK. I'll see what flight I can get to Chiredzi. But I won't be able to make it until tomorrow at the earliest."

"Tomorrow will be fine. But if you can't get seats on the plane tomorrow, I'd suggest you arrange to drive down."

John Fynnes-Clinton and I arrived at Chiredzi's Buffalo Range Airport on Rhodesia Airways' 10 AM flight the following day. We were dressed in military camouflage and armed with our FN rifles. My .458 magnum was secure in its leather gun case, hidden from prying eyes.

John Davey was there to meet us, and he promptly whisked us off through the vast sugar plantations to his home on the outskirts of Chiredzi. He introduced us to his lovely wife and two young daughters, then excused himself and disappeared for the rest of the day. Young John and I spent the day kicking our heels and reading *Reader's Digest* magazines, of which there was a plentiful supply in the house.

Davey came back after five that afternoon. He refused to tell me anything about the urgent need to bring me down to the lowveld.

"All in good time," he said. "I'll tell you all about it in good time."

This is all I need right now, I thought, *a primo uomo* (a male prima donna) *SB controller who treats the whole exercise as a big game.* I didn't need the theatrics, and I was getting both frustrated and cross at Davey's secretive attitude. But I kept my mouth shut and accepted all that he had to give—or not give. *After all,* I thought, *I don't yet know the man, so I must reserve my judgment.*

Detective Inspector John Davey was not at all what I had expected. He was about my own height and well built, but softer in the flesh than I felt was good for any man. He would have to watch his weight, I thought, for if he relaxed just a bit he would become pudgy. He was soft-spoken, of a calm disposition, and I was to discover that nothing ever riled him. Anger seemed alien to his makeup. I never once saw him cross.

Over the next few days I was to come to know John Davey very well and like him immensely. On that first day of our acquaintance, however, I had to forcibly hold my tongue, for a pressure was building up inside that threatened to explode.

"All you need to know at this time is that we're going down to the Sabi-Lundi junction, where, I hope, we'll meet up with Shadrek."

"You've arranged a meeting?" I asked excitedly. All was suddenly forgiven.

"Well, maybe. It's all still a bit up in the air."

"And Josiah?"

"We'll be picking him up at his kraal in the Sangwe in the morning. We'll travel down together to Tamboharta through the northeastern gate in the tsetse fence."

"So we'll be traveling down, east of the Sabi and inside the Gonarezhou?" This was a road parallel to the one we had used to get to Mahenya's. It traversed the Chihunja Hills on the opposite side of the Sabi.

"Affirmative," he said, the military jargon coming naturally to his lips. "And in case you're worried about it, I've 'frozen' the area for our little exercise."

"You've *frozen* it?"

"After a fashion. I've had the game warden at Chipinga Pools pull his game scouts out of the area for the next two weeks."

"Does he know what we'll be doing?"

"'Of course not," John said with some derision. "And your name wasn't mentioned. But he does know that what *I'll* be doing has Dr. Graham Child's blessing."

"Good. That sounds OK."

Fynnes-Clinton and I had dinner with John and his family that evening and spent the night in their suburban home. The next morning we were up at the crack of dawn, and the three of us left Chiredzi at first light.

It took us an hour to get to Josiah's village. He was waiting for us. When we stopped, he immediately dumped a bedroll and some blankets in the back of the Land Rover. He greeted me with a huge grin and shook my hand vigorously through the open window. Then he climbed onto the open back of the vehicle and sat down on our camping *katoonda* alongside John Fynnes-Clinton.

"And John Chauke?" I asked Davey as we set off once again.

"He's out of it. Permanently."

"Oh?"

"Josiah tells me he was bitten by a puff-adder inside Mozambique—when he was coming back from carrying your tusks to Shadrek. He says Chauke's in a very bad way."

"I'm sorry to hear that," I said. And I was honestly sorry. Chauke was the second member of our team, after Don Boyd, to fall by the wayside. And it seemed that he had truly fallen by the wayside.

A serious puff-adder bite results in the destruction of tissue all around the site, followed by the gradual sloughing off of skin and flesh. If the bite is not treated promptly, gangrene sets in. If the gangrenous limb is not amputated, death often comes slowly and painfully after many months of heavy suffering. I felt deeply sorry for John Chauke. I had no particular love for the man, but he did not deserve such a fate.

Thereafter John Davey became surprisingly uncommunicative. We both gazed through the windscreen, lost in our own thoughts, examining the bumpy dirt track ahead of us. I felt disappointed. Davey's lack of explanation and his avoidance of any kind of discussion regarding the joint venture we were embarking upon were off-putting. We had a lot to talk about. *If we are going to work together,* I thought, *we really must be able to at least speak to each other.*

Then we came to the northeastern Sabi gate in the outer tsetse fence. John stopped his Land Rover in front of the gate and waited. Presently a black man emerged from nearby bushes and opened the gate for us. I thought this unusual since I had never enjoyed such a courtesy when I was the game warden at Chipinga Pools. Perhaps being an SB police officer had its advantages! I paid the black man scant attention. But when I glanced at my companion I saw that he was looking at me intently, with a strange smirk on his face.

Davey drove through the gate, and the man closed it behind us. Then he climbed onto the back of the vehicle and sat down alongside Josiah and young John.

We seemed to have a plethora of Johns on this exercise—John Davey, John Chauke, and now John Fynnes-Clinton. I thought again of poor John Chauke, the second member of the original team to bite the dust. *Two down—two to go,* I thought, then immediately checked myself. Thinking along those lines was bad luck.

Davey drove off, but he kept looking at me sideways, quizzically.

"What's the matter?" I inquired. "Why are you looking at me like that?"

"You're not very observant, are you?" came the retort.

Not very observant? Observant about what? I thought. Suddenly it dawned on me. I turned and looked through the back window of the cab. The strange black man grinned back at me. It was Shadrek. I immediately recognized him from his photograph. A great emotion overwhelmed me. Goose bumps ran up and down my arms. After all these years. After all our efforts to get to him. Here he was—finally—in the flesh.

"I'll be damned," I exclaimed, laughing at John. "Stop the vehicle!"

I climbed out of the cab and shook Shadrek's hand. We grinned at each other but otherwise had nothing to say. I was clearly the happier man—or was it the more smug?—because I knew all about Shadrek but he knew precious little about me. Nevertheless, something of my expertise as an elephant hunter must have filtered through to him because he was obviously pleased to have met me, too. Josiah must have given our man a great sales pitch.

Josiah looked at us both grinning inanely at each other. He shook his head and exclaimed, *"Hah!* Now we've got the two biggest *mscabenga*s in the country together. Now we're gonna see lots of trouble." *Mscabenga* in many African languages means scoundrel. He was not far wrong.

"OK, John," I said with some degree of determination as I climbed back into the cab, the grin still painful on my face. "Now tell me what the hell is going on."

John Davey laughed. This was what all the cloak-and-dagger secretiveness was about. This was the moment he had set up—"all in good time." This was the moment he had been waiting for to offer me an explanation. It broke the ice between us.

"Would you believe," he said, laughing, "that two days ago Shadrek walked into the Chiredzi police headquarters and demanded to see me?" He looked at me, challenging me to call him a liar.

I shook my head. "Cheeky bastard." But somehow I wasn't at all surprised. Such temerity was the measure of the man. It was the reason he had been such a successful poacher and had never been caught.

"He walked right into my office, bold as brass, and he asked: 'Are you Mr. Davey?' I said I was. He then said: 'My name is Shadrek. I believe you want to speak to me?'" John grinned. "How d'you like that?"

"I don't believe it. After all the years we've tried to catch him."

"You've got to admit he's got balls!"

"He sure has. And then what?"

"Well, I told him that we would have to get him and you together, so I suggested this little camping trip to the junction area. I told him you had a plan to make us all very rich but that he would need to discuss it with you." John looked at me almost for approval. "And I thought it might be nice for the two of you to shoot a jumbo or two together—to break the ice, as it were. I've brought along my own .375 magnum for Shadrek to use."

"Great," I said. The grin on my face was now an ache. I could have hugged John Davey at that moment. My plan was working. *Our* plan was working! Shadrek was at last in our company. It was all going according to plan. And I was looking forward immensely to hunting elephants with this legendary poacher over the next few days.

Shadrek and I were two men with the same great passions. We both loved elephants, and we both loved hunting them. Yet in many other ways we were as different as chalk and cheese. Nevertheless, our lives were about to become inextricably intertwined in a manner that neither of us could ever have expected. The game warden and the poacher were about to join forces. Together we were about to rock the Rio Save in Mozambique, to rock FRELIMO and ZANLA, and to rock Mahenya's, too, as the region had never been rocked before.

We camped at Hohveh Pool, a large, crystal-clear body of water at the upper end of the Sabi-Lundi flood plain. Nestled up against the flood-plain bank, the pool is shrouded in tall reedbeds on the riverside and hidden by a broad blanket of *mlala* palm thickets on the land side. The riverbank at that point is high above the water. There is a ribbon of forest trees on the high bank under which we made our camp. We had a good view across the half-mile-wide reedbeds that stretched across to the Marhumbini Hills, a little downstream.

No sooner had we unloaded our meagre camping kit and selected our sleeping sites under the trees than John disentangled the bunch of fishing rods he had thrown onto the back of the Land Rover. Among his kit was a grimy old coolbox, which I now discovered contained heavy clay-loam soil and a squirming mass of small red earthworms. He had certainly come well prepared for what he had fully intended should be a leisurely few days of camping at government expense. War was hell for John Davey! In next to no time, he had scampered down the sloping, crumbling bank and, standing at the water's edge, cast out his line.

One thing about the Lundi surpassed all other Rhodesian rivers that I have ever fished in: There was no shortage of fish. The lower Lundi was home to two varieties of freshwater bream, the black and the red-breasted, both of which were excellent eating. There were also tigerfish and barbel—Africa's ubiquitous catfish—and a host of other species. The presence of tigerfish with their heavy, sharp-toothed jaws necessitated the use of a wire trace (leader) above the hook.

An interesting fact about the Sabi-Lundi junction was that although it was four hundred miles from the sea, it was only some four hundred feet above sea level, and the Rio Save's sluggish journey to the Indian Ocean was impeded by no rocky rapids at all. This meant that during the floods, sea fish could penetrate inland right up to the two waterfalls on the Sabi and Lundi Rivers inside Rhodesia. Sawfish of immense size—to name but one large species that penetrated inland—were sometimes trapped in the deeper pools of both rivers when the floods subsided. The National Museum in Bulawayo is in possession of several "saws" recovered from Mahenya's people that are between six and eight feet in length. Some people claim to have seen Zambezi sharks at the junction. Other, more regular, visitors include tarpon and one species of sea bream. Indeed, on this visit to the Lundi I was to catch a sea bream, which I gutted and salted and later presented to the museum.

Using a bubble-float half filled with water—which enabled him to cast right across the pool—John Davey had five bream flopping on the bank by the time young John Fynnes-Clinton and I joined him to fish for our breakfast. Within half an hour we had more than enough fish for our purpose. I don't think that either Shadrek or Josiah had ever had a fried-fish breakfast of the likes we all enjoyed that morning.

Chapter 13

The next several days were marked by a very leisurely approach to our task. We fished often and had crisp fried-bream fillets with our eggs every breakfast and served them as snacks with our beers in the evenings. That first evening I shot a young warthog, which kept our three-legged iron stock-pot full. We lamented the fact that we had not brought along a shotgun or a .22 rifle, for guinea fowl sported all around us everywhere we went.

We talked a lot—and walked a lot, looking for suitable elephant bulls to shoot. Early on the second afternoon we came across a number of big bulls out on the open plains of Tamboharta. Among them was a large tusker carrying some sixty pounds of ivory a side. He was good enough for Shadrek.

"OK," I said to Shadrek. "You take this one, and I'll back you up. The next one will be mine."

I was keen to witness the great Shadrek in action—and I was to be disappointed.

Shadrek clearly had no fear of elephants, for his approach was direct, bold, and without any outward sign of apprehension. He tested the wind by breaking off dry grass leaves and casting them into the air, or by picking up the crumbling soil, powdering it between his fingertips, and watching which way the dust traveled in the air currents as it spilled to the ground. But he failed to close the final gap as I believe all good elephant hunters should. Instead, at a range of about forty yards he stopped and fired a single shot into the elephant's side, low down behind the shoulder. He declined to place second and third shots into the beast as it ran away, although he could have done so.

The elephant ran off—fast, furiously, and silently. Letting a wounded elephant run out of range without doing something about it was just too much for my soul to bear. Agitated as hell, I let the animal run for fifty yards, then brought it down in full flight with a bullet angled into its brain. The bullet passed through the neck and entered the head at the back of the skull. The big bull crashed to the ground amid tall grass.

Shadrek looked at me askance. Our eyes locked for a second. Then he turned away silently to watch the other elephant flee across the flood plain and disappear into the tree line beyond.

"That was a good shot," Shadrek said, not shy about the compliment. "Josiah and Chauke told me you were good with elephant."

I nodded, acknowledging the compliment. Then I asked: "Why didn't you shoot it again when you had the opportunity?"

"There was no need," Shadrek said calmly and confidently. "My bullet was in the animal's heart. It would have fallen down dead before it reached the trees." He smiled at me in the sure knowledge that I understood what he was talking about.

We had different hunting styles, and we each knew that both were effective. I had perfected the brain shot, which Shadrek never used. He had perfected the heart shot, which I rarely used. He shot only one bull elephant at a time, so one shot to the heart was all he needed to achieve his purpose. I often shot out whole herds of elephants, so I needed the brain shot, for I had to be quite sure each elephant was dead before I moved on to the next one.

We were different. We were both good in our own right, and I was humbled by the quiet understanding that Shadrek brought into the equation. My initial disappointment turned quickly to respect, and I was shamed by my earlier arrogance. I quickly saw that Shadrek had understood the difference between us long before my own comprehension dawned, and that fact seemed to level the playing field. He knew that

I had conjured up a contest in the hunting we had begun, and he had quietly put me in my place.

We took many photographs of Shadrek and the elephant, and of Shadrek and me on the elephant. We also took many other photographs to record every aspect of our short hunting trip together. All I wanted was something to remind me of our time together, for I already had a vague notion that one day I might need those photographs to write up Shadrek's story. Not many months later, however, those same photographs were to become an important factor in Shadrek's fortunes.

I shot *my* elephant the very next day. It was not nearly as big a bull as Shadrek's. Indeed, it was hardly worth killing for its ivory, but it was good enough for my purpose. I had by then abandoned the hunting competition and had no wish to outclass Shadrek again. In fact, I felt ashamed at ever having had the gall to conjure up the one-upmanship in the first place.

We again found a group of elephants out in the open grassland of Tamboharta. Shadrek looked them over and screwed up his nose. Nothing in the herd interested him. But at that stage I was impatient to get the task over and done with because I had started to record Shadrek's story—and to me that was now far more important an objective.

I approached very close to an elephant—perhaps closer than was prudent—and dropped the bull with a single bullet through its temple. It collapsed where it had been standing.

That hunt was something of an anticlimax. Both Shadrek and I had shot enough elephants to be unimpressed by the killing of yet another one. But it did demonstrate to Shadrek again the efficacy of the brain shot. This was important because at that time we were still labouring the point that we could make a lot of money out of poaching elephants. We had already discussed in some detail the proposition that I would do the shooting—with Josiah at my side—and Shadrek would do the marketing of the illegal ivory.

Back in camp that night we sat around the log fire sipping beers from dumpy brown bottles and chewing on kudu biltong that John Davey had brought along. That was one good thing about the Rhodesian lowveld—everyone always had access to good biltong. We had eaten much earlier, before the sun had set, for we did not want to use our paraffin lamps in the night. A paraffin pressure lamp would have been a beacon for any terrorist group that might pass by. In those days we were forever conscious of the fact that we were fighting a bitter war. And in the junction area of the Gonarezhou, we were particularly aware that the enemy's safe haven, the Mozambique border, was not ten miles away, just across the now-much-depleted Sabi River.

During those first days of our camp together, Shadrek and I struck up a unique friendship. He still had no idea that I was a senior officer in the Department of National Parks and Wildlife Management, or that I had spent many long years trying to apprehend him when I was the game warden-in-charge of the Gonarezhou. To him I was just another soldier, and my camouflage fatigues and my camo-painted automatic rifle were proof enough of that fact. Even Josiah, whom I had personally arrested and sent to jail not too many years earlier, still failed to recognize me. So I was truly incognito, and my cover held.

Shadrek fascinated me, for much of his character was contradictory. Despite his often wise and quiet inner self, he was a total extrovert and a rabid egotist—in short, a show off. When we took pictures of him on the elephant, we had to ask him to stop posing every time we lifted the camera. So it was a simple matter to get him to start talking about himself.

I had come unprepared to record all that he told me, but I did have a small notebook in my pack that allowed me to write down the outline of his personal history. When he understood that I had a genuine interest in his life story and might one day write a book about him, Shadrek opened up to me completely. For hours each day we sat in the shade on the riverbank, him talking and me writing. Below us, Josiah and the two white Johns fished away the hours.

On the night of my own elephant kill, after again belabouring the point that we could make a lot of money out of poaching elephants, I decided the time was right to expose Shadrek to our real purpose. It was a touchy subject that had to be handled with great care. We had come a long way to get Shadrek to share a camp with us on the Lundi, and I knew I could blow all our hard work if my approach were insensitive.

It was with some trepidation, therefore, that I reached for my pack jacket, which lay on the ground behind me. I dragged it across the ground toward the campfire. Everyone sat on their camp chairs around the fire, silently watching my every move and wondering what was about to happen.

I rummaged inside the pockets and found my diminutive travel light. Then I withdrew my wallet and extracted a photograph from one of its sleeves. I switched on the light and handed both the torch and the photograph to Shadrek.

The photograph was a blurred black-and-white of Shadrek himself, an extract from the photo that Charles Mackie had retrieved during his raid on Shadrek's Madjwisanga village in 1969, nine long years before. The whole photograph had shown three men, the middle one being Shadrek. The picture I now handed to Shadrek was a blowup of his own image only.

He looked at the photograph in the torch light. Slowly he raised his eyes to meet mine. "*Ghauh!*" he exclaimed gutturally. "Where did you get this?"

"Johannesburg," I lied.

"Johannesburg?" He looked back at the photograph, examining it carefully.

Shadrek was looking at a photograph that was out of context. Had he seen the complete picture, he would have known it was the one that had been stolen from his village by Charles Mackie. He would have known, too, that I was somehow linked to that raid on his home. That knowledge would have made what was to come much more difficult. I watched Shadrek's reaction and waited, patiently but apprehensively.

Josiah moved to look over Shadrek's shoulder. "*Ghauh!*" He, too, exclaimed his surprise. He looked back at me with some consternation. I saw distrust in his eyes for the first time. Josiah was no fool. He suddenly realized that this caper was a lot deeper than he had ever imagined.

"How did you get this?" Shadrek asked cautiously, gesturing with the photograph.

"From the South African Security Police on the mines," I lied again. I was treading on thin ice because I had no idea in which group of gold mines Shadrek had worked, so my answer was vague and open.

Shadrek nodded. He recognized the leather jacket he was wearing in the photograph, and the dark porkpie hat. "When?"

Shadrek was no fool, either. He had now put together the facts as he recognized them in the picture. He knew when he had owned that leather jacket and porkpie hat. He was testing me. One lie now and all would be lost.

"I obtained the picture in 1974," I responded, careful with my words. "But I was told that it was even then an old picture. The Security Police told me it had been taken several years before—maybe in 1966 or 1967. They weren't sure."

"Nineteen sixty-seven," Shadrek confirmed. "It must have been taken in 1967. I had that jacket and that hat when I worked for Rand Mines in 1967."

I smiled. The tension was easing. "You were quite good looking as a young man, Shadrek. You must have been one hell of an attraction with the Jo'burg girls." I stretched out my hand and retrieved first the photograph and then the torch, both of which I returned to my pack. When they were safely stored away, I heaved an internal sigh of relief.

The first hurdle was behind me.

John Davey and John Fynnes-Clinton never said a word. They watched the proceedings with both interest and concern, for they both knew that the future of Operation Poacher hung on every word uttered between Shadrek and myself. One wrong word, one wrong answer to a pointed question, and I'd blow the gaff.

Shadrek remained silent as he watched me store away the photo.

When I sat up straight in my chair again, he asked: "Why? Why did you go to Johannesburg to get a photograph of me?"

"Nineteen seventy-four was the year FRELIMO took over from the Portuguese in Mozambique," I responded. Now I was on safer ground. I had rehearsed this argument time and time again. I had my routine fully sorted out in my mind, but I still had to choose my words carefully. "It was obvious," I plowed ahead slowly, "that once they had power in their hands, FRELIMO would allow ZANLA to operate all along the border with Rhodesia." All these facts were based on the absolute truth.

"So?"

"So I knew that we would soon be needing friends in Mozambique," I answered seriously. "Friends like you."

"Friends like me?" Shadrek looked perplexed.

I nodded. "I work for army intelligence," I said. It was only partly a lie, for I did sometimes work for the Rhodesian Intelligence Corps. "And I have regular contact with the police Special Branch—like Mr. Davey here." John Davey said nothing but looked at Shadrek and nodded his head in confirmation.

"I knew all about Shadrek the great elephant poacher in the Gonarezhou. I also knew that you were a good capitalist because you shot elephants to sell their tusks. And I knew that you would not like working under communist FRELIMO."

Shadrek laughed out loud, bouncing his head up and down vigorously. "Sure. Sure!" he confirmed that fact emphatically.

I had to smile at that. I could feel the tension easing. "I also knew that FRELIMO would not like you crossing the border into Rhodesia to hunt elephants. That would have made you a security risk."

"True. True!" Shadrek was seemingly beginning to enjoy himself. Everybody was beginning to relax.

"Then I heard that the great Shadrek was being forced to work like a garden boy in the FRELIMO mealie fields every week, digging out the weeds with a *badza* like a woman." I was taking a chance. I had heard that *all* Mozambican citizens were required to work in the FRELIMO fields for one day in every week. I had merely assumed that Shadrek would not have been an exception.

I looked at Shadrek carefully as he slowly shook his head. "Every Thursday," he confirmed. "Every Thursday." I breathed a sigh of relief when his statement contradicted his silent head movements. "My day is Thursday."

"So I said to myself, *Shadrek won't like that!* Then I knew it was time to bring you on board."

Shadrek looked at me without understanding."Bring me on board?"

I smiled and nodded my head. "Yes, Shadrek. It is time you began living like a man again. It is time you started working for me."

"I don't understand," he responded. "I thought you asked me to come here to talk about us working *together*—you shooting the elephants and me selling the ivory?"

"Where and how are you going to sell the ivory, Shadrek?"

"I don't know yet," he responded honestly. "But I'll find a way."

"Shadrek," I said, looking at him with an open, honest face. "In the past you sold your ivory to the Portuguese and to the South African helicopter crews who serviced the Cabora Bassa hydroelectric power lines. The Portuguese are now gone. So are the South African helicopters. I'll hazard a guess and say that you have lost all your ivory markets!"

"*Ghaauuu!*" Josiah exclaimed at my bold revelations, and he sat there looking at me, shaking his head. His guttural pronouncement clearly implied: *How do you know these things?* He had forgotten that it was he himself who had told me about the South African helicopters.

"That is true," Shadrek answered honestly. "But how do you know these things?"

I ignored his question and continued with the thrust of my argument: "You really joined me here, Shadrek, because you are bored with your life under FRELIMO. You are a capitalist, not a communist. And, like me, you love elephants and you love hunting elephants."

Shadrek nodded his head in agreement.

"You came here because you wanted to hunt elephants again and because you were curious. You wanted to know more about me and why I had invited you to hunt with me. It was not because you wanted the ivory."

"There was another reason," Shadrek said. "I have nothing left in Mozambique—which is something I'll tell you all about later."

"*Haaiee!*" Josiah intervened at that point, shaking his head and looking at me in amazement. "You knew all along about Shadrek?"

I smiled and nodded my head. "Yes, Josiah. I knew all about Shadrek, and I knew all about you and John Chauke, too."

"You used us!" It was a statement, not a question.

"Yes, Josiah, I used you and John Chauke. I used you to get to Shadrek."

"*Mscabenga!*" Scoundrel! But Josiah was clearly now more amused than annoyed. "And shooting those elephants with *Baas* Don? And giving us the ivory?"

"It was all part of the plan, Josiah. All part of the plan."

"And the elephants we have shot on this trip?"

"Them, too," I answered honestly. "And you can take their ivory, too, if you want to, Josiah," I added. "It is all part of the price we've had to pay to get to Shadrek."

"And just why do you want to get to me?" Shadrek asked.

"Because I need you to help us in Mozambique," I answered honestly.

"You want me to help you fight ZANLA?"

"Yes and no," I responded. "I want you to help me get information about ZANLA bases in Mozambique."

"No fighting?"

"No fighting."

"And why should I do that?"

"Because I can make you a very rich man if you help me."

"How?"

I reached over to my pack jacket again. This time I extracted a wad of wall posters, each about three feet square. One by one I unfolded them and laid them out on the ground in front of Shadrek. "You can look at these again tomorrow in the daylight," I said. I played the light beam from my little torch over them as I unfolded each poster. John Fynnes-Clinton stoked up the fire with some new logs to increase the light from the flickering flames.

"What are these?" Shadrek asked in puzzlement.

"These are reward posters that the Rhodesian government is displaying on the walls of all government buildings throughout the country," I explained. "You will see them, for example, on the walls of every post office." I handed the little torch to Shadrek.

"What he says is true," Josiah said to Shadrek. Both he and Shadrek began examining every detail on the posters. Josiah, of course, was exposed to this kind of Rhodesian propaganda every time he visited a post office or police station, and every time he had tribal business to address in the local district commissioner's office or veterinary department station. The posters were displayed openly everywhere. Shadrek, however, may have seen them but once—on the day he had visited John Davey in his police station office. It was doubtful, however, that he had had the opportunity to examine them or to understand their importance.

The posters showed pictures of land mines and grenades, of AK-47 assault rifles and RPD machine guns, and of RPG rocket launchers. And against each picture was a reward price. One thousand Rhodesian dollars was offered for information leading to the recovery of a land mine, $500 for an AK-47 or RPD machine gun, and so on. Any information leading to the recovery of any of these arms-of-war would bring the informant the prescribed reward. Confidentiality and anonymity were guaranteed—a good thing, because if an informant's name were ever released he would be found the next day with his throat cut.

Other posters offered even greater rewards for information leading to the arrest or killing of terrorists. A ZANLA sectorial commander or officer of higher rank was worth $5,000. Detachment commanders were worth half that amount. Ordinary rank-and-file cadres were worth $1,000. Again, the poster guaranteed confidentiality and anonymity.

Shadrek examined the posters with obvious interest and questioned Josiah about many things, asking him for explanations time and time again. I let the two of them talk, for Josiah was clearly doing a better job at convincing Shadrek than I could ever have done. Finally Shadrek looked up at me and asked: "What does all this mean?"

"It means that you can make far more money helping us to hunt down ZANLA in Mozambique than you ever could by hunting elephants."

"You want me to *hunt* ZANLA for you?"

"No! All I want is that you get information for me that will help us—the Rhodesian security forces—to hunt down ZANLA." I explained the difference. "I don't want you to fight ZANLA in any way. That is the last thing I want you to do."

"And what is there in it for me?"

"You can see the reward structure yourself," I said, gesturing to the posters. "I am authorized to tell you that you will receive rewards according to the results we achieve. For every terrorist we kill or capture as a result of the information we receive from you, you will receive the appropriate reward. Five thousand dollars for a sectorial commander—captured or killed. Two thousand five hundred dollars for a detachment commander. One thousand dollars for an ordinary soldier. One thousand for a land mine. Five hundred for an AK-47. And so on."

Shadrek thought deeply about these prospects. I remained silent to let all the implications sink in.

"And I won't have to fight?"

"Not at all. I will need you to locate for us the ZANLA bases in the Rio Save area of Mozambique. The Rhodesian army and air force will then attack those bases and you will be rewarded according to how many terrorists we kill or capture and how much of their arms we recover."

A slow smile crept over Shadrek's face, and I knew we had him firmly in our net—and that my instincts about him had been correct. His eyes were already turning over like the dollar signs on a cash register. "And Josiah? What will he get out of it? And John Chauke?"

I suddenly understood why so many of Shadrek's cronies stood by him so stoically. He truly was a fine leader of men. He was just as concerned about his people's interests as he was about his own. Again I felt humbled. I had given no serious thought to what Josiah would get out of the effort. I knew he was getting a stipend from John Davey's SB coffers, but beyond that I had not enrolled him as a participant in the bigger picture at all. Now that we had reached this stage of the game, Josiah's purpose, in my book, was largely over. Clearly that was not to be—Shadrek was not about to let me discard either of his stalwarts so easily.

John Davey, seeing my hesitancy, jumped in to fill the gap. "Josiah will get a proportion of the reward monies," the policeman assured Shadrek. "So will John Chauke—if he recovers from his snakebite. Both are part of our team."

"How much of a proportion?" Shadrek asked pointedly.

"Enough," John stated stoically. He was not about to let Shadrek intimidate him. "We can discuss their remuneration later—once you, Shadrek, have agreed to help us."

Shadrek nodded and smiled. John Davey, too, could draw a hard bargain.

"I am authorized to tell you, too, Shadrek," I continued, "that you will be given amnesty for all your past poaching activities. And should you serve us well, the Rhodesian government will give you a farm in Rhodesia to live on. You will then be able to leave Mozambique and FRELIMO, and you can come and live with us in Rhodesia."

Shadrek beamed. That information clearly clinched the deal, and I felt the tension suddenly lift from all our shoulders.

"Hah! You are a *skellum* (rascal)," Josiah said, settling down again into his camp chair across the fire from me. He looked me in the eye and smiled in a conspiratorial fashion through the heat waves above the simmering coals, shaking his head all the time.

"What do the black people call you?" Shadrek asked suddenly.

I dared not reveal my real African honour name, Mahohboh, to our visitors. My good friend Volker Grellmann in Namibia had conjured up the name's gentile interpretation as meaning: "The great slayer of elephants." Literally translated, however, it implies: "He who leaves elephant in heaps behind him." Every black man in the district had once known the name Mahohboh, even if they had not known me personally. Mahohboh had been the big chief game warden of the Gonarezhou National Park. Both Shadrek and Josiah would have known that much.

So, for the sake of my continued anonymity with my newfound black friends, I poached the African honour name given to my late good friend Rupert Fothergill. Rupert had been the game warden-in-charge of Operation Noah—the rescue effort mounted in the late 1950s to save thousands of game animals marooned on the islands of the then newly formed Lake Kariba. He was also an experienced government elephant hunter.

"They call me Katasohroh," I answered.

"Katasohroh!" Shadrek repeated the name, seeming to turn it round and round in his mind. "He who shoots in the head." He looked at me and smiled in a friendly manner. "It is a good name," he opined, "and very apt."

"Anyone for coffee?" John Davey asked, changing the subject. He got up and withdrew a bottle of brandy from his patrol box. "And I think we all need a nightcap before we go to bed." A *dop* of brandy in his coffee was a Davey necessity—the last thing before the policeman went to bed.

The reined-in tension over the last several minutes had gotten to me badly. I suddenly felt exhausted and knew that tonight I would sleep like a log.

John winked at me and said under his breath: "I think a little celebration is called for, too, don't you?" I smiled and nodded silently. Shadrek was now definitely *on board!*

PART II

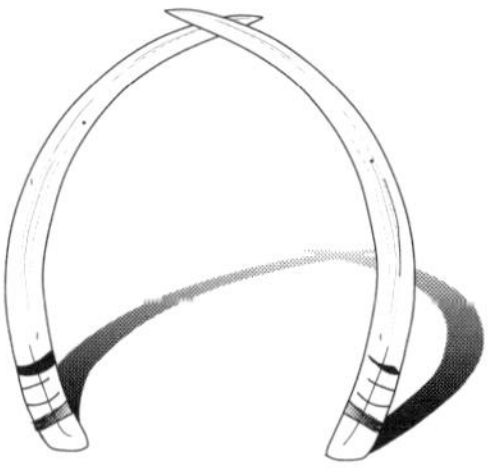

Chapter 14

When Nandi, mother of King Chaka of the Zulus, died in October of 1827, Chaka declined into a state of depressed melancholia. He decreed that no crops be grown for a whole year and that the milk produced by cows be poured upon the earth. People who showed no sadness over Nandi's death were viciously killed. Women who gave birth during that fatal year were killed, together with their babies and their husbands, and any woman who became pregnant met a similar fate.

Individuals took advantage of the situation by reporting their enemies for showing no remorse, and the king ordered their immediate execution. This period in Zulu history is known as the *fecane*—the time of Chaka's mourning for his mother, the period of Chaka's madness. It brought great dissension within the Zulu nation and eventually led to Chaka's assassination. But it was only one of many excesses that marked Chaka's rule and drove several of his military generals to flee the country.

The Zulu people live in Zululand in the province of Natal, South Africa, now known as KwaZulu-Natal. It is a long, long way from the Gonarezhou region, but the *fecane* had repercussions that were to rock south-central Africa until the end of the millennium.

The three most notable generals to escape Chaka's wrath during the 1820s were Mzilaghazi—who escaped from Zululand and founded the Matabele nation in Rhodesia (present-day Zimbabwe); Zwangendaba—who founded the Ngoni people of Malawi; and Soshangane—who was founder of the Shangaan people.

Bvekenya country was Shangaan country, for Soshangane's people settled in the general area of the Limpopo River straddling

South Africa's far north, Rhodesia's southeastern corner, and adjacent territories in Mozambique.

Ngungunyane was one of Soshangane's generals, and he battled the Portuguese as far north as Espungabera. In their bid to contain Ngungunyane, the Portuguese enrolled the help of the chieftains of the Ndau tribe. Together the Portuguese and the Ndau defeated Ngungunyane, who was killed in one of the battles. This brought a halt to Soshangane's northward advance and forced him to settle his people on the Limpopo River.

Later the Shangaans insinuated themselves northward to the Rio Save, where they intermingled with the resident Ndau people, the mixture becoming known as the Mhlengwe. More often than not, however, the Mhlengwe people called themselves Shangaans, which is why all the black peoples in the Gonarezhou region were incorrectly called Shangaans by the Rhodesian administration.

As a gesture of thanks for Ngungunyane's defeat, the Portuguese appointed the most senior of the Ndau chiefs, Garawa, as the paramount chief of all the Ndaus. This status remained in force from the 1830s to the early 1900s, when the international boundary commission defined the border between Southern Rhodesia and Mozambique. The new boundary split the Ndau people between the two countries, and the paramount chief found himself living inside Southern Rhodesia.

The Portuguese tried to get the chief to move his kraal into Mozambique, since the majority of the Ndau people lived in Portuguese-controlled territory, but the old chief declined. He preferred to live on the rich alluvial plains of the middle Sabi valley in British-ruled Southern Rhodesia rather than in the barren mountains of Mozambique. So the Portuguese appointed his younger brother, who lived on the Portuguese side of the border, as the new paramount chief of the Ndau tribe in Mozambique. He, too, was called Garawa. It was the name of the family dynasty. So there came into being two paramount chieftaincies of the Ndau people, one in Rhodesia and one in Mozambique.

The new Mozambican paramount chief Garawa (Mugonda Kumbuya) presided over many more people than did his Rhodesian brother. He was

Shadrek's grandfather, and he lived a long life lasting into the 1950s. After his death, Shadrek's father, Muteruko Kumbuya, became the new paramount chief.

At first Shadrek's family lived in Garawa province at the Mugonda kraal, for this was the centre of the old paramountcy. In 1956, however, the Portuguese asked Muteruko to move his kraal from Garawa to Madjwisanga on the Rio Save. At that time the Rio Save area was becoming a focus for European hunting and prospecting parties, and the administration wanted someone there they could trust to control and supervise the growing European interest.

The new chief visited the Rio Save area and liked it. So it was that the seat of the paramountcy moved to Madjwisanga. Once he had settled down on the Rio Save, Muteruko never entertained any regrets about leaving Garawa.

Shadrek's father was a great hunter, and he discovered game aplenty in his new domain. There he killed many elephants using the .303 rifle he had been given by the Portuguese authorities. The soil was fertile, the rainfall fair, and the climate conducive to agriculture, so his people grew magnificent crops on the rich alluvial soils along the banks of the great river.

Muteruko had nine wives, the most senior of which was Mdhlayi Mave, Shadrek's mother. Altogether, the chief had thirty-five children. Shadrek was the second oldest, and he was, therefore, second in line to the paramount chieftaincy. His elder brother, Mishek, was born also to Mave. At birth Shadrek was named Gocalves Muteruko Kumbuya.

Shadrek had no connection whatsoever with Bvekenya Barnard. He was not a coloured but a purebred Ndau—and one of noble birth to boot. Just where the myth began that he was Bvekenya's grandson I have no idea, but it led us all off on a wild goose chase. Shadrek himself had nothing to do with it because he was totally unaware of the story.

Shadrek's family was associated with mining in many ways. Mishek, for example, had worked at the Shabani asbestos mines in central Rhodesia for more than twenty years at the time Shadrek told me his life's story in 1978. At that time, too, Shadrek's uncle, Josepha Mugonda Kumbuya—one of his father's younger brothers—had been working at Ntabazimbi iron mine in South Africa since long before Shadrek was born. There, Shadrek told me proudly, Josepha had been "chief of the underground mineworkers." He lived, he said, in a mine location called Skopplaas.

Josepha visited Garawa before the family moved to Madjwisanga, and there he met young Shadrek, then age fourteen, for the first time. Shadrek was dazzled by the tales his uncle told him, and he pleaded with Josepha to take him back to South Africa when he returned.

Shadrek's father raised no objection, so Josepha took his young nephew to Espungabera to get travel documents for the boy to visit South Africa. However, the *chefe de posto* there said: "No. The lad will learn *tsotsi* ways if he goes to Johannesburg." In other words, he suspected that Shadrek would become criminally inclined like many other local young black people had after experiencing the "city of gold."

Shadrek returned to Garawa very dejected. Josepha and his father discussed the matter, and Muteruko told Josepha to take the boy into South Africa without papers—for Josepha had said it could be done.

They traveled by bus the one hundred miles from Massangena on the Rio Save to the South African Limpopo border post at Pafuri. There, Josepha led Shadrek through the bush and across the border into South Africa. Josepha left his young nephew with an English-speaking white family at Pafuri and returned the same night to Mozambique. The next day, Josepha crossed through the border post, presenting his papers in the proper fashion. He came to see young Shadrek the next day before leaving for Johannesburg, alone, by bus.

Josepha had just been appointed a recruiting officer for Rand Mines in Johannesburg. He had left the iron-mining town of Ntabazimbi and was in the process of moving to Johannesburg. He wanted to set up his family in their new accommodations before introducing his country-bumpkin nephew to the delights and hazards of the city lights.

All Shadrek could remember about the white man at Pafuri—Josepha's friend—was that his name was Jimmie. He could not remember the man's surname, but he did know that Jimmie and Josepha had had a longstanding relationship. At one time Jimmie had worked at Thabazimbi with Josepha and had been responsible for promoting him to the position of underground boss-boy. Now Josepha was to receive the Shangaan recruits that Jimmie would send to him for the gold mines, and they would both profit by the arrangement.

Shadrek believed that Jimmie was a medical doctor because he physically examined all the new mine recruits that came out of Mozambique, accepting those who were fit and rejecting those who were not. He may or may not have been a medical doctor, but he certainly had something to do with the recruiting procedures at the border post.

Shadrek told me that he had been very proud of his uncle when he realized that, in addition to his own native language, Josepha could speak three European languages fluently—English, Afrikaans, and Portuguese.

Whether all these facts are true or not is really unimportant. I believe Shadrek tried to tell me what he believed to be true. His own experiences were undoubtedly factual, but for the rest, he was relating to me information he had been told by Josepha many years before when Shadrek first came to South Africa at age fourteen.

Shadrek stayed with Jimmie and his family for two weeks. The house servant was a Shangaan woman called Sara, and Shadrek shared her quarters, located in the garden at the back of the house. During those two weeks Shadrek played with Jimmie's son, who was his own age, and his daughter, who was a little younger.

Then the whole family, including Sara, went by car to Johannesburg, where they met Josepha. Shadrek stayed with Josepha and his South African-born wife in their home in a black Johannesburg township. Shortly after Shadrek's arrival Josepha took him to his mine's Germiston office. This was where incoming foreign labourers were processed by government officials and mine authorities. There Shadrek was given a temporary schoolboy resident's permit, with Josepha listed as his guardian.

It was in Johannesburg that young Gocalves Muteruko Kumbuya was given the name Shadrek. It happened in this manner: Every morning he attended school and every afternoon he worked in a white man's kitchen to earn some pocket money. Josepha arranged the afternoon job for him with *Baas* Piet, an underground manager for the same mine in which Josepha worked. Shadrek earned two pounds a month for his afternoons in the kitchen, and he described *Baas* Piet as a good *baas*. *Baas* Piet, Shadrek recalls, had a wife and six children. But *Baas* Piet could not pronounce Shadrek's Portuguese names, so he called him Shadrek.

Not long afterward, Shadrek met a young Zulu girl at the school he attended. She was called Tandayana. Her father, Sigauke Simbine, worked in one of the gold mines of the Witwatersrand. The Simbine family lived just three houses away from Shadrek. At first the two teenagers had a strong but distant mutual attraction, and for many weeks their respective school friends passed letters between the two. Finally they met outside the school grounds.

As they came to know each other better, Shadrek and Tandayana planned nocturnal meetings.The first time this happened, Tandayana left the window of her bedroom open and at ten o'clock young Shadrek climbed inside the Simbine house. There the two lovers, both virgins, made love until one in the morning. Many other such meetings took place.

A year later young Shadrek, hopelessly in love, went to his uncle and told him he wanted to marry Tandayana Sigauke Simbine. Josepha approached Tandayana's father and the two men discussed the matter, realizing that the youngsters' relationship had reached a serious point. Simbine told Josepha that he wanted a Zulu man as his daughter's husband, and he removed Tandayana from the school. The two young lovers never saw each other again.

Johannesburg was the young Ndau's first experience of school and of the big world outside rural Mozambique. Nevertheless, he excelled in the classroom, and during the three years he stayed in Johannesburg he passed his Grade Two examinations. The teaching was in Afrikaans.

Then Josepha received a letter from Shadrek's father, who requested that the boy be sent home. Josepha waited until some mine workers from the Rio Save were due to return home, and he sent young Shadrek back with them, knowing that the miners would make sure the paramount chief's son returned home safely.

The homebound miners set off from Johannesburg laden with goods for their homes and families—clothes and blankets and suitcases full of fascinating trinkets. Shadrek himself carried a suitcase packed with clothes for Muteruko from Josepha. He also carried a handbag stuffed full with his schoolbooks. Shadrek and the miners traveled together in a steam locomotive as far north as Mtuzi Siding, where they took a bus to Pafuri.

At Pafuri, Shadrek went to visit Jimmie and his family. Jimmie could not conceive of Josepha's letting his young nephew return home on his own, so he accused Shadrek of running away. He insisted that Shadrek stay with him at Pafuri until he had time to telephone Josepha to confirm that it was all right to send Shadrek on his way. By the time Josepha gave Jimmie the assurances he needed, however, the mine workers had continued their journey to Massangena on the Rio Save.

It must be said at this point that shortly after Shadrek had passed through Pafuri en route to Johannesburg three years before, Jimmie had received word that Shadrek's father had gotten into serious trouble with his Portuguese masters for letting young Shadrek proceed to South Africa without a passport. So now, rather than just letting Shadrek cross the border and go on his merry way, Jimmie went to see the Portuguese officials on the Mozambican side of Pafuri. There he explained the details of Shadrek's story and his lack of a passport.

By doing this, Jimmie unknowingly added grist to the Portuguese government's mill. Had he allowed the boy to sneak across the border and continue his journey, perhaps Shadrek's life story would have been very different. Jimmie interfered with the best of intentions, but in the process he opened an old wound and alerted the Portuguese authorities to Shadrek's imminent return.

While he waited for the Pafuri official to clarify the situation with his government superiors, Shadrek stayed with Jimmie. As before, he lived with Sara in the servant's quarters at the back of Jimmie's garden. Now, however, he was seventeen years old and had had a taste of making love to a woman. This time he and Sara whiled away the long hours of darkness making love.

Finally, Shadrek was summoned to see the Portuguese *chefe de posto* at Pafuri, and Jimmie saw him through all the necessary formalities. The Portuguese official gave Shadrek a dressing down, but because he was the son of the paramount chief Garawa, he arranged temporary papers to get Shadrek through the border without a passport. Eventually Shadrek was placed on a bus that took him back to Massangena.

When the bus arrived, the local police were waiting and immediately placed handcuffs about his wrists. Shadrek did not even have the opportunity to send a message to his nearby parents, let alone see them. Instead, the police sent him on the very next bus to Espungabera, where the selfsame *chefe de posto* who had originally refused Shadrek his travel documents was waiting for him. He was not impressed with the young man's defiance of his orders three years previously. He expected better behaviour from Gocalves Muteruko Kumbuya, son of the greatest paramount chief in the land.

The official refused to send Shadrek home. Instead he sent the boy to nearby Msawu, where officials put him into a boarding school. They informed him that he would remain there until he had attained an education up to the level of Standard Seven, after which he would be press-ganged into the Portuguese army.

Shortly thereafter, Shadrek's father and mother came to see him. Because the elder Muteruko was a big chief in Mozambique, he was given a furnished house on the school grounds to stay in. Shadrek stayed in that house with his parents for ten days. At the end of his parents' stay, the baggage that Shadrek had brought with him from South Africa was surrendered to him; and only then was he able to give his parents the presents Josepha had sent.

During the chief's stay at the school, Portuguese officials questioned him as to why he had sent Shadrek to South Africa without a passport—particularly after the *chefe de posto* had specifically refused the boy travel documents. Muteruko stated that Shadrek had absconded in the night, and so his son's movements had been beyond his control. The officials finally accepted this story but informed the chief that, as a punishment, Shadrek would be conscripted into the army after he had finished his schooling.

Msawu was a very large school, with students attending their lessons in three shifts: from 6 AM to 10 AM; 10 AM to 2 PM; and 4 PM to 8 PM. They followed similar shifts in tending the school's croplands—maize and coffee. In every respect Msawu was a military school; both boy and girl students received training for an eventual career in the army.

Shadrek, in fact, enjoyed Msawu. With the pocket money he had earned in South Africa, he was able to enjoy a few extra luxuries that his companions could not afford. He would buy sweets and Coca-Colas at the school tuck-shop for his new girlfriend, Maria; for Maria's girlfriend, Saramoyo; and for Shadrek's closest male friend, Phineas Sithole. The girls, when confronted about fraternization with the boys, called them their "uncles" to sidestep a confrontation with the teachers.

In the fields the boys mixed with the girls, and Shadrek and Maria would find ways to slip away together to make love in the nearby bushes. A common ruse was to plead diarrhea with their respective supervisors and return to the barracks after having had their rendezvous on the way home.

All was not work at Msawu. The school boasted a very active football team, and Shadrek became one of its champions. He was called "Posta" because he kicked the ball very hard, and when he ran in to make a kick the crowd would shout "*Pohhhhstaaaaa!*"

After passing his Standard Four examinations, Shadrek received permission to go home to see his parents. It was the first time in four years that he had been allowed to leave the school, and the first time in seven years that he had been home. But home was not the same home he had left. When he had accompanied Josepha to South Africa, he had departed from the old family seat at Mugonda village in the Garawa district, which was in the mountains. Now he was going home to Madjwisanga on the Rio Save. It was a place that he had never seen.

Chapter 15

Shadrek stayed with his parents at Madjwisanga for a month before heading back to Msawu to start his last three years at the military school. He traveled on foot to Garawa with a party of five older men. In reality, however, he was very much alone, for he fought with his conscience all the way. He had no wish to spend six years in the army fighting FRELIMO in the far north of the country. At the same time, he did not want to cause his parents any more grief with the Portuguese authorities. In the end, his survival instincts got the better of him.

Shadrek left the group at Garawa and crossed the border into Rhodesia. Asking directions along the way, he proceeded to the kraal of the Rhodesian paramount chief Garawa, his great uncle. There he stayed a few days with his relatives, then walked to Chipinga, more than a hundred miles to the north. He was told that black people could always find work there on the white man's farms.

Just across the border from Chipinga was the Portuguese post of Espungabera. Shadrek was quite sure that the *chefe de posto* there would have had apoplexy had he known how close Shadrek was. That particular Portuguese was a tyrant. He could not abide anyone who disobeyed his orders and thereby made a fool of his authority. Shadrek had done just that and had paid the price. Now, for a while at least, Shadrek was free of the man's Draconian rule.

Shadrek obtained work with an Afrikaans farmer whom the local natives called Maqwah. The farm was in the Mount Selinda area, and it, too, was called Maqwah. The farmer was married and had six children.

His eldest son, Rosey, who lived and worked on the farm, was himself married with one child.

Shadrek worked for Maqwah as a policeboy for six months. Armed with a spear and a knobkerrie, his job was to keep the farm labourers in order. It was also his responsibility to see that no strange people came onto the farm to do mischief.

At the end of every month, Shadrek went with Rosey to Nyanyadzi in the middle Sabi valley, west of Chipinga's Chimanimani Mountains. There they hunted impala. At first Shadrek used Rosey's shotgun while Rosey used a .22 Hornet rifle. Shadrek claims that he and Rosey shot the same number of impala, but that Rosey claimed all the kills as his own to impress his father. They made biltong out of the meat, and Shadrek made a little extra pocket money by selling the leftover scraps. On their last hunting trip to Nyanyadzi, Rosey taught Shadrek to use the .22 Hornet, and he shot a kudu and an impala with it.

Shadrek tired of the routine of his policeman's job, but he persevered because he was afraid to return home. Then he heard that the official at Espungabera had been recalled to Portugal. Immediately he asked to be released so that he could return to Madjwisanga. Rosey, however, did not want Shadrek to leave. He told him that if he stayed he would give him a good job. Shadrek was adamant. He wanted to return home.

Finally, when it became apparent that Maqwah himself would not let him leave the farm, Shadrek absconded. Alone, he traveled southward on footpaths through the hills, keeping the Sabi River valley faraway to his right.

He received hospitality at the villages he passed, on the strength of his claim to be the Muteruko's son and the grandnephew of the Rhodesian paramount chief Garawa. He turned to the east only when he reached Mahenya's. Within a matter of hours he was back home with his parents at Madjwisanga. The journey had taken him five days.

The transfer of the Espungabera tyrant made Shadrek's position in Mozambique a lot easier, for the new *chefe de posto* had no interest in continuing Shadrek's heavy punishment. Nor did he see any need to force him to return to the military school at Msawu. In fact, at first he had no interest in Shadrek at all.

Shadrek liked Madjwisanga much better than his old home at Garawa, for he was able to fully express there the hunter that was inside him. There was a lot of game on the Rio Save, and the new official had given his father a 10x75mm rifle by the new official. The Portuguese administration gave most native chiefs shotguns, but Muteruko was an exception. He knew how to use a rifle, and he was required to shoot crop-raiding elephants and buffaloes on the Rio Save on behalf of the government. All the ivory from the crop raiders shot by Muteruko went to the new *chefe de posto.*

Shadrek was now able to put to good use Rosey's recent rifle instruction. He showed his father that he knew how to handle a rifle and could aim it properly. He was not put off by the tremendous recoil of the 10x75mm, though the heavy kick of the big weapon had surprised him.

Consequently, Muteruko allowed Shadrek to take the weapon to hunt a buffalo that had been raiding some nearby crops. He told Shadrek, however, that should he wound the buffalo, under no circumstances was he to follow it up. A wounded buffalo, his father said, was far too dangerous an animal to hunt, and such animals were best left alone to die in the bush.

Not one but five buffalo bulls had been responsible for the crop raiding, and Shadrek had no problem tracking them. He found them lying up in some thick *mzimbiti* ironwoods south of the river, but they bounced to their feet at his approach.

Shadrek's heart was beating fast as he threw himself to the ground behind some thick cover. He had heard many terrible stories about how dangerous buffalo were and how they attacked people without provocation. He did not know what to expect. He lifted his head and peered through the top leaves of the bush he was hiding behind. The buffaloes had not run away and were not about to charge. He relaxed a little.

The five big bulls were all standing with their heads held high, peering down their noses in his direction. One of them was pawing the ground and snorting loudly and sibilantly through its nostrils. This meant that the buffalo had seen Shadrek's movement behind the bush and was worried. The young hunter was intimidated by the bull's menacing behaviour. The fact that none of the group had run away, however, meant that they were not sure what had caused the disturbance. But they were clearly ready to run off at a moment's notice.

None of the bulls presented a good enough target, so he waited. *If they run off,* Shadrek thought, *so be it.* If they did not, he knew that sooner or later one of them would change its position.

When Shadrek told me this story, I asked him how he knew that one of the buffaloes would change its position. That, after all, was his first buffalo hunt. He shrugged and stated: "All animals will change position if you wait long enough." He was right, of course—or they will run away. But I also believe that Shadrek's sense of the animals' behaviour

was largely instinctive. During our brief sojourn together, I learned that Shadrek was truly a "natural" hunter.

The buffaloes became more and more agitated, since they could not confirm if the movement they had seen was a threat or not. They were clearly making ready to run away. Then one turned sideways, presenting Shadrek with a perfect shot to the area behind its shoulder. The range was no more than fifty yards.

Shadrek shuffled himself into a comfortable, prone position behind his bush and pushed the rifle barrel through the branches, propping the front end in a convenient fork. He was quivering with buck fever as he lined up the iron sights. The front sight wavered around the fold at the back of the buffalo's shoulder. He could not keep his aim steady, but he squeezed off the shot anyway.

The recoil was vicious. That one shot taught Shadrek that firing such a heavy-calibre rifle from a prone position was just not a good idea. His shoulder hurt and his cheek felt bruised, and it took many days for the soreness to dissipate.

The buffalo dropped where it had been standing. The bullet had hit too far forward but had broken both shoulders below the blades. It was not an ideal result, but it did the trick. The rest of the herd stampeded off into the brush and left their fallen comrade to its fate.

The mortally wounded buffalo took over an hour to die. It lay where Shadrek had dropped it, bellowing and moaning as the life slowly ebbed out of it. The young hunter sat down behind his bush, watching and waiting until there was no further sound or movement from the stricken beast. That buffalo kill was Shadrek's introduction to big-game hunting.

Whenever Muteruko went hunting, young Shadrek went along. He begged his father to allow him to shoot an elephant. The big pachyderms held a huge fascination for the young Ndau, and it was his greatest ambition to kill one of them. His father, however, refused, saying that he was too young to tackle such large and dangerous quarry.

One day, however, Shadrek and his father were on the tracks of buffalo when they came across the spoor of an elephant cow herd.

Muteruko was reluctant to abandon the buffalo, but Shadrek's pleading changed his mind. They could, after all, come back to find the buffalo if the elephant hunt proved futile.

Shadrek was armed with his father's old Tower musket, an ancient muzzleloader that his father had taught him to use. Muteruko was armed with the 10x75mm. They started on the elephant tracks at 7 AM and found the animals in the Ruwanje thicket at 9 AM. The herd was screaming and trumpeting in the thick bush ahead of them, and there was the sound of breaking branches. Muteruko climbed a tree and discovered that there were a couple of mature bulls in the herd. The one he selected to shoot was at the edge of the herd on the downwind side. This meant he did not have to venture into the herd to shoot it.

Cow herds, his father told him, were called *mabfangwe.* Bull herds were called *mujindi kambako. Kambako* herds, Muteruko told Shadrek, were normally silent. At that stage of his career Shadrek had a lot to learn, and like a sponge he soaked up every snippet of information his father told him.

Muteruko climbed down from the tree and made an approach to the bull of his choice. At a range of about fifty yards, he climbed onto a fallen log to elevate himself above the understory bushes. Shadrek remained on the ground, his ancient muzzleloader at the ready.

Muteruko's bullet smashed the elephant's near shoulder, and it fell to the ground screaming. The herd ran off in a cloud of dust, breaking branches and tumbling rocks down the hillside. The stricken bull maintained its loud trumpeting and screaming for some time. It was not going to die quickly. Muteruko knew that he would have to put a stop to the noise or it would encourage the other elephants to return. He urged Shadrek to follow him, and they ran in close to the downed elephant. Standing in front of the struggling beast, Muteruko gave Shadrek the 10x75mm and instructed his son how to dispatch the elephant with a frontal brain shot. Shadrek killed the beast with one bullet.

The two then began to chop out the tusks, Shadrek's first such experience. As always in Africa, it did not take long for the local people to come filtering in through the bush to collect the meat. By then Shadrek and his father had removed the tusks, and Muteruko gave instructions to have the ivory carried back to his village. He also press-ganged several of the villagers to bring the meat from one entire leg to his village—the rest he made available to the people.

Leaving Shadrek with the 10x75mm to supervise the cutting of the family's meat, Muteruko returned to his village with the muzzleloader. The attraction at the village was Mave's recent brew of fine sorghum beer.

At 4 PM, with most of the meat now stripped from the carcass, Shadrek heard elephant screaming and trumpeting in the distance. His father was by then back home drinking his wife's excellent home brew, so Shadrek had no one to gainsay his actions. He and an old man named Tauzan Simango decided to go see the elephants they had heard. Tauzan was a veteran hunter himself, having shot many buffaloes with a muzzleloader, so he was the right companion for Shadrek to have on his quest. The elephants had gone by the time the two hunters reached the place where they had heard them screaming, so they took up the tracks and followed. It did not take them long to find the animals. They were spread out, feeding heavily, and not really moving at all.

The sight of feeding elephants and the feel of a heavy weapon in his hands were just too much of a temptation for Shadrek. His delivering of the *coup de grâce* to his father's elephant earlier that day had whetted his appetite. Without hesitation, he made up his mind to kill his first elephant. Tauzan made no attempt to dissuade him.

There were no big bulls in the herd, so Shadrek stalked a large and very old cow sporting long, thin tusks that nearly reached the ground. He had never seen an elephant cow with such long ivories, and that made her a good substitute for a mature bull. For the second time that day, Shadrek felt buck fever shaking his body, but he was resolute: Today he was going to shoot his first elephant. Nothing was going to stop him.

There were elephants all around him. To get within a reasonable range of his target, he would have to insinuate himself into the herd without being detected. He had no idea what the rest of the herd would do when he fired, but that did not deter him. He had made up his mind and was determined to follow through.

Standing with his legs braced wide to offset the heavy recoil, he aimed two-thirds of the way down the big cow's body to a point behind its shoulder and pulled the trigger. The recoil kicked him backward, and he saw a puff of dust erupt from the cow's hide at the point where he had aimed. He felt confident that the projectile had flown true. He loaded another round into the breech, and then crouched in the bushes to hide from the alarmed cows cruising around him in search of the human intruder.

The cow Shadrek had shot rushed off silently into the bushes. Strangely, none of the others followed her. Instead they paraded through the undergrowth, looking for the source of the disturbance—all the time growling aggressively as they gathered their youngsters closer about them.

Shadrek experienced great fear for the minute or so that it took for the elephants to understand that they would not quickly find their adversary. He watched apprehensively as the cows raised their trunks to test the wind, and he resisted his great desire to get up and run. People had told Shadrek of the terrible rage of elephant cows that knew they were being hunted, so it took all his courage to sit tight and wait out the drama. Despite his uncertainty and fear, he told me later, the adrenaline rush of those few haunting moments was exhilarating and intoxicating. This was the very essence of the elephant-hunting experience.

Suddenly one of the big cows turned and, with a heavy growl, ran off into the bush. Her string of calves took off after her in hot pursuit. The other cows followed her lead, and in an instant all were gone.

Shadrek stood up, shaking from the encounter but relieved that the elephants had all run off. He stood in the haze of dust they had left behind and listened as their noisy departure faded away.

Tauzan appeared from the bushes behind Shadrek. "Where did you hit it?" he asked.

"Behind the shoulder," Shadrek said, lifting his arm and pointing under his armpit.

"Did you see where it ran off?"

"Over there," Shadrek said, walking off toward where he had last seen the stricken elephant. He did not know if he had killed the animal, but he did know that he had hit it well.

They found the spoor but no blood. Tauzan was skeptical but said nothing. The spoor was easy to follow, as the elephant had run straight and hard, off on its own to the south, the direction the rest of the herd had run. One hundred yards farther on they came across the elephant, lying dead under some trees. It had collapsed in full flight and ended up propped upright on its brisket, its front legs splayed out on either side of its body, pointing backward, and its trunk flailed forward. It looked like a large collapsed tripod.

Shadrek was jubilant, shouting loudly and dancing for joy. He and Tauzan examined the animal in great detail, and Shadrek showed Tauzan just where his bullet had struck. It had been a perfect heart shot.

The two men then returned to the bull that Muteruko had shot. A mass of humanity still crawled all over the carcass, which was now much reduced in size. The families were lined up behind the men doing the cutting, passing back every bit of meat that the head of the family could carve loose. At the end of each line, people were cutting the large lumps of coarse red meat into long ropes as thick as a man's wrist.

Shadrek told the people about the elephant cow he had shot and instructed them not to touch that carcass, for he wanted to show the animal to his father. Despite Shadrek's tender years, this instruction was almost a royal command since he was an influential member of the paramount chieftaincy.

Shadrek ran most of the way home, arriving exhausted but triumphant just after sunset. He told his parents of the killing of his first elephant. His mother was ecstatic. She ululated so loudly that everyone in the village must have heard her. His father was equally pleased with his son's accomplishment. It was Shadrek's dream, Muteruko knew, to shoot an elephant. Though Shadrek had not received permission to shoot the elephant, Muteruko was not about to diminish his son's achievement by issuing a rebuke.

The next day the whole family and all the villagers went to see Shadrek's first elephant. Shadrek reenacted the hunt for them, telling his mother and father of his courage and his hunting prowess. After removing the tusks, the villagers stripped the carcass and carried the meat back to the village. There they cut it into ropes and smoked and dried it over a period of six days.

When the meat was cured, the family and villagers carried it, on their heads or strapped to bicycles, to faraway Garawa. There they crossed the border and presented the meat to the Rhodesian paramount chief Garawa—who just happened to be another Mugonda Kumbuya. Even the Mozambican Ndaus recognized the supremacy of the Rhodesian paramountcy.

Shadrek's father had recently abdicated the Mozambican paramount chieftainship. The new Portuguese *chefe de posto* at Espungabera had demanded that he return to the old seat of the paramountcy at Garawa because it was more convenient for the Portuguese administration. Muteruko had refused, stating his wish to remain on the Rio Save, where he was now happily settled. His younger brother, Zhumile Kumbuya, had been appointed the new paramount chief in his stead.

Muteruko had received a new commission in recognition of his long and faithful service to the Portuguese. He was to retain his chief's status and from thence forward was to be called Chief Madjwisanga of the Rio Save.

Mugonda Kumbuya summoned his cousin Zhumile and his family to his kraal in Rhodesia—nobody in those days bothered about crossing the border illegally. There the whole extended family feasted and danced and drank great quantities of beer for many days to celebrate Shadrek's first elephant. The special occasion was fitting for a young man who was so close to the throne of the Garawa Ndaus. At the same time, Mugonda dispatched carriers to take a large quantity of the dried meat to Zhumile's village at Garawa in Mozambique.

At the end of the feast, Mugonda hosted a ceremony that marked Shadrek's coming of age. At that time he was still called by his juvenile name, Gocalves. Now he was given his two adult names: Mundete—a war cry much the same as the Zulu royal salute, Bayete—and Mukwame, which meant "sheath of spears." He was also presented with a Ndau ceremonial spear called Mkonto-ka-loh-Mudzwiti, literally meaning "the *chefe de posto's* spear." The Ndau people, however, preferred to think of it as "the spear of the warrior who killed Ngungunyane."

Neither then nor during the period we worked together did Shadrek drink the strong African home brew we Europeans called Kaffir beer. But he did drink the white man's bottled beer, as well as *mlala* palm wine (*uchema*) and *marula* beer (*ankanyi*). At the ceremony Shadrek drank only *mahgehwu*, a sweet drink made from maizemeal that did not make him drunk.

The presenting of the ceremonial spear was the pinnacle of the ceremony, and it was conducted in the dead of night. Shadrek was required to sit on a small stool, with the spear stuck in the ground in front of him. Strings of beads and special *mutis* (medicines) were hung around his neck, and a cape made from a leopard's skin (back) and a lion's skin (front) was set upon his shoulders, while the elders sat around him drinking beer. The dried nerves from inside the elephant's tusks were then cooked by Mugonda's wives, and Shadrek was required to eat a major part of the nerves. Since that time no elephant meat ever passed between Shadrek's lips. The two paramount chiefs sat on either side of Shadrek and counseled him into the early hours of the morning, repeatedly instructing him to fear nothing in this life.

After the five days of celebration, all the meat from Shadrek's elephant had been consumed and all the beer Mugonda's wives had made had been drunk. Those realities, more than anything else, brought the festivities to an end.

Shadrek's family returned to Madjwisanga, and he and his father immediately went on a buffalo hunt together. Shadrek shot two buffaloes with Muteruko's 10x75mm. The family then had its own private ceremony to mark Shadrek's coming of age. He was then twenty-one years old. During this ceremony Muteruko gave Shadrek the 10x75mm rifle and told him he could now use the weapon to shoot whatever he wanted without his father's permission.

The next day Shadrek went out on what he considered his first real elephant hunt. Over the next several days he shot four elephant bulls—each with a single shot to the body—and brought the tusks and a large quantity of meat back to his father as a special present. Thus began Shadrek's elephant-hunting career.

This is the photograph that Charles Mackie recovered from Shadrek's Madjwisanga village in Mozambique in 1969. Notice the centre-block portrait of Shadrek. The author showed Shadrek this portrait, claiming he had obtained Shadrek's picture from security at the Rand Mines in Johannesburg. Separated from the greater picture, this centre-block picture confused Shadrek and helped to get him to cooperate with the author.

The abandoned ruins of the Assembly of God Church at Marhumbini Mission after John Osborne had scavenged all the usable building materials—seen through what was once a classroom window. Game scout Tivani is shown in a Department of National Parks and Wildlife Management uniform. The broken-down mopane trees are the result of an invasion of elephant bulls.

Another view of the ruined classrooms with Tivani looking up at the rafters. It was in this classroom that Shadrek met his wife-to-be, Tabita.

This elephant bull is shoulder-deep in a wet-season pan (pond) located in the ecologically rich Sabi-Lundi junction area. He is eating water grasses that grow in abundance there during the rains.

Shadrek and the author with the smaller elephant killed by the author.

This belligerent black rhino cow was looking for trouble. Upon release, she tried to get at the Land Rover shown here, and later she repeatedly gored holes through the radiator of a tourist's Land Rover..

Josiah Chiranzwa and Shadrek (on right).

This black rhino has just emerged from the crate that transported it to the Gonarezhou. It is about to enter the holding pen before being released. John Osborne sits on the poles on the left. The author is standing on the crate in the background.

Shadrek and the author.

John Fynnes-Clinton and Shadrek on right. John is wearing a Rhodesian army camouflage shirt and army chest webbing, which has four canvas pouches to carry four loaded magazines for the FN military rifle. Tragically, shortly after we returned to Salisbury from this phase of the operation, John was involved in a motorcar accident that left him a paraplegic. Note how Shadrek, the great extrovert, is posing for the camera with two rifles.

Shadrek and the hollow baobab tree located just north of Tamboharta Pan. This was his retreat during times of inclement weather. He often slept inside this arboreal "cave," and he stockpiled his ivory here until he could transport it across the border into Mozambique.

Shadrek on the author's elephant.

A bull elephant in a clearing in the Sabi-Lundi junction forest. Notice how thick the forest was in that part of the Gonarezhou. Elephants are preferential grazers, eating very little other than lush grasses and annual forbs during the wet season. During the dry season they eat woody plants.

Shadrek and the author. Note the author's Rhodesian military camouflage shirt, the importance of which is explained in the text. This was the elephant Shadrek shot at Tamboharta Pan, Gonarezhou, with the author.

Kambaku, one of the bigger elephant bulls in the Gonarezhou during the author's service there. Such big bulls were Shadrek's prime targets. Fortunately, Kambaku lived a solitary life in the thickets of the Sibonja Hills, so he was outside of Shadrek's regular hunting territory, which was near the Sabi-Lundi River junction.

Shadrek loved to be p
graphed and was quit
pared to pose all day lo
front of a camera.

The western end of the spectacular Chilojo Cliffs. They rise six hundred feet and run for five miles along the southern bank of the Lundi River—seen here at the height of the dry season.

You can see forever from the tip of the Chilojo Cliffs. This photograph was taken in the middle section at the point where the cliffs start to move away from the riverbank. Looking north, this view takes in the lower foothills of the Chihunja range and the dry bed of the Lundi River (center foreground).

Charles Mackie (circa 1970) crossing the flooded Lundi River, at Fishans, on the shoulders of a black game scout. During the rains, the lower Lundi was not negotiable by vehicle. Note the Chilojo Cliffs in the background.

Shadrek, Josiah, and John Davey with the ivory from the elephant that Shadrek and the author shot together in the Gonarezhou. John Davey was the author's police Special Branch "controller."

These tusks and the .375 H&H Magnum rifle were recovered by game ranger Glen Tatham from John Chauke's Mahenya village. They all belonged to Shadrek.

Top & bottom: The author shot 160 hippos in the Lundi River in 1973. These brain-shot hippos would sink to the bottom, and after about twenty minutes, their bodies would rise to the surface. The carcasses were dragged to the bank, where they were transported to a central point for processing. Shadrek told the author that many hippos moved downriver into the Rio Save in Mozambique after this culling exercise.

A large bull elephant photographed by the author in the Chihunja Hills.

John Osborne (circa 1972), in National Parks uniform, skinning an elephant with one black game scout (in uniform) and three black labourers.

Even some of the Gonarezhou's cow elephant carried magnificent ivory. The matched tusks of this culled cow each measured 5 feet, 7 inches and weighed 28 pounds—although they were no thicker than the author's wrist. This is the heaviest ivory that the author ever recovered from a cow.

The author and Shadrek (on right), the two biggest mscabengas *in the country. This photo was one of many that Shadrek asked to be taken. He never saw any of the photos.*

Game Ranger Mike Bromwich stands next to his Land Rover, which, while standing unattended on a quiet road in the game reserve, was visited by an elephant cow herd and seriously damaged. This will give readers some idea of the belligerent nature of the Gonarezhou elephants.

In Africa, generally, when elephants are downed by a hunter's bullet, it does not take long for every villager in the vicinity to reach the carcass and begin vying with each other for the meat. Literally within minutes of an elephant kill at Mahenya's, the first of the villagers were on the scene. This means they started on the hunter's trail from the very beginning of the hunt, following the human tracks just as avidly as the trackers followed those of the elephant. And when the hunter gives his permission for the people to start cutting, they swarm around the carcass like bees about a honey pot.

The author's faithful Bushman tracker, Ben, was not allowed to participate in Operation Poacher because Josiah Chiranzwa and John Chauke undoubtedly would have recognized him, and that would have blown the author's cover. Here Ben stands next to an elephant cow that was part of the cull that Shadrek watched from Kundani Hill—the pimple in the background. As this photograph was taken, Shadrek was sitting near the top of Kundani watching the culling process.

Shadrek and his sixty-pounder.

Kambaku was by no means the only big tusker in the Gonarezhou. He was also not necessarily the biggest. In an effort to save these big elephant bulls from Shadrek, the biggest tuskers were darted and fitted with radio collars, which enabled the department to find them from the air and keep tabs on their welfare. This bull was collared in the Mabalauta Sector.

In the beginning we had
idea what Shadrek looked li
Legend had it that he was t
grandson of the great Bveken
Barnard, which meant he wou
be one-quarter European.
reality, we had no idea wheth
he was big or small, short or ta
fat or thin, fair-skinned or dar
skinned. We could have employ
the man and not known who
was we had engaged.

Chapter 16

About this time (circa 1960), Shadrek had a yen to visit Shabani and see his elder brother, Mishek, who had not been home for many years. Shadrek had last seen Mishek so long ago that he had forgotten what his brother looked like. So Shadrek went to Marhumbini Mission to meet a white man named Blake Thompson. He was the resident recruiter of black labourers for the Rhodesian Shabani asbestos mines. And Marhumbini was one of the main sources of black mine workers.

Years earlier the mine management had constructed a well-formed road that ran from the west right through the Gonarezhou. The road's purpose was to transport new recruits to the Shabani Mines, and it terminated right at the mission station. To this day that track is still called the Shabani Road.

The Shangaans who lived in the vicinity of Marhumbini all thought that Blake Thompson was a little mad because he gave the black children one penny for every dead tsetse fly they brought him. It was Blake Thompson's belief that if enough youngsters caught flies, the menace could be brought under control at minimal cost. In those days the tsetse infested the Gonarezhou. It was eradicated only in the middle 1960s, when the Rhodesian Tsetse Department sprayed the land with DDT.

Chief Muteruko of Madjwisanga, previously the paramount chief of the Ndau nation, was well known at Marhumbini. He was also a renowned and respected hunter. And something of Shadrek's reputation as a promising young hunter—a chip off the old block had preceded him to Marhumbini. Upon hearing that Shadrek was Muteruko's son and knowing a little about Shadrek's elephant-hunting exploits, Blake Thompson gave Shadrek his old

.303 rifle and asked him to shoot an impala for him. This was several years before the Gonarezhou was declared a game reserve, let alone a national park. Even then, however, game abounded in the area.

Shadrek went off into the bush with a man named Mufundjwa Mek Chauke. Mek was John Chauke's father, but at that time Shadrek and John Chauke had not yet met. John Chauke was away most of the time in those days, working on the gold mines of the South African Witwatersrand. Mek told Shadrek to shoot more than one impala so that everyone could get a bit of meat. Shadrek shot six.

Blake Thompson, together with four Shangaan helpers, accompanied Shadrek back to where he and Mek had hung up the impala carcasses. They brought back only those parts of the six carcasses that Blake Thompson wanted for himself. Shadrek and Mek and the four black labourers were allowed to take whatever meat was left. Blake Thompson gave Shadrek four Rhodesian pounds for his work that day.

Strangely, throughout my later discussions with Shadrek, he always referred to his finances in terms of "pounds"—even when speaking of his monies in Mozambique, where the currency was escudos. This may have been because he grew up understanding the relative values of South African pounds and Rhodesian pounds, which were comparable in those days. Also, the local black men from the Rio Save area of Mozambique went on regular pilgrimages to the gold mines of South Africa and to Rhodesia's Shabani asbestos mines, where they were all paid in "pounds."

Even after South Africa changed its currency to the rand (and one of the old South African pounds became two rands) and when Rhodesia converted to dollars (and one of the old Rhodesian pounds equaled two dollars), the local black people still referred to both currencies as pounds. Thus thirty rands and thirty dollars were still both referred to as fifteen pounds. How the people equated this terminology with Portuguese escudos I have no idea. Since Shadrek always referred to his finances in terms of pounds, I have not tried to change his terminology.

Shadrek was unable to go to Shabani. When he arrived at Marhumbini, the single lorry that transported the mine recruits had recently left. Blake

Thompson explained to Shadrek that the lorry would return only when there were enough new recruits to warrant the journey.

Then a bus came to Marhumbini—a very rare event—and Blake Thompson boarded it to visit Shabani himself. Others at Marhumbini had pre-booked their passage and there was no room for Shadrek. So the bus left without him.

Shadrek was at loose ends. He was still determined to visit Shabani but had no means of getting there. So he went to the white man who was head of the Assembly of God mission station at Marhumbini, the Reverend Coopman. He explained his predicament and asked the churchman for a job. He said he needed to earn some money and did not want to waste his time while waiting for transport.

The Marhumbini mission station in those days was not a thriving metropolis but a rather ramshackle outfit with one or two creature comforts installed for the two white men who lived there. The missionary himself lived on the very top of the Marhumbini hill in a small, cement-blocked house roofed with asbestos and painted a yellowish cream. It commanded a fantastic view overlooking the Sabi-Lundi River junction, and from the veranda you could see the wide Tamboharta flood plain between the two rivers. Below the house stretched the Marhumbini flood plain, and upstream the picturesque Chilojo Cliffs. Behind the house lay the vast expanse of Mozambique and the Rio Save, and the panoramic view from the kitchen seemed to stretch to eternity.

Drinking water on top of the hill came from rain that ran off the house's roof and collected via a gutter system and a series of pipes. It was stored in large cement-lined cisterns dug into the ground next to the house. A galvanized iron water tank was under the eaves.

Halfway down the hill was the cottage in which Blake Thompson lived. At the bottom of the hill, on the edge of the flood plain flats, was a thatched church and a small row of school classrooms. Scattered about behind the church were a number of dilapidated thatched huts that housed those itinerant black men who came to Marhumbini in search of work at Shabani.

Reverend Coopman offered Shadrek a job in which he would help make bricks for a planned extension of the mission station. Shadrek readily accepted, and he also arranged to attend the mission school to continue his education. His routine involved going to classes in the morning and making bricks in the afternoon.

Although Shadrek had already passed his Standard Four examination at Msawu, the language there had been Portuguese. In South Africa, the teaching medium had been Afrikaans. Now he was going to be taught in English. He had picked up only a smattering of English along the way, because in South Africa Shadrek had moved in circles where Afrikaans was the local lingua franca. Because his command of English was poor, Reverend Coopman was obliged to drop him one class. Learning anew in a foreign language did not worry Shadrek unduly because he enjoyed learning about new things—even new languages.

In school Shadrek met John Chauke's sister, Tabita, and that changed his plans about going to Shabani. He was immediately attracted to the young woman, and from the glances he received from her, he understood the attraction was mutual. Day in and day out they bumped into each other inside the classroom and out of it—for Marhumbini was a tiny mission station not much bigger than Shadrek's home village.

Shadrek and Tabita contrived to sit next to each other in the classroom, and prior to a school test one day, Shadrek slipped a note into one of her books. When she opened the book and found the note, she secreted the folded piece of paper in her knickers. She had no intention of letting the teacher find the note and take it from her.

There were no toilets in the school, so after they had written their tests, the girls dispersed into the nearby bush to relieve themselves, and there Tabita read Shadrek's note. In the note Shadrek told Tabita that he loved her and that they should marry. She quickly wrote a reply, suggesting that Shadrek visit her in her nearby home village.

The mission station served the many Mozambican families who had moved to Marhumbini and to the lower Lundi flood plains to live. They had done so in order to claim token Rhodesian residency because it was government policy that Shabani mines employ no foreign labour. Everybody knew full well that the mine recruits from Marhumbini really all hailed from Mozambique. But appearances were all that mattered. In fact, the whole Marhumbini complex was a setup to subvert Rhodesian laws, and none of the many black people living there were Rhodesian Africans. They were all Mozambican Shangaans, Ndaus, and mixtures of the two called Mhlengwes. Even the mission had been built on dubious credentials.

Tabita's father, Mufundjwa Mek Chauke, was a Mozambican Ndau who technically fell under the hegemony of Shadrek's father. Now that he lived on the Rhodesian side of the border, however, Mek was considered by the people of Marhumbini to be the local chief, and he adopted all the trimmings of chieftainship.

Unlike Shadrek, who lived in one of the huts near the church, Tabita lived at home in her father's village on the banks of the Lundi River, some five miles from the mission station. She walked from her village to school and back again every day.

Having received Tabita's positive response, Shadrek told her that on Saturday he would dig up some worms on the river's edge and go fishing in the big pool below her father's village. He told her to meet him there midmorning. They met as arranged and discussed Shadrek's proposal. Tabita agreed that they should marry, but first she wanted to pass her Standard Two examinations at the end of the year. Their courtship, in fact, lasted two years. In 1962 Shadrek went to his father at Madjwisanga and told him he wanted to marry Tabita.

Muteruko summoned Mufundjwa Mek Chauke to his kraal at Madjwisanga, where the two fathers conferred. Because the proposed marriage would involve the son and the daughter of two chiefs, there were no insurmountable obstacles. Muteruko gave Mek sixty-seven Rhodesian pounds as Tabita's bride price, after getting assurances from his son that he would work to pay the money back.

During his two years at Marhumbini, Shadrek went home periodically to Madjwisanga (and during those visits he shot six elephants and four buffaloes). When Tabita had completed her education, Shadrek collected his bride from Mek's village and took her home to Madjwisanga. There Shadrek's parents prepared a huge feast for the new couple. Muteruko went out and shot three buffaloes and Shadrek bought fifteen cases of Portuguese *cerveja* (Laurentina beer) and four cases of Coca-Cola. Mave, Shadrek's mother, made a huge quantity of home-brewed beer. The feast lasted several days.

It was not the Ndau custom, Shadrek told me, for young people who seriously planned to marry to sleep with each other before the ceremony. Shadrek solemnly swore to me that, despite his several previous sexual encounters, he never made love to her or even petted her over the two years he waited to claim Tabita as his wife. Nor did he sleep with any other woman. Just why Shadrek insisted on telling me these intimate details I shall never know. Perhaps he was proud of his self-imposed celibacy.

The young couple settled into their new home at Madjwisanga, and Shadrek took up the job of killing elephants and other game. He sold the meat and ivory to any and all willing buyers. In this way he quickly accumulated the money he needed to pay his father back the *lobolo* (bride price).

During the next two years, Shadrek shot fifteen elephant bulls inside Mozambique and sold all the tusks to Portuguese store owners. He did not have to look for buyers for his ivory, he told me, for the Portuguese came to Madjwisanga to collect it. He named all the store owners who bought ivory from him: Kamali Jhivana from Madjwisanga store near his home; Vuyeka and Parasi from Malvernia; Francisco from Lourenço Marques; and Juse' Moyana from Chimoio and Vila Pery. Shadrek claimed to have received between fifteen and twenty pounds for each tusk.

In 1966–67, Shadrek was plagued by a sudden urge to return to South Africa. He wanted to work underground in the mines, as had his uncle, Josepha. Miners returning home from the Witwatersrand all spoke of their high wages and the high life they had led in Johannesburg. Besides, I think that life as a married man at Madjwisanga—even with the elephant hunting—had become a bit commonplace for the always-adventurous Shadrek.

He traveled to Espungabera and met the new *chefe de posto,* Alberto. Alberto knew all about Shadrek and tried to dissuade him from going back to South Africa. He offered Shadrek good prices for his ivory if he would concentrate on shooting elephant for him alone. He also promised to give Shadrek complete immunity from prosecution inside Mozambique and said he would supply him with all the weapons and ammunition that he would need.

Shadrek said he would think about it—but first he wanted to go to South Africa. The official, realizing the young man was dead set on going to the mines, provided Shadrek with a passport—but when he handed it over, he asked Shadrek to think deeply about his offer. "When you come back from Johannesburg," Alberto said, "come to see me and we will talk some more."

Shadrek caught a bus to Pafuri, where he was officially recruited to the Rand Gold Mines by Dr. Jimmie, who gave him R2,000 to purchase food en route. Shadrek inquired about Sara, but Jimmie told him she had left his employ. From Pafuri, Shadrek traveled by bus with other recruits to Mtuzi railway siding, and then headed southward to Pretoria on an old steam locomotive. At Pretoria railway station they took a bus to the Rand Mines' Pretoria recruiting office. Three busloads of Mozambican recruits arrived at the same time, and they all had to be examined by another doctor.

A European mine official, whom Shadrek called *Baas* Jan, then questioned each of the men to ascertain his experience and to determine what kind of work he could perform best. During the interview, one of the Shangaans from the Rio Save area told *Baas* Jan that Shadrek was a great elephant hunter. Jan then took Shadrek to one side and questioned him about his hunting experience. Satisfied that Shadrek did indeed know how to shoot elephant, he told Shadrek that he had a very special job for him.

All the other recruits were allocated specific jobs—mostly as underground workers—and told on which mine they would be working. They left that same afternoon by bus. Shadrek remained at the recruiting office for most of the afternoon until a taxi arrived to pick him up. The taxi took him to *Baas* Jan's house in the suburb of Pretoria North. There he was shown to a vacant room in the servants' quarters at the back of the garden. Jan worked for the Rand Mines Security Branch. He arrived home just after five that evening and tasked Shadrek to work in his garden.

Shadrek protested, saying that he had come to work underground in the mines. *Baas* Jan told him that the garden-boy job was only temporary—he had a much better job lined up and Shadrek just had to be a little patient. *Baas* Jan did not say what that special job was going to be.

Shadrek worked for a whole month in the garden. Then, one Saturday, two white men came to the house with *Baas* Jan, and they took Shadrek to a quiet farm out in the bush. There they sat around a campfire in the evening, drank beer together, and spoke about hunting elephant.

They told Shadrek that his special job was going to be shooting elephant for the three white men—not legally but *ku-injonja* (to steal them). The place they would take him, they said, was the Sangwe area south of the Gonarezhou in Rhodesia. The price they would pay him would depend upon the results he produced. Would Shadrek agree to this kind of employment? Yes, he said, he would *njonja* elephant for them. They then broke camp to return to their various homes in Pretoria.

Shadrek continued to work as *Baas* Jan's garden boy for another month, all the while chafing at not being able to fulfill his ambition to work in the mines. Then one day Jan came home and told him that he would start the elephant-hunting job the next day.

Baas Jan and Shadrek traveled by Land Rover to the farm they had visited and there met one of the two white men Shadrek had been introduced to on their previous visit. He was a South African Air Force helicopter pilot, and together the three of them worked out a plan of action. Shadrek would not hunt in the Sangwe area of Rhodesia after all but in South Africa's Kruger National Park.

Jan and Shadrek returned to Pretoria, where Jan purchased a number of things for Shadrek's expedition: an ax, a hunting knife, a black shirt, a pair of black slacks, and black tennis shoes. Back at the house, Jan picked up a rifle in a leather case and some boxes of ammunition. Finally they returned to the farm.

That evening Shadrek was allowed to inspect the rifle, a brand-new .375 magnum. He felt its weight and balance and brought it up to his shoulder. It fitted him well, and he was pleased with the weapon.

Very early the next day, a South African Air Force helicopter arrived at the farm, piloted by the man they had met the previous day. He, *Baas* Jan, and Shadrek took off and flew for about two hours. Shadrek knew they were traveling east because the rising sun was positioned on the right front quarter of the machine. Finally, the helicopter began circling and then descended rapidly.

Jan pointed out some elephants in the mopane bush below, and he showed Shadrek the snaking path of a dirt road to the south of their position. Below them was a small hillock that seemed to be the only feature in a vast expanse of mopane scrub.

They landed in a grassy clearing, and Jan helped Shadrek unload his katoonda from the helicopter. Besides the rifle and two packets of ammunition, Jan had provided Shadrek with a cartridge belt containing another twenty-five rounds, a bag of mealie meal, a jerry can of water, one pot, one blanket, a bag of salt, two loaves of bread, a packet of sugar, and two bottles of concentrated orange drink. When the meagre supplies and equipment had been unloaded, the helicopter quickly rose and headed off low over the trees in a westerly direction. It was clear to Shadrek that the pilot was nervous about being spotted by people on the ground.

After the helicopter disappeared over the treetops, Shadrek looked around him at the surrounding bush. He had been dropped right in the middle of the game reserve. His instructions were to shoot as many big elephant bulls as he could find. "If you see five or six, kill them all," were the exact words *Baas* Jan had used. Shadrek recalled Jan's instruction that he should sleep in a big tree to avoid being eaten by lion. When telling me this, Shadrek smiled at the memory, but he ignored the advice. He was familiar with lion from his many encounters with them on the Rio Save. They represented no danger to the intrepid hunter.

Shadrek was much more conscious of the danger of being caught by the game reserve's antipoaching patrols. Jan had briefed him in great detail about the sophistication of Kruger National Park's administrative systems, and about the large number of tourists who used the game reserve each day. He knew, too, of the reserve's well-developed road system and that the patrols used both fixed-wing and helicopter aircraft to combat poachers.

Shadrek sought out a suitable location for his base and hid all his equipment under the trunk of a large fallen tree. Then he went hunting. Within an hour he came across the spoor of a large lone elephant bull. Inside another hour he had tracked the animal down and killed it with a single shot through the heart. The stricken beast ran only fifty yards before collapsing. Shadrek had fired his shot just before 10 AM.

Shadrek explained to me his strategy to elude being captured in Kruger National Park. The practicality and efficiency of his plan were

remarkable. He had never needed to hide from anyone on any of his previous elephant hunts. In Mozambique there had been no one in authority to apprehend him. Nobody had wanted to. Indeed, all his hunting, although carried out without a license, had been conducted aboveboard and in the full knowledge of everyone in the district. In fact, as the son of the senior Ndau chief on the Rio Save, he had had virtual carte blanche authority to shoot whatever he liked.

Shadrek created his plan of action almost on the spur of the moment, yet it was full of common sense logic. When he told me about it, I was dazzled by its simple brilliance, for it revealed why we had so much trouble trying to catch Shadrek in later years in the Gonarezhou.

Shadrek knew he was operating illegally inside Kruger National Park. *Baas* Jan had also stressed that many white game rangers and even more black game scouts were patrolling the game reserve all the time. Shadrek was well aware of the dangers facing him, so he set about minimizing his chances of being discovered.

When his first elephant collapsed that morning, Shadrek went nowhere near the carcass. Had he done so, he explained to me, he would have left tracks about the body for anyone to follow. Being a good tracker himself, he knew that human tracks around a dead elephant would be a dead giveaway that a poacher was operating in the game reserve. On the other hand, should a game ranger find the dead elephant with no human tracks around it, he would probably conclude that after being shot by a poacher the elephant had run off, only to die later. Given that scenario, immediate pursuit of the poacher was unlikely.

Shadrek also knew that his shot might have been heard by a passing patrol, causing the game scouts to focus their attention on the general area in which he was operating. A patrol might not be able to pinpoint the shot's location, but it would cause the men to scout about in the general vicinity.

So Shadrek did not chop out the tusks immediately; the sound of an ax hacking at the bone of an elephant's skull would draw any human presence within miles. Shadrek sat quietly in the shade of a tree, watching the elephant from a distance and letting the hot hours of the day pass him by. And he listened for voices and watched for movement in the bush all the time. At 4 PM he was convinced that nobody had heard the shot and nobody was coming to investigate. Having slept in the bush on hunting trips many times in the past, he knew that any game patrols in the area would by 4 PM have selected their camping place for the night. They would be gathering wood for their fire and preparing their evening meal. Game scouts patrolling on foot would not be carrying lamps!

Sometime after four o'clock Shadrek emerged from his hiding place and approached the elephant. Immediately he set about chopping out the tusks. It was dark by the time he finished, and he spent the early hours of the night cutting down saplings to cover the carcass.

Baas Jan had agreed that Shadrek would operate in the game reserve for three days only—after which the white man would pick him up by vehicle and get them both out of the game reserve as quickly as possible. So Shadrek had to reduce the chances of vultures quickly finding each carcass—many vultures flying in the sky would act as a beacon for vigilant game scouts.

Shadrek was several miles from his base camp, but he carried the tusks, one by one, back to the hillock that loomed against the midnight sky. He hid the ivory under bushes some distance from his sleeping site. It was past midnight by the time he had cooked and eaten a meal. Then he lay on the ground under his single blanket and went to sleep. A low fire smouldered away at his head.

Before the sun rose over the eastern skyline, he had already rejected two young bulls that he found in a small breeding herd. Just after sunup he found a very large lone bull and killed it with a raking shot into the body behind the rib cage. As usual, his bullet found the heart.

Again Shadrek did not approach the carcass. Instead, he sat in the shade and waited until late afternoon before starting to cut out the tusks. This he accomplished before sunset. He then covered the carcass with branches, and he opened the gut to let out the air in the distended belly, which he had not done to the first elephant. He carried the tusks one by one back to his camp and secreted them in different places under nearby bushes. It was again past midnight before he had eaten and retired to his blanket.

The next day he woke up very tired, so he rested in his makeshift camp until 8 AM. Then he went hunting. By ten o'clock he had followed the tracks of a lone bull to a pan, where he found it bathing in the water. Not waiting for the elephant to leave the water, he placed a shot into its chest. The bull stormed out of the mud and dropped dead on dry ground next to the pan. He was fed and sleeping under his blanket by one o'clock the following morning.

The next day he waited for *Baas* Jan and the helicopter pilot to arrive. It was midmorning by the time he heard the drone of the Land Rover plowing through the mopane scrub toward the small hillock. Shadrek remained in hiding and refused to answer the cooing calls the two men made. Only when he heard them use his name, and he recognized *Baas* Jan, did he reveal himself. Nevertheless, not knowing what to expect, he kept his rifle at the ready just in case their arrival was a trick to apprehend him. Despite his agreement to hunt elephants for these men, he was still ultracautious about everything he did with them.

Eventually they came together, and Shadrek shook their outstretched hands. They asked how the hunt had gone. Then they retrieved the ivory and Shadrek's gear, and loaded everything onto the back of the Land Rover. The two white men covered it all with a heavy tarpaulin and placed their own baggage on top. Finally, they tied branches behind the vehicle to obscure their tracks and journeyed back to the dirt road. Before reaching it, they cut loose the branches.

The trio passed through Numbi Gate, one of the main tourist entrances to the game reserve, without any trouble. Then they drove on a tarred road for a long way before turning off onto a dirt road that took them to a white man's farm. There they dug a deep hole in the garden behind the farmhouse and buried the six big tusks. Then they returned to Pretoria. At the end of the month, Shadrek received thirty-five pounds

for his hunting endeavours plus an additional ten pounds representing his monthly "ticket"—his garden-boy wages.

Shadrek immediately requested of *Baas* Jan an underground worker's position in one of the mines, but *Baas* Jan refused. Shadrek insisted, saying that he had come to South Africa to make lots of money working in the mines and was wasting his time as a garden boy. In response, *Baas* Jan increased his monthly stipend to fifteen pounds, and he told Shadrek that he was planning another hunting trip for him into Kruger National Park.

This time Jan and another European transported him into the game reserve by Land Rover. One of *Baas* Jan's security guards, Enoch Sithole, came along, tasked with helping Shadrek to remove the tusks of the elephants he shot. Like Shadrek, Enoch was a Ndau, and he came from a place called Chibababa in the Garawa area. *Baas* Jan dropped them off near a large baobab tree on a dirt road, one of the minor tourist routes. They made their camp not far from the road.

Over the next three days, Shadrek shot six elephant bulls using exactly the same modus operandi he had employed before, only this time he had Enoch to help him chop out and carry the tusks back to camp. On the fourth day *Baas* Jan returned, parked his vehicle under the baobab tree, and set his red emergency lights flashing. This was Shadrek's signal to come out of hiding. Jan was jubilant at Shadrek's great success.

They loaded the tusks and followed the same routine as before, passing openly through Numbi Gate and proceeding to the same farm, where they buried the tusks. Then they returned to Pretoria.

Again Shadrek began agitating for a transfer to the mines. Again *Baas* Jan refused. This time he paid Shadrek fifty pounds for his hunting success and gave him a transistor radio. It was the radio Shadrek was holding in the photograph that Charles Mackie removed from Shadrek's village in 1969. One of the two other men in the photograph was Enoch Sithole.

Baas Jan also procured a woman for Shadrek and employed her in his kitchen. Her name was Mary. "She was very good in bed," Shadrek told me with some glee. Sharing the servant's quarters with Mary placated his chagrin somewhat.

Once the novelty of having Mary as his constant bedmate had worn off, however, Shadrek again began to feel claustrophobic in what amounted to his captive position. He was a prisoner in more ways than one. *Baas* Jan held an important security position within the Rand Mines organization, and if he chose not to deploy Shadrek in the mines, there was nothing Shadrek could do about it. He also could not leave, for Bass Jan was the only person in South Africa who could issue him a written pass.

There was no more talk of Shadrek's returning to Kruger National Park. It seemed that *Baas* Jan felt they should lie low for a while. Finally, having had enough of the stalemate, Shadrek demanded that *Baas* Jan sign him off and allow him to return home. This Jan also refused to do. And since he was in possession of all of Shadrek's recruitment papers, including his passport, there was little Shadrek could do about it. Remember, this period of South Africa's history was the zenith of Verwoerdian apartheid. To be arrested as a foreign African without employment papers in that era meant immediate incarceration.

Shadrek's agitation became palpable. He was seriously contemplating fleeing and risking being picked up by the South African police. A short period in jail seemed, at that time, preferable to the monotony of working as *Baas* Jan's garden boy. Even Jan could see that something was wrong and that he would have to do something if he were to retain Shadrek's services. And he did not want to lose those services, for he had great plans for his elephant poacher.

So *Baas* Jan came up with a plan of his own. How would Shadrek like a two-week holiday at Durban, on the shores of the Indian Ocean? There were inexpensive facilities for black vacationers on the Natal North Coast. *Baas* Jan would pay for the train fare and the accommodation. Shadrek had never seen the sea, he told Jan. Yes, he said, he would appreciate a holiday by the sea.

Jan made all the arrangements, and to facilitate Shadrek's movement about South Africa he provided him with written confirmation of his employment—as a mine worker! Another certificate stated that Shadrek was on official leave of absence from his work. *Baas* Jan, however, retained Shadrek's passport.

But Shadrek had no intention of going on holiday to Durban. The papers he received from *Baas* Jan were all that he needed to facilitate his safe return to Pafuri. Once there, he sneaked across the border into Mozambique and caught a bus back to Massangena. So it was that Shadrek escaped *Baas* Jan's employment and returned home to Madjwisanga.

Chapter 17

When Shadrek returned home from South Africa he was laden with suitcases and presents for Tabita and his parents. His pockets, however, were not jangling with extra change. He was smarting because he had been unscrupulously abused by *Baas* Jan in South Africa. In his position as a senior officer in the recruiting section of the Rand Mines, the white man had held Shadrek over a barrel. Shadrek had been a virtual captive.

His agitation continued long after he returned home, and he tried to work off his frustration by hunting elephant. He soon discovered, however, that his old stamping ground, the Ruwanje Shati—the big thicket—on the sandveld south of the Rio Save, had changed drastically during his absence. The Rhodesian Tsetse Department had bulldozed many roads through the thick bush in their programme to rid the land of the tsetse fly. The once pristine and almost limitless sandveld thickets between the Rio Save and the Malvernia railway line to Lourenço Marques had been divided up into five-mile-wide strips. The whole bushveld was now crisscrossed with bulldozed lines running east-west and north-south. Every tree trunk and bush, every log and antbear hole, even the bare ground was stained white and reeked of pesticide. The elephant and the buffalo had all gone. And the land was totally silent, for even the birds had disappeared—they had either died or flown away.

Tabita told Shadrek that other changes, too, had taken place in his absence. The Rhodesian National Park authorities, in creating a national park in the Gonarezhou, had evicted all the Mozambican squatters from the lower Lundi and from the Sabi-Lundi junction area. Some of the people had been moved into Rhodesian Tribal Trust lands to the north and west

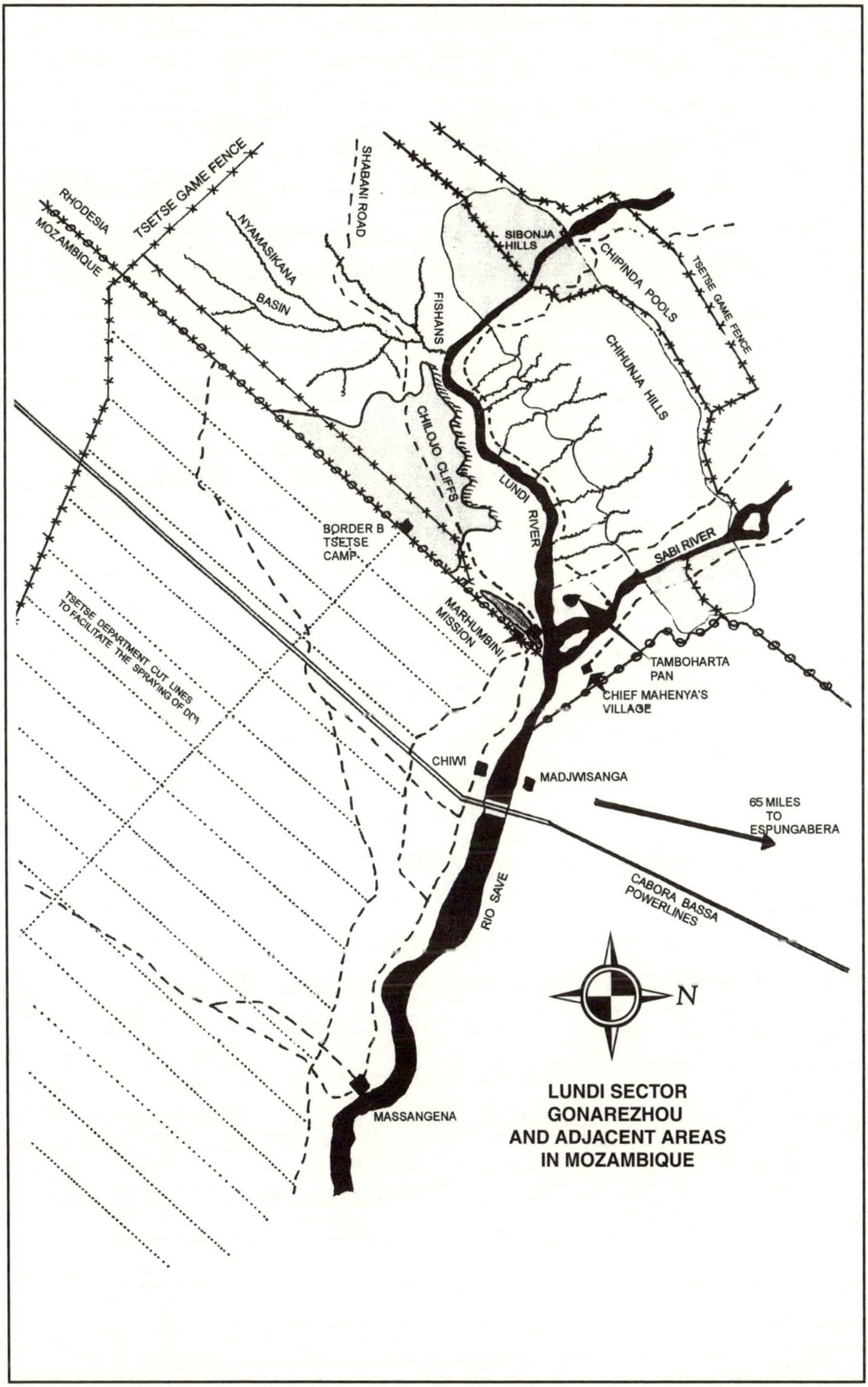
RHODESIA
MOZAMBIQUE
TSETSE GAME FENCE
NYAMASIKANA
BASIN
SHABANI ROAD
FISHANS
SIBONJA HILLS
CHIPINDA POOLS
TSETSE GAME FENCE
CHIHUNJA HILLS
CHILOJO CLIFFS
LUNDI RIVER
SABI RIVER
BORDER B TSETSE CAMP
TSETSE DEPARTMENT CUT LINES TO FACILITATE THE SPRAYING OF DDT
MARHUMBINI MISSION
TAMBOHARTA PAN
CHIEF MAHENYA'S VILLAGE
CHIWI
MADJWISANGA
65 MILES TO ESPUNGABERA
RIO SAVE
CABORA BASSA POWERLINES
N
MASSANGENA
LUNDI SECTOR
GONAREZHOU
AND ADJACENT AREAS
IN MOZAMBIQUE

of the game reserve. Some had moved to Mahenya's. Others had elected to return to Mozambique, from whence they had come originally. Tabita's father, Mufundjwa Mek Chauke, was one of those who had moved to Mahenya's. In the process he had lost his status as a chief.

The Marhumbini mission, with no parishioners to serve, had closed down, and the national park authorities had stripped the buildings of all usable materials. Shadrek was horrified. As soon as he was able, he traveled to Marhumbini to see for himself.

He walked the derelict mission station, feeling deep remorse and melancholy. The asbestos roofs had been removed from the houses once occupied by Coopman and Blake Thompson. A concrete roof covering one of the water cisterns on the hilltop had collapsed when a national parks lorry had driven over it. On the flood plain below, the thatched roofs of the church and the school were in tatters and the huts that had once housed itinerant visitors to the mission, including Shadrek's old hut, had been burnt to the ground. And the elephant had moved in and pushed over large numbers of the big mopane trees that had once provided summer shade at the mission station.

Marhumbini was like a ghost town. The land was deserted.

Shadrek walked to Tabita's old home on the nearby banks of the Lundi and discovered that it, too, had been razed. All over the land, the villages lay in ruins or ashes.

There was now elephant spoor everywhere. The pachyderms' great footprints were visible all along the riverbanks, in and around the burnt huts, and all over the derelict croplands. In the mile-wide reedbeds of the river junction, Shadrek could see the backs of many elephant bulls as they fed on the lush young reeds growing in the damp sands.

So this is where the Ruwanje elephants have come! Shadrek thought. The animals had abandoned the disturbed and stinking thickets in Mozambique and joined the already excessive numbers of elephants in the Gonarezhou. After the squatters were evicted, the game reserve became a haven of peace and tranquillity for wildlife. Shadrek realized

that if he continued hunting, he would have to become more and more reliant on the game reserve's elephant herds.

He returned to Madjwisanga with a burning anger in his heart. The interfering Rhodesians had turned his whole life upside down, and he needed some solace for his soul. He remembered his last conversation with Alberto, the new *chefe de posto* at Espungabera, and decided to pursue the man's suggestion. So he journeyed up to Espungabera, high in the mountains beyond Garawa, and went to see the new *chefe de posto.*

"Certainly I meant what I said," Alberto told him. "If you want to hunt elephant on the Rio Save, or even in the Rhodesian game reserve across the border, I shall guarantee you immunity inside Mozambique—provided, of course, you sell the ivory to me."

"And a rifle? You said you would provide me with a rifle?"

"Yes," the man replied, "and ammunition. As much as you will need."

Alberto was as good as his word. He excused himself and left the room, returning in a few minutes with a used but well-kept .375 Holland & Holland Magnum. This he placed on his desk along with two boxes of solid ammunition—forty rounds in all. Shadrek beamed and shook Alberto's hand to seal their agreement.

Exuberant at his new prospects, Shadrek boasted to Alberto that he had poached elephant in Kruger National Park. And he told him all the circumstances surrounding that experience. Alberto was impressed, and the story sowed the seeds of an idea in his mind. Alberto discussed his idea with the chief of police at Espungabera, who would later make an approach to Shadrek. That, however, was something for the near future.

For the present Shadrek was again in business—proper business. Now he had a beautiful weapon that he felt was truly his own. He had unlimited ammunition. He had an abundant supply of elephant and a ready market for his ivory. What more could a man want?

Shadrek's first excursion into the Gonarezhou, however, nearly ended with his arrest. He knew that the Gonarezhou was completely undeveloped and, unlike Kruger National Park, had a pathetically inadequate antipoaching force. Too bold and cocky for his own good, he failed to consider that a game patrol might be in the area and he brazenly shot a big bull elephant alongside the road near Tamboharta pan. Disdaining the strategy he had used to avoid detection in Kruger National Park, he immediately set about cutting out the tusks. This was the procedure he had adopted previously when hunting elephant on the nearby Rio Save, and without thinking he had fallen back into his old way of doing things.

Four armed game scouts surrounded him before he realized his predicament. They were right on top of him, rushing to close the last few yards and arrest him, when he first heard the noise of their passage through the tall grass. He had just enough time to snatch up his rifle before the first scout reached him.

"*Ehmah wena!*" the man shouted at him. "*Ehmah!*" (Stop you! Stop!)

The lead scout made a grab for the poacher's weapon, and Shadrek smashed the butt into his face, knocking him to the ground. Another scout was running at him like the first, and another was heading around the back of the elephant. A fourth stood on the far side of the carcass, blocking his escape in that direction.

Shadrek ran like a weasel, twisting and turning and spinning round and round to avoid contact with the second scout, whose hands were outstretched trying to get a hold on him. He struck the man on the side of the head with the rifle barrel. He went down.

Then Shadrek was gone, running like the wind through the tall grass with two of the game scouts in hot pursuit. He was much fitter than any of his adversaries, however, and soon left them far behind.

When he realized he had outpaced them, Shadrek stopped and looked back. He laughed as the two men shook their fists at him and made gestures with their old .303 rifles. They made no attempt to use the weapons. Instead, they shouted some serious abuse—but Shadrek

laughed all the louder. His laughing derision made the scouts even angrier, but they knew that this time Shadrek had got the better of them. At that stage the scouts did not know who Shadrek was because his poaching career in the Gonarezhou had only just begun. They were very soon to find out!

Shadrek came away from that encounter without his ax and his hunting knife, and with his pride a little bruised. But he still had his rifle, and he had learnt a valuable lesson. Never again would he be so casual when hunting elephant in the Gonarezhou. But the game was on. And as we now know, it was to develop into a major confrontation between Shadrek and the game rangers of the Gonarezhou.

Shadrek decided to leave the Gonarezhou alone for a while to let the dust settle. So, after his encounter with the game scouts, he passed straight through Mahenya's and went home to Madjwisanga. Upon his arrival, Tabita handed him a note from a man named Fror, the chief of police at Espungabera; it was a summons to visit Fror.

The note puzzled Shadrek. It could not possibly have anything to do with his recent encounter with the Gonarezhou game scouts. There simply had not been enough time for them to report the matter and for the Rhodesian police to lodge a complaint with the Portuguese authorities in Mozambique. He was not unduly worried, though, because he had been assured of immunity from prosecution in Mozambique by the *chefe de posto.*

At Espungabera, Fror took him to his home. There he spoke of Shadrek's reputation as an elephant hunter and about elephant hunting in general. He said that Alberto had told him all about Shadrek's exploits in Kruger National Park, and he questioned him about that. Shadrek, believing that Fror had no intention of arresting him for his poaching offenses, was openly boastful about his exploits. In fact, Fror was testing Shadrek to determine his real ability to hunt elephant and to see just how bold a hunter the young Ndau really was.

The conversation turned to the war the Portuguese had been waging against FRELIMO in the far north. Fror told Shadrek that FRELIMO had crossed the Zambezi in its drive to the south and that the guerrillas, for the first time, had set up bases in the Tete province of Mozambique. This, Fror said, had caused a great deal of trouble in Portugal, where the people were beginning to question the wisdom of maintaining colonies in Africa. Far too many young Portuguese lives were being lost in a costly war in a faraway land that brought few, if any, returns to Portugal. There was great resistance in Portugal, therefore, to sending out more young men to face death in the African bush—especially when FRELIMO's advance seemed to indicate that the guerrillas were winning the conflict.

It was clear to us Rhodesians at the time that when FRELIMO crossed the Zambezi and set up major bases in the Tete province of Mozambique, the Portuguese lost both their confidence and their desire to continue fighting the war. For most Portuguese, home was not Mozambique but Portugal, and when their spirit was broken by FRELIMO advances, they began looking forward to abandoning Mozambique and returning home.

During the several years it took to disengage, however, those Portuguese who were in positions of authority in Mozambique began fleecing the country of all its riches. Because everyone was doing it, the process continued openly without any kind of censure. That is what Alberto, the *chefe de posto*, and Fror, the chief of police, at Espungabera were doing when they enrolled Shadrek to obtain ivory for them from Mozambique's vast elephant herds.

Much of Fror's discussion about FRELIMO and the war went high over Shadrek's head—except when it came to the punchline, the reason Fror had summoned Shadrek to Espungabera.

"Alberto and I would like you to hunt some elephants for us in Gorongoza," Fror told Shadrek at last.

"Gorongoza. Where and what is that?" Shadrek asked.

"It is a large national park west of Beira," Fror told him. "It is a very long way from Espungabera."

Shadrek shook his head. "I have already been away from home in South Africa for far too long. Besides, I have all the elephants I need in the Gonarezhou."

"But very soon the Rhodesians will be looking for you, Shadrek," Fror said, as if he were looking into a crystal ball. Fror was clearly a policeman who understood the way international police forces worked together. "Once you start killing lots of elephants in the Gonarezhou, you will need our support. I can tell you now that one day the Rhodesian police will ask me to help them arrest you. Then what should I do, Shadrek?"

It was a veiled threat. Shadrek recognized it. He also understood that Fror's prediction was probably quite accurate. He would then truly need the protection of both the *chefe de posto* and the chief of police. Fror had him over a barrel, and he knew it. So Shadrek capitulated.

"I would like to spend two weeks at home with my family," Shadrek told the dark-skinned, thickset policeman. "I have been away for a very long time."

"Things are heating up in the Gorongoza area," Fror retorted. "FRELIMO have already set land mines on the roads in the game reserve, so we cannot waste any more time. You will have the rest of your life to be with your family after we return."

"So when do you want me to go to Gorongoza?" Shadrek asked.

"Tomorrow morning," Fror said, beaming at Shadrek. "All I need to do is make one or two phone calls." Obviously, Fror and Alberto had already prepared the ground for his hunting trip to the Gorongoza.

The next morning Fror took Shadrek to Alberto's house, and there they loaded up all their gear in a Land Rover. Alberto took Shadrek's .375 magnum from him and secured it in his gun safe. Then they set off for Beira, which they reached in late afternoon. They went directly to a senior government official's house, where they stayed the night. Shadrek slept on the kitchen floor.

Early the next morning, Shadrek was given another .375 magnum rifle and thirty-eight packets of ammunition, each containing twenty rounds of solid cartridges. He had brought blankets and cooking utensils. They then departed for the Beira air force base, where Shadrek, Fror, and Alberto boarded a Portuguese air force helicopter for the flight to Gorongoza National Park. Shadrek called it "a huge swamp in the bush." It was like Tamboharta and the Sabi-Lundi junction forest, he said, only much bigger. They landed and off-loaded Shadrek's gear.

From the helicopter they had seen lots of elephants, so Fror suggested that Shadrek show them how he killed one. Shadrek agreed. He moved off into the bush with the two Portuguese following. The pilot and a technician remained with their machine.

It did not take the hunting party long to locate a suitably large bull, and Shadrek walked right up to it and fired a bullet into its heart. The elephant ran off and collapsed dead a little way off. Shadrek climbed on top of the elephant's back, and Fror took a picture of him. Then Alberto took a photograph of Shadrek and Fror together, sitting on the elephant's back. Finally, a picture was taken of Alberto and Shadrek.

Shadrek cut out the elephant's tusks, finishing the task a little after midday. They returned with the ivory and rested in the shade of the helicopter. Fror broke out some *cerveja* and wine. Shadrek drank the beer but not the wine. The Portuguese roasted some elephant meat and ate it for lunch. Shadrek declined the meat. At four o'clock, the helicopter took off with Fror and Alberto along with the two elephant tusks on board, and Shadrek was left standing alone in the dust of Gorongoza.

He arranged a makeshift camp and hunted elephant in the late afternoon. All he saw, however, were cow herds, and those he left strictly alone. Shadrek was not afraid of elephant cows, but he respected them and rarely interfered with them.

He shot an impala and cut off both the back legs and cut out the backstrap and liver. He carried the meat back to his camp, leaving what he did not want for the hyenas and jackals. He spent an hour collecting dry wood for his campfire, and at dusk he roasted the liver and several slabs of impala meat over the hot coals. Then he snuggled down under his blanket next to the fire and slept his first night in the Gorongoza bush.

He woke early and soon found what he was looking for—a herd of big bulls. From this group he selected and shot dead two big tuskers. It took him until 4 PM to remove all four tusks, which he hid near the carcasses. He left the carcasses open for the vultures.

Fror had said that in Gorongoza there were no longer any game scouts to catch Shadrek because the escalating war had driven away the entire national park administration. Hiding the carcasses of the elephants that he shot, therefore, was not necessary.

He had little to worry about from the FRELIMO freedom fighters, either, because at that stage of the war they visited Gorongoza only on rare occasions in order to lay land mines on the roads. Then they returned to the north, where they had more secure bases. The plethora of land mines that booby-trapped the roads prevented the Portuguese authorities from patrolling the game reserve, so the game rangers had left. Shadrek had the game reserve virtually to himself.

The next morning he hunted again, locating another bull herd at their siesta in the heat of the day. He killed three bulls with three clean heart shots. Shadrek rested throughout the remaining hot period of the day and began cutting out the tusks in the cooler hours of the afternoon. He finished his task in the moonlight around 1 AM. Then he slept, hungry and dead tired, not far from the carcasses.

The next day he carried back to his camp all the tusks from the elephants he had killed so far. He hid them in the bushes nearby. And again he slept like the dead that night. The whole of the next day he remained in camp, resting and sleeping, and slept soundly again throughout the night.

The next morning he found two big bulls not far from his camp, both of which he killed. By sunset he had all the ivory safely stashed away in the bushes.

At six o'clock the following morning the helicopter returned. Immediately Fror and Alberto questioned Shadrek about how many elephants he had killed.

"Seven," Shadrek told them.

"Seven! Is that all?" Fror was unhappy at the number. "Why have you killed only seven? You had enough ammunition to kill many more."

"Yes, Fror," Shadrek responded, "but I am alone, and not only do I have to shoot the elephant, I also have to cut out the tusks and carry them back to camp. I think that seven elephants is a lot for one man to have killed and processed in just six days."

Fror and Alberto conferred under their breath, all the while casting surreptitious glances at Shadrek. Finally Fror turned and said: "You are right, Shadrek. Alberto and I agree. It has been a hard job for you both to hunt and take care of the ivory. We now have another plan."

Another plan? Shadrek was not sure what that implied, but for the moment he remained silent.

"Where is the ivory?" It was Alberto who spoke this time.

Shadrek led them over to the pile of tusks he had hidden away behind some bushes. Fror and Alberto and Shadrek then loaded the ivory into the helicopter, and the two Portuguese made ready to leave.

"Am I not going with you?" Shadrek asked when he saw that they intended leaving without him.

"No, Shadrek," Alberto said. "You must stay. We want you to shoot many more elephants while you can. Use up all your bullets."

"I told you, Alberto, it is too heavy for one man to do all these things," Shadrek said. "It would be better if you brought another man to help me cut out the ivory and carry the tusks."

"We will bring you more than one man to help you," Alberto said, clapping a hand on Shadrek's shoulder. "We want you just to shoot the elephants. Don't cut out any of the ivory or carry the tusks back to camp. We will bring you people to do that work for you. Please. You just kill the elephants."

Fror then off-loaded a small bag of mealie meal, another of salt, and a case of Coca-Cola.

"When will you be back?" Shadrek asked, beginning to feel vulnerable. He was, after all, completely at the mercy of these two Portuguese men and was not sure he could trust them. He believed they were quite capable of abandoning him in the Gorongoza.

"We'll be back the day after tomorrow," Alberto said. "And we'll bring you some help."

The helicopter left with Alberto and Fror and Shadrek's fourteen elephant tusks.

Shadrek rested for the remainder of that day and ate hugely from the mealie meal, which he cooked into a stiff porridge just before dark.

He ate it with strips of half-dried impala meat roasted over the hot coals, washing it all down with several bottles of warm Coke. Once again he slept soundly through the night.

The next morning he again found the resident herd, from which he shot four big bulls. This time he made no attempt to cut out the tusks. Late in the afternoon he found a lone but very large tusker, which he also killed. He returned to camp and had another dinner of stiff mealie meal porridge and impala meat.

Shadrek left very early the next morning, hoping to find elephants before the helicopter returned. This time he found three tuskers feeding on an open flood plain, and he killed them all with well-placed heart shots.

Alberto and Fror showed up with a much bigger helicopter, an army troop carrier. In its hold were ten black labourers armed with knives and axes. This time they off-loaded a two-hundred-pound bag of mealie meal and a hundred-pound bag of salt, together with three cast-iron, three-legged cooking pots and an old five-gallon paint tin with a wire handle. The purpose of the tin was to carry water to the camp from a puddle on the edge of the swamp.

The two white men had brought along a third Portuguese, and those three, together with the pilot and his technician, settled down to await the hunter's return. During late morning they all heard three shots in the near distance. Shadrek returned at midday.

"How many elephants, Shadrek?" Fror asked.

"Eight," the young Ndau replied. "Eight in two days' hunting time."

"Good. And you haven't cut out the ivory?"

"No!"

"That's OK. All you have to do is show these men the elephants," Fror said, indicating the ten labourers.

Shadrek looked the men over and shivered. They were all city slickers—*tsotsies* that Fror had obviously picked up off the streets of Beira.

"All you have to do is kill the elephants—as many as you can. These guys will cut out the tusks and carry them back to camp for you."

"How much longer is this hunting going to go on?" Shadrek asked Fror directly.

"You are tired?" Alberto responded. "I can see it in your eyes."

"And I want to go home," Shadrek added truthfully.

"Two days," Fror cut in quickly. "All you have to do is keep going for another two days. But you mustn't let up with your hunting. We want as much ivory as we can get over the next two days."

Shadrek and his merry men left camp at three o'clock that afternoon and walked to the carcasses of the three elephants he had shot that day. He showed them how to cut the tusks from the skulls.

He had been right in his assessment of these men. They were indeed city slickers and hadn't a clue what they were doing. Shadrek was afraid they would run off into the bush the first time they heard a lion roaring or a hyena snickering in the night. So he stayed and worked with them deep into the night to remove the six tusks.

They slept alongside the carcasses for what remained of the night, and early the next morning Shadrek guided his labour gang to the five other carcasses. Then he left the men to remove the ivory and went off hunting on his own.

The herd had moved, and Shadrek found them five miles from where he had last seen them. He dispatched five of the remaining bulls with five clean heart shots and returned to camp. He hadn't had a filling meal since the morning the helicopter had departed, so he was ravenous and very tired. He ate and he slept. At two that afternoon he led his gang of labourers to the five bulls he had shot that morning. It was nearly midnight by the time they had cut out all the tusks. Shadrek made a big fire, and they all slept there.

The next morning they carried the tusks back to camp. While en route they ran into a lone buffalo bull, which Shadrek shot. After depositing the tusks at the camp, the labourers went to fetch the meat from the buffalo. This they shared among them. They spent the rest of the day cutting the buffalo meat into long ropes, which they cured with salt and dried on pole racks over a smoky fire. Shadrek promised the men they could return home with this meat when the helicopter came to collect them.

Shadrek expected the helicopter to fetch them the next morning, but it did not arrive. So they wasted a whole day sitting around camp waiting for their transport.

The helicopter arrived the next day, and Fror emerged to ask immediately: "How many elephants?"

"Thirteen," Shadrek responded.

"That's not enough," Fror said.

This made Shadrek very angry. "Not enough! Not enough? Do you know how much work there is in shooting and processing thirteen bull elephants in three days?"

"OK, OK," Fror replied, holding his hands out in a supplicatory manner. He could see his remark had angered Shadrek, and he was truly sorry. "I understand, Shadrek, I understand. You've done a good job all round. Really you have."

"Come, Shadrek," Alberto said then, pouring oil on troubled waters. "We're finished here. Let's load up the ivory and go home." Shadrek had been in the Gorongoza for twelve days. In that time he had shot and recovered the ivory of twenty-one elephant bulls.

The helicopter transported them all back to Beira. The same day, Fror, Alberto, and Shadrek set off for Espungabera by road, leaving the tusks behind. They arrived well after midnight, and Shadrek spent the rest of that night at Alberto's house. The next morning Alberto directed his driver to take Shadrek back to Madjwisanga in the government Land Rover.

Alberto gave Shadrek a measly fifteen pounds for the ivory he had collected in Gorongoza. He also held back the rifle he gave to Shadrek, saying that he wanted to clean it properly.

Shadrek did not complain about any of these things, for he knew that he had now well and truly ingratiated himself with both the *chefe de posto* and the chief of police. In the next few years that indebtedness was to pay handsome dividends for the intrepid hunter.

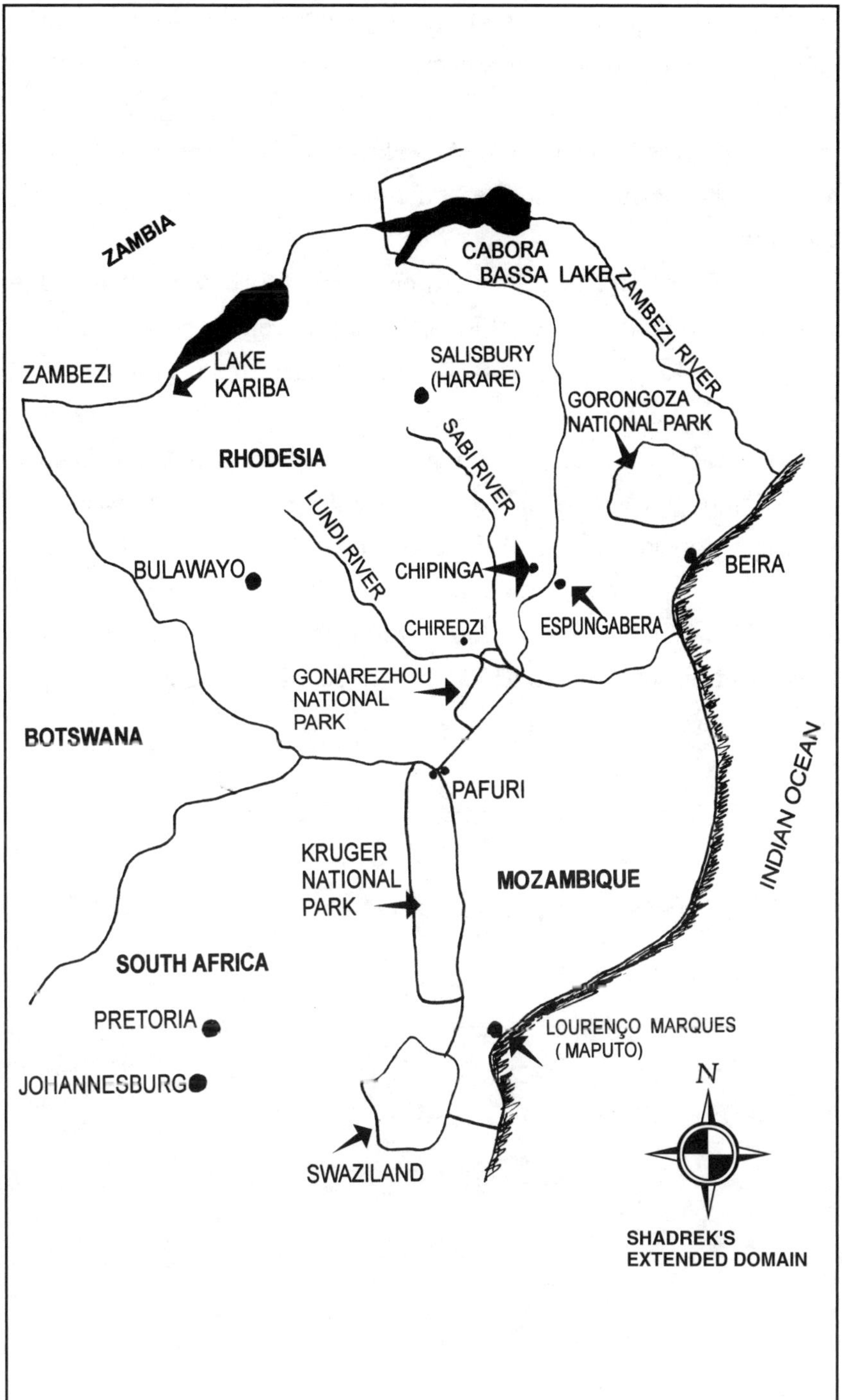
ZAMBIA
CABORA
BASSA LAKE
ZAMBEZI RIVER
ZAMBEZI
LAKE
KARIBA
SALISBURY
(HARARE)
GORONGOZA
NATIONAL PARK
RHODESIA
SABI RIVER
LUNDI RIVER
BULAWAYO
CHIPINGA
BEIRA
CHIREDZI
ESPUNGABERA
GONAREZHOU
NATIONAL
PARK
BOTSWANA
INDIAN OCEAN
PAFURI
KRUGER
NATIONAL
PARK
MOZAMBIQUE
SOUTH AFRICA
PRETORIA
LOURENÇO MARQUES
(MAPUTO)
JOHANNESBURG
N
SWAZILAND
SHADREK'S
EXTENDED DOMAIN

Before his departure from Espungabera, Fror told Shadrek that he must rest at home for a full week. Then he was to return to Espungabera by bicycle because Fror and Alberto had other jobs lined up for him. When he returned, Alberto told Shadrek, he would get the .375 magnum back. In the meantime Alberto would give the weapon a good cleaning and oiling.

Shadrek told Fror that he would need at least two weeks to rest. The policeman grudgingly agreed. Indeed, he had little option because Shadrek was adamant. So Shadrek returned home to Tabita and his parents.

It should be now apparent why, sometime later, the *chefe de posto* and the chief of police at Espungabera failed to apprehend Shadrek in Mozambique at the behest of the Rhodesians. Not only were they Shadrek's principal source of weapons and ammunition, and his chief market for ivory, but they also were enriching themselves grandly through his elephant-poaching activities. It certainly was not in their interests to arrest Shadrek, and, consequently, these men did nothing more than pay lip service to their agreement with the Rhodesians.

Chapter 18

One week later Fror pitched up at Madjwisanga in his police Jeep. He arrived in late afternoon and stayed the night with Shadrek and Tabita. The purpose of his visit was to ply Shadrek for more ivory. He was clearly convinced that FRELIMO would soon defeat the Portuguese in Mozambique, and he intended to use whatever time was still available to him in the country to enrich himself any way he could. Obviously, Fror saw Shadrek's passion for elephant hunting as one way to achieve that end.

It took the Portuguese another five years to capitulate, and with Alberto's and Fror's background support, those five years were to be Shadrek's golden era.

"You know this area, Shadrek," Fror said. "Where is there a place with lots of elephants?"

"Mahenya's . . . Marhumbini . . . the Gonarezhou. All in Rhodesia."

Fror smiled and said, "I don't think that will be a problem for you, Shadrek. I want you to go there and kill as many elephants as you can. Alberto and I will buy all the ivory you can get."

"I can't," Shadrek replied. "Alberto took my rifle back, and my father is out of ammunition for his 10.75mm."

"I'll get the .375 back for you," Fror replied immediately.

"And there is one other thing," Shadrek said determinedly. "We need to agree on a price for the tusks that I sell to you. Fifteen pounds for all the elephants I shot for you and Alberto in the Gorongoza is not enough. When I sell my ivory to the storekeepers around here, I get more than that for just one tusk."

"You must remember, Shadrek, that Alberto and I provide you with your weapon and your ammunition. And we paid for the journey to Beira out of our own pockets, and also for the helicopter. That was very expensive." Shadrek had not thought about such expenses, and he grudgingly had to admit that there was some logic in Fror's explanation—although he had a feeling that the government in Portugal had paid for most of that expense.

"But you won't have to pay for any helicopters when I go into the Gonarezhou," Shadrek said, using an argument equally sound and logical.

"How much do you want for your ivory?" Fror now had a serious frown on his face.

"Fifteen pounds a tusk," Shadrek responded. "That is a reasonable price considering I get twenty when I sell ivory to local storekeepers."

"Fifteen pounds?" Fror was taken aback. He had not thought to pay such a high price for a single tusk.

"You forget two things, Shadrek. I must tell you again that Alberto and I provide you with the weapon and the ammunition. That is the first thing. The second thing is that we will guarantee you immunity if, or rather when, the Rhodesian police ask us to arrest you."

Shadrek thought about that for a while, during which Fror looked searchingly at Shadrek. Finally Shadrek shook his head and asked: "How much do you want to pay me for a tusk?"

"Five pounds."

"No," Shadrek replied immediately. "I cannot do business with you for such a low return."

"Seven pounds, ten shillings," Fror retorted.

"Ten pounds." It was Shadrek's final offer.

"And what if you bring me small tusks?" Fror asked.

"I do not shoot elephants with small tusks," Shadrek retorted, his pride pricked by the suggestion.

Fror thought through the cost-and-return implications. The young Ndau drove a hard bargain, but he had sympathy for him. He himself would not shoot an elephant for ten pounds a tusk. "OK," Fror said at last. "Ten pounds a tusk."

They shook hands on the deal, and Fror left immediately for Espungabera, returning the next day with Alberto's .375 magnum and fifteen packets of ammunition. There were twenty rounds in each packet. Having completed his business with Shadrek, Fror returned to Espungabera. One thing about the Portuguese administration in their African colonies: The officials hated being without their creature comforts and spent as little time as possible in the bush.

The next day Shadrek went to Mahenya's by bicycle, traveling the well-worn path that joined Mahenya's in Rhodesia to all the Mozambican settlements along the Rio Save. The path went as far as Massangena and then a good bit beyond.

South of the chief's village he entered the dense thickets and encountered a large bull herd. He shot three. Then he went to the villages and invited the people of Mahenya's to come and take the meat. He also visited the old chief and promised him his chiefly due—a goodly supply of meat and the three elephant hearts. The people, in gratitude, helped Shadrek cut out the tusks, and four of the men agreed to carry a tusk back to Madjwisanga. Shadrek took two tusks, one hanging on either side of his bicycle.

They all returned to Mahenya's, where Shadrek was determined to kill yet more elephants. But the big bulls had vacated the area, crossing the Sabi and entering the Gonarezhou.

At this time Shadrek still had not met John Chauke, Tabita's brother, or Josiah. Both these men were to become Shadrek's companions on many hunts in the game reserve over the next several years. Shadrek explained all this to me, then told me two other things: that Tabita's father had recently died, and that the last of the Shangaan and Mhlengwe people had finally been evicted from the Gonarezhou.

His storytelling was like that—disjointed and fragmented. Because it is impossible to insert this kind of background information into Shadrek's story in a chronological sequence, I must recite these tales in the order he told them to me.

Shadrek was by then just starting to enjoy the fruits of his growing reputation as a daring elephant hunter. However, he was still a greenhorn youngster in the eyes of the Mahenya veterans. Many of Mahenya's people had suffered from John Osborne's irregular eviction strategies, and they knew that Shadrek had not come up against this spirited and highly dedicated senior game ranger. They preferred to wait and watch and see how Shadrek would fare when the weight of the Rhodesian antipoaching machine leant against him. So it was on this occasion that Shadrek could find no volunteers to accompany him across the Sabi into the Gonarezhou.

He was alone when he crossed the river in the cold light of dawn. By eight o'clock he had located a large herd of bulls, from which he killed six animals in a running hunt. Working determinedly on his own all day long, his eyes this time continually canvassing the surrounding bush, he cut out the twelve tusks and, exhausted, laid the last of the great ivories on the ground just before it grew dark. He spent the night transporting the tusks across the Sabi to Mwachimeni Island, where he buried them in the river sands under shallow water.

The next day he took two tusks, one strung on either side of his bicycle, back to Madjwisanga. He slept at home that night and the next morning returned with two friends and their bicycles. Between them they managed to get the remaining ten tusks back to Shadrek's home by nightfall.

Fror was waiting for Shadrek, and took all the tusks from him. He had brought four cases of *cerveja*, two cases of Coca-Cola, and a bag of salt as presents.

The chief of police suggested to Shadrek that after such a successful visit, he should give the Rhodesian game reserve a break for a while. He suggested that Shadrek try Mapani Game Reserve, which was relatively near Lourenço Marques. Shadrek said he had not heard of the Mapani and suggested that if Fror really wanted him to hunt elephant there he should supply some transport.

Four days later a Jeep arrived at Madjwisanga, driven by Fror's driver, Manweri. On the back were three black labourers whose job it was,

Manweri told Shadrek, to chop out tusks. Manweri then took Shadrek to Mapani, a long way from Madjwisanga. They traveled all day and all night. The following midday they entered Mapani and hid the Jeep deep in the bush. They saw lots of elephants but made no attempt to hunt that day. Instead they lazed away the afternoon hours and had a good sleep that night.

The next morning Shadrek shot seven bulls. Another he wounded. By 3 PM all fourteen tusks were safely stowed away in the Land Rover. They then packed up their *katoonda* and headed out of the game reserve. On the way out they encountered another big bull, which Shadrek shot. The removal of this animal's tusks kept them in the game reserve well into the night. They moved out in the dark and drove all night toward home.

An interesting aside about this little escapade is that Fror had instructed his driver, Manweri, to tell Shadrek that if he encountered any game scouts in Mapani, he was to shoot them. No one would think Shadrek had killed them, Fror had said, because by then there was a new FRELIMO presence in the Mapani area. The game scouts' deaths would be put down to terrorist action. They never encountered any game scouts, so Shadrek did not even have to think about following Fror's instructions—thank goodness. Shadrek told me, however, that he had no intention of shooting anybody.

They arrived in Espungabera about 10 PM. Shadrek delivered the tusks directly into Fror's care.

"Why have you returned so early?" Fror asked.

"The place is crawling with policemen, Fror," Shadrek lied easily. "They were looking for FRELIMO people. They thought we were FRELIMO."

"Humph," grunted the policeman. "Listen, Alberto and I would like you to go back to Gorongoza."

"No!" Shadrek responded immediately. "I'm not going back there. We have already killed many elephants in the Gorongoza, and FRELIMO might be expecting me to return."

"Mmmm. OK," the policeman said finally. "But where can you go now to shoot elephant?"

"How about Muzamani?" Shadrek suggested. "It's near Kapiteni and well within my reach from Madjwisanga."

"Are there many elephants there?" Fror asked dubiously.

"So I have been told," Shadrek answered with apparent confidence.

"Mmmmm."

"There is one thing, Fror," Shadrek said. "I wounded an elephant at Mapani. It ran away after I shot it in the heart. There must be something wrong with the rifle."

"You were just unlucky," Fror said derisively. "Or you shot it in the wrong place."

"No," Shadrek was adamant. "I shot it in the right place, but the bullet wasn't strong enough. There must be something wrong with this rifle. I want you to change it."

Fror gave a loud sigh. "OK, then. Give me Alberto's weapon." He went into the house and came out with another .375 magnum. "This is my own gun, Shadrek," Fror said authoritatively. "I want you to look after it." It was an older weapon than Alberto's, but it felt better in Shadrek's hands. He smiled his pleasure at Fror.

Manweri drove Shadrek back to Madjwisanga that night, and Shadrek spent the next two days resting at home.

Shadrek had no intention of going to Muzamani since it, too, had been disturbed by Rhodesian Tsetse Department activities. Instead, he cycled to the junction area, crossed the Rio Save inside Mozambique, and entered Rhodesia south of Marhumbini. Early the next morning, he located a very large herd of bulls near Machaniwa in the game reserve. These he pursued for most of the morning. By ten o'clock he had accounted for nine bulls—five of them lying out in the open and the remainder in thick bush.

He realized that he would have great difficulty in cutting out all the tusks and transporting them back home, so he returned to Mozambique and came back with some three hundred people, to whom he gave the meat. They cut out the tusks under his direction and transported the ivory back to their homes inside Mozambique. While the people were stripping the carcasses, Shadrek stood guard just in case a Rhodesian game scout patrol should venture by.

When the volunteers had shifted all the tusks and meat back across the border, Shadrek walked across the Lundi into the junction flood plain. Then he crossed the Sabi at Mwachimeni Island to visit Mahenya's, where he was to meet with Tabita's brother, John Chauke. Chauke had been employed by the Rhodesian Tsetse Department as a *magotsha*, a black hunter. It had been his job to eliminate game in the tsetse corridors of the middle Zambezi valley. *Magotsha* literally translated means "butcher."

John Chauke's village was at Mahenya's. It was the home that Mufundjwa Mek Chauke had built after he had been evicted from the Gonarezhou. After Mek's death, John Chauke had assumed ownership of the kraal. His father's recent death was the reason he had returned home.

At the time of Shadrek's visit to the village, John Chauke's cousin, Josiah Chiranzwa, was staying with him. Josiah had recently returned from the gold mines in South Africa. Shadrek slept at John's house, and the next day they all went fishing together on the Sabi. The following day the three men crossed the Sabi and started hunting elephant in the Tamboharta Pan area. This was the start of a notoriously successful poaching partnership that brought much fame and fortune to Shadrek and many spin-off financial benefits for both John Chauke and Josiah Chiranzwa.

As the three men were hunting elephant at Tamboharta, a strong force of John Osborne's game scouts were looking for Shadrek in the vicinity of Machaniwa on the far side of the Lundi beyond the Chilojo Cliffs. The game ranger had been alerted by a tsetse department fence guard, who had seen the meat being transported across the border into Mozambique. The guard had questioned the people carrying the meat, and they had told him that Shadrek had killed nine elephants. The tsetse guard had passed that information on, and John Osborne's hunt for Shadrek began in earnest from that moment on.

That morning Shadrek shot two bulls east of Tamboharta. It was not far from the Sabi, so Shadrek called upon Mahenya's people to come and collect the meat. The tusks of these two bulls were left at John Chauke's house at Mahenya's.

Thus began the rumour that Shadrek had a "home" at Mahenya's. Shadrek never lived at Mahenya's, but he often used John Chauke's home there as his base. Shadrek's home was *always* at Madjwisanga. Tabita often visited John Chauke's home at Mahenya's because it was, after all, her paternal kraal—which is why the national park game rangers sometimes found her there. None of these facts, however, were ever known to the Gonarezhou staff. To this day, whatever records remain of that era will tell you that the Gonarezhou staff believed Shadrek had his home at Mahenya's until our antipoaching efforts drove him into Mozambique—which is untrue.

After dropping the tusks at Chauke's, Shadrek went back into Mozambique and visited the villagers who had collected meat from his Machaniwa bulls. He secured volunteers to carry those tusks to Chiwi, which was at the end of the official road from Massangena on the south bank of the Save. Chiwi was only a mile or so from Madjwisanga, which was on the north bank. He stashed the tusks away under the sand in shallow water near the riverbank. Then he returned home.

The next day he press-ganged two of his friends to visit Mahenya's with him to recover the tusks from John Chauke's village. By the time he got back home that night, Fror was waiting for him.

"You've stirred something of a hornet's nest, Shadrek," Fror advised him with a laugh. "The Rhodesian game rangers and police want your hide. They have asked Alberto and me to help catch you on this side of the border."

"But that won't happen—right, Fror?" Shadrek asked with a hesitant confidence. This was really the first time the two white men's loyalty to him had been put to the test, so Shadrek was a little anxious to hear Fror's reply.

"You've got nothing to worry about, my friend," Fror replied, "as long as you keep supplying Alberto and me with your ivory." It was a veiled threat, and Shadrek understood the implications immediately.

At that point in Shadrek's revelations to me, I asked him about his reported supply of ivory to the South African helicopter crews on the Cabora Bassa power lines. He just smiled at me and said, "Sometimes they got more ivory from me than did Alberto and Fror. They paid better money, so why shouldn't I sell my ivory to them, too? I also sometimes sold ivory to my old customers in the local stores."

"But weren't you afraid Fror or Alberto would find out?" I asked—feeling a little frightened for Shadrek at the prospect.

"Who would tell either of them?" Shadrek retorted. "The people had more loyalty to me than they ever had to the chief of police at Espungabera. I was not only the son of the big Ndau chief at Madjwisanga, I was also a favourite grandson of the great paramount chief Garawa in Rhodesia. I was never in any danger of being betrayed to the Portuguese by our own people."

Fror crossed the Rio Save at Madjwisanga and collected the ivory from Shadrek's cache under the sand at Chiwi. He loaded the tusks Shadrek had at his home, too. On that occasion Fror left two cases of cerveja and six bags of sugar. Half of this, Fror said, should be given to Shadrek's father, Muteruko Kumbuya, the big chief at Madjwisanga.

A week later Shadrek was back in the Gonarezhou, entering the game reserve at Marhumbini. He walked to Kundani Hill and found no fresh sign of elephant. He hunted the south Lundi area extensively without success, then at 4 PM he crossed into the junction area and shot a waterbuck bull for meat. He cut off as much meat as he could carry and hung the rest up in a tree. Then he crossed the Sabi at Mwachimeni Island and slept at John Chauke's house that night. John was not present, but his brother Phineas was, and the two men talked deep into the night.

Early the next morning, Shadrek and Phineas and seven other men crossed the Sabi into the junction area to collect the rest of the waterbuck meat. On the road they came across the fresh tracks of a Land Rover. This, they knew, meant that a European game ranger was in the junction area. Phineas and the other men became apprehensive and suggested that they should get back to Mahenya's while the going was good. Shadrek pooh-poohed the idea.

"What can he do—this white game ranger?" Shadrek said. "We have my rifle."

They proceeded to the place where Shadrek had hung up the waterbuck meat and spent some time cutting it up into equal loads, which the men could carry back across the Sabi. They then went to a secluded pool on the Lundi to have a drink of water. It was about 11 AM.

Two of the party preceded Shadrek to the pool, which was well hidden and on the edge of a *mlala* palm thicket. The leaves of the palms came right down to the ground, and visibility was no more than ten feet. Just as they emerged at the water's edge, the two men in front of Shadrek stopped dead in their tracks. The next thing he knew they were running back past him as fast as they could go. This scattered those behind Shadrek, too. The hair on the back of Shadrek's neck rose. He stood his ground, however, his rifle at the ready, expecting a buffalo or an elephant to come charging through the thick foliage. Instead of an animal, a bullet whistled past his head, followed by the loud report of a rifle. At that point a white man in a game ranger's uniform materialized on the path in front of him. His rifle, too, was at the ready. No more than fifteen yards separated them.

"*Eenie endabah?*" (What's going on?) Shadrek asked angrily.

The white man did not reply. Instead he said to the black game scout at his side: "Arrest him."

When the scout started toward him, Shadrek lifted his weapon and said to the black man: "If you come any closer, I'll kill you."

The game scout stopped in his tracks, turned to the white man, and said: "*Baas* . . . he means it. He'll kill us all."

The European then fired a shot, but Shadrek could see that he had no intention of hitting him. It was a shot to frighten him into submission. But Shadrek was not intimidated. As the white man was reloading, Shadrek fired a warning shot at the game ranger, intentionally putting the bullet close to the man's ear. The white man ducked, turned, and ran back down the river to a point where the bank afforded him some cover. When he looked up, Shadrek was gone, racing away through the *mlala* thicket.

The white man fired another shot at the noise of Shadrek's retreat, and Shadrek heard the bullet plow through the heavy foliage at his side. He turned and fired another shot. Then he ran away as fast as he could go.

Once Shadrek was away from the thicket country, he stopped running and proceeded at a fast walk. He headed north, skirting Tamboharta pan, and in the forest immediately beyond he encountered two large elephant bulls. At that point Shadrek's blood was up, and he felt a little bloody-minded. Throwing caution to the wind, he killed both elephants with clean heart shots. By then he was five or six miles from the site of his confrontation with the game ranger, so he felt reasonably confident that he had given his pursuers the slip. He immediately set about cutting out the ivory and moved it, one tusk at a time, to the nearby Sabi River and buried it in the sand.

At dusk he set off again back across the flood plain to the Sabi-Lundi junction and crossed the Lundi in the dark. He knew there was a good chance that the game ranger and his scouts were camped nearby, but he continued undaunted. At Marhumbini he retrieved his bicycle from the thicket in which he had hidden it and cycled home along one of the many paths that ran along the south bank of the Rio Save.

The next day he returned to Mahenya's with a helper, and they recovered the ivory from its watery hiding place in the Sabi. Using their bicycles as beasts of burden, with two tusks per vehicle, they were back home before dark.

Four days later Shadrek was walking along the track between his home and Kamali Jhivana's store at Madjwisanga. Tabita was out of groceries, so he had volunteered to go to the store and collect what she needed. A Land Rover with Rhodesian number plates raced past him coming from the direction of the store. A white man was driving the vehicle, but Shadrek paid it scant attention, assuming it was a tsetse department man returning home from some errand.

At the store, the Portuguese, Kamali, told him that a white man who spoke English had left there only minutes before. The man, Kamali told Shadrek, was dressed in a khaki uniform and had asked, in English, for the whereabouts of Shadrek's village, saying that he wanted to buy ivory from Shadrek.

Flashes of a recent memory came to Shadrek—of a young white man wearing a khaki shirt with green tabs on the shoulder. In his mind's eye this man was confronting him on the banks of the Lundi River. Shots were exchanged. Shadrek realized that this was the same man he had encountered in the Gonarezhou—the game ranger who had tried to arrest him and later tried to kill him.

Shadrek ran out of the store and along a narrow path to his father's house. From his father's gun cabinet he retrieved his .375 magnum, grabbed a handful of cartridges, and ran back to his own village, only to see the Land Rover racing off back toward the store. Tabita and his son, Johan—then seven years old—were sitting on the back of the vehicle between three black game scouts.

It had not been Shadrek's intention to harm the white man but rather to put a solid bullet through the vehicle's engine block. The white man would then have been immobile and at Shadrek's mercy, and Fror would have done the necessary in Shadrek's behalf.

Shadrek went into his village, where the huts were in disarray. One of several local villagers informed him of what had happened. He quickly inspected his ransacked possessions. Among sundry other things, the game scouts had taken his radio, his Shangaan hunting bow and several arrows, and thirty pounds in cash. Two elephant tusks were also gone. His mattress had been ripped open. But that seemed to be all.

Shadrek came out of his huts and stood fuming. He looked in the direction the vehicle had gone. At last his mind began to function properly. The Land Rover had gone toward the store, so the white man had probably crossed the river below Madjwisanga to Chiwi. If so, Shadrek surmised, he would return to Rhodesia on the track that ran west from Chiwi along the far riverbank opposite his village.

Shadrek took off like a hare, running as fast as he could across the deep sand and shallow waters of the Rio Save. The river here was a mile wide, however, and he was still some distance from the south side when he heard the Land Rover droning its way past him high up on the bank. Frustrated, he stood in the middle of the river and cursed the white man profusely.

Author's Note

Shadrek's record of Charles Mackie's raid on his Madjwisanga village is different in many respects from Mackie's version. Mackie, for example, made no mention of taking Tabita and her son prisoner. John Osborne never mentioned anything to me about Charles Mackie taking any captives, and there was no report on it from the police at Chiredzi. I do not mean to imply that Charles did not take these two people with him. It is quite possible that he did take them prisoner and that both Charles and John Osborne decided together not to tell me about it.

John was not one to cross t's and dot i's in such matters, and he may well have decided to let sleeping dogs lie. There are, in fact, many differences between what Shadrek told me about himself and what I knew of his exploits at the time of my service in the Gonarezhou. By the time of Charles Mackie's raid on his home, for example, Shadrek was reported to have killed well over a hundred elephant bulls in the Gonarezhou. Yet if you add up those that he admitted to me he had killed up to that time, it comes nowhere near one hundred. And when one considers that Shadrek was very much an egotist, it is unlikely that he would have intentionally sold himself short.

Theoretically, someone other than Shadrek could have been shooting large numbers of elephants in the Gonarezhou at the same time Shadrek was active. That would account for the discrepancies in the figures. However, consider the legend that grew up around Shadrek. The people at Mahenya's and in the communities across the border in Mozambique spoke of nobody but Shadrek. There is really only one answer: Shadrek told me about only a small fraction of the elephants that he had actually killed in the Gonarezhou. Perhaps he purposely told me about only those kills that he considered important.

Shadrek also stated that he had sold a considerable amount of ivory to the South African helicopter crews who maintained the Cabora Bassa power lines. He also sold large numbers of tusks to Portuguese storekeepers who came to him for ivory from hundreds of miles away. Yet the stories he related to me about his poaching exploits seemed to indicate that most of the ivory went to Alberto and Fror. Clearly he did not tell me about every hunt he had made. Taking all these facts together, I believe that Shadrek had forgotten about many of his elephant hunts—as I myself have forgotten the bulk of my own. People with such vast experience remember only the most significant incidents. I believe that Shadrek had indeed shot as many elephants as the legends surrounding him said he did.

Another part of Shadrek's story that did not gel was his assertion that Fror had told him about the Rhodesians' asking the chefe de posto to help with Shadrek's arrest before he had wrought retribution for Mackie's raid on his home. In fact, it was as a consequence of Shadrek's killing an extraordinary number of bull elephants immediately following Charles Mackie's raid on his village that I arranged for the police Special Branch to visit Espungabera.

Shadrek's version of his confrontation with Charles Mackie on the Lundi is also at variance with the written report I obtained from Charles himself, which I believe to be the true version. Shadrek said, for example, that he went to the river pool to have a drink. In fact, he went to lift his gillnets. There is no reason he should have omitted this information, or fabricated a different story. The truth, I believe, is that he had forgotten the details.

None of these variances represent contradictions, and they do not mean that Shadrek lied to me. It is more likely that, looking back ten years and more, he had forgotten a lot of the details of what really happened.

In my opinion, the differences in the various versions of Shadrek's story add to, rather than detract from, its authenticity because they show that Shadrek—like all of us—was fallible. I genuinely believe he tried desperately to tell me his story as he remembered it. So I do not believe it is my place to try to correct his story or marry together all the various versions told to me by different people. After all, what most people told me about Shadrek was second-, third-, and fourth-hand information. What Shadrek told me about himself came straight from the horse's mouth!

When I wrote my book Mahohboh, *I had great difficulty in remembering the details of my own elephant-hunting exploits and the sequence in which events took place. I therefore sympathized with Shadrek when he tried to piece together for me the various facets of his own life's story from memory. That was one of the reasons why many elements were so disjointed. I ask the reader to bear with me as I try to write down the facts as Shadrek told them to me. I have not tried to judge who was right and who was wrong in this narrative, but rather to reveal the heart and the soul of its chief character.*

The reader must also remember that I never revealed my true identity to Shadrek. So I could not ask him to explain the many discrepancies I picked up between his version and other versions I had heard—and certain other facts that I knew to be true. Regrettably, I did not have the opportunity to "come clean" with Shadrek before his mysterious disappearance several years later. Had that been possible, I am sure I would have been able to fit together the pieces of the jigsaw puzzle in a much more coherent and understandable manner.

Chapter 19

Shadrek was confident that the Rhodesians would not hold Tabita and that she would very soon be returned to the border unharmed, probably at Mahenya's. Or they would take her to Espungabera and hand her over to Fror at the police station there. So he was not unduly worried about his wife's safety or that of his young son. He would just have to wait out the Rhodesian charade.

Back at the store, Shadrek had Kamali Jhivana write a letter to Fror explaining what had happened. Kamali's son took the letter to Espungabera on a motorbike. When he returned, he told Shadrek that Fror had gone to Beira, so he had left the letter with Fror's wife. All Shadrek could do now was wait.

But he could not just wait. His blood was up, and he was furious at the temerity of the young white game ranger. He traveled by bicycle to Mahenya's, left his cycle at John Chauke's village, and walked alone across the Sabi into the Gonarezhou. At a place he called Tamaquindi, Shadrek shot two elephant bulls, cut out the tusks, and hid them in the Sabi's sands. He went to Chauke's house, recovered his bicycle, and went back to where he had hidden his ivory. With one tusk secured on either side of the frame, he pushed his cycle back to Madjwisanga. Later that same night he returned to fetch the second pair of tusks.

On this visit to the game reserve Shadrek had flaunted himself—inviting a confrontation with the administration. Had he been accosted by game scouts, he probably would have shot them. Shadrek was angry and wanted to vent his wrath on any elephant he encountered, or on any game scouts he might come across. He was a virtual time bomb looking for a place to explode.

At 6 AM Shadrek returned with the last pair of tusks, just before Fror and eight soldiers pitched up at Shadrek's village. Fror recorded a full statement from Shadrek, omitting, of course, any reference to poaching in the Gonarezhou. Fror then invited Shadrek to accompany him and the soldiers into the Gonarezhou.

Shadrek guided them through the tsetse gate in the border fence south of Marhumbini. Inside Rhodesia they visited the Lisodo Tsetse Department camp and spoke to the two cattle guards there. The young game ranger, they were informed, must have come from the game reserve's Lundi headquarters at Chipinda Pools. Chipinda Pools was deep inside Rhodesia, and Fror was hesitant about traveling that far into the country illegally. It was too far to write off as a hot-pursuit exercise.

They made further inquiries at the Chitove Tsetse Department camp near Machaniwa. Guards there confirmed that a day or two before, the young white game ranger from Chipinda Pools—whom they knew as "*Baas* Charrels"—had passed by their camp traveling toward Chipinda. A black woman and a young boy had been on the back of the vehicle, they said, and the woman was sitting between three or four game scouts.

"Let's go back," Shadrek suggested. "I'm sure the Rhodesians will let Tabita go. She has done nothing wrong, and they cannot charge her with anything." At that stage, Shadrek told me, he was beginning to feel very vulnerable.

Back at Madjwisanga, Fror gave Shadrek fifty-five pounds in compensation for his troubles, and Shadrek gave Fror six large tusks, for which Fror paid Shadrek the sum of sixty pounds. Before leaving, Fror told Shadrek he would do all he could to get Tabita released quickly, and he suggested that when she returned, he should bring her to Espungabera.

A week after her abduction Tabita returned home, having been released at Mahenya's by the white game ranger. Shadrek said she had been badly beaten by the white man called "Charrels," which made Shadrek even more angry.

I doubt if that is true. Charles Mackie is not the kind of man who would have assaulted a woman prisoner. I also do not think he would have allowed his scouts to beat up an innocent black woman because her husband had poached elephant in the Gonarezhou. Nevertheless, I must admit that when Shadrek told me his version of the story, I felt that anything was possible. Again, what I relate here is what Shadrek told me.

Tabita told Shadrek that they had stayed for three nights at Marhumbini—she, her son Johan, the white man called "Charrels," and four black game scouts. There she had been fiercely interrogated by the white man. This included being slapped heavily about the face. She said that the four scouts had lain in ambush day and night on their back trail in the hope that Shadrek would follow them into Rhodesia. When Shadrek did not turn up, they had journeyed to Chipinda Pools and then on to Chiredzi, where they took mother and son to the police station. After further interrogation there, a senior policeman had told "Charrels," in front of Tabita, that he must take his captives back to Mahenya's and release them.

The white game ranger was very angry. As they drove the one hundred miles from Chiredzi back to Mahenya's, Tabita alleged, "Charrels" had his scouts interrogate her in the back of the Land Rover. Throughout the journey, the black game scouts had beaten Tabita in an attempt to get her to tell them what she knew about her husband's operation, where he got his weapons and ammunition, and where he sold his ivory. She told them nothing.

Tabita's most serious injuries, Shadrek asserted, were those she received from the scouts on the return journey to Mahenya's. The police at Chiredzi, Shadrek asserted pointedly, had no knowledge about what had happened to Tabita between the time she left there and the time she was released at Mahenya's.

Upon their return home, Shadrek took Tabita and Johan to Espungabera, where they went immediately to Fror's office at the police station. Shadrek asked Fror to lay an official charge of assault against the game ranger called "Charrels." The chief of police agreed to do so, but first he arranged for the treatment of Tabita's wounds at the local hospital.

Although Shadrek told me that Fror had definitely filed an official charge of assault against Charles Mackie and his four game scouts, the Rhodesian police never received such a communication from Espungabera. This whole incident, therefore, is probably surrounded by untruths, untold truths, and contradictions. It is doubtful we shall ever know what really happened.

Of course, it is possible that Tabita was beaten by the scouts, but Fror declined to take the matter beyond his own office for fear of stirring a hornet's nest. He was, after all, deeply implicated in Shadrek's poaching, and he would not have wanted that fact to emerge from any official investigation.

After taking Tabita's statement, Fror gave her fifteen pounds in compensation and Johan ten pounds as a special present. But that was not all. Fror's wife took Tabita to a local store and purchased six dresses and four skirts for her, and seven shirts and seven pairs of shorts for young Johan. Shadrek was also given 250 pounds in cash from the police funds.

Alberto, the *chefe de posto*, asked Shadrek and his family to call upon him at his home. There Shadrek was given an additional sixty pounds from government funds. Alberto's wife rummaged about in her closets and came out with a whole range of used clothes for Tabita and Johan. Then Alberto and Fror threw a party for Shadrek and Tabita.

All this unasked-for largess suggests to me that Alberto and Fror were perhaps trying to placate Shadrek into not making a big issue of Tabita's alleged beating at the hands of the Gonarezhou staff. Certainly they had a great deal to gain if Shadrek would just let sleeping dogs lie and continue with his poaching. They also had a great deal to lose if the matter blew up into an international incident. The next day the Portuguese provided transport to take Shadrek and Tabita back home to Madjwisanga.

Two weeks later Shadrek visited Mahenya's again. The rains had started, and he knew that the game rangers at Chipinda Pools would be having a hard time getting vehicles through the Chihunja Hills. The chances of being surprised by a game scout patrol, Shadrek surmised (correctly), were remote.

During the next week Shadrek shot twelve big elephant bulls along the Lundi River between the junction and Fishans. They were blatant kills, many of them within sight of the main track along the river. Fishans was the closest to Chipinda Pools that Shadrek had ever killed an elephant. His intent was clear: He wanted to tell the Rhodesian national park authorities that he was angry and that these kills were in retaliation for Charles Mackie's raid on his Madjwisanga home.

It took Shadrek the better part of two weeks to move the ivory from these elephants into Mozambique. But he was not yet finished. No sooner did he have the ivory safely home than he returned to Mahenya's to the village of a man called Msimbi, who possessed a muzzleloading musket of great vintage. The Sabi was in early flood, and Shadrek had been told that Msimbi knew all the best crossing points. Shadrek was not concerned about crossing the flooded river at its then-current state, but he was worried that the river might rise while he was working on the far bank. Msimbi was Shadrek's assurance for the return trip, not the outgoing one.

Shadrek was in luck, Msimbi informed him, for he, Msimbi, planned to go net fishing the next day on the Lundi, which was not yet in flood. He told Shadrek that he could cross over into the game reserve with him in the morning. Shadrek stayed the night at Msimbi's village.

They rose at 4 AM and went to John Chauke's home to collect a tin of fresh gunpowder that John had manufactured for Msimbi. The Chauke brothers joined them, and they all went off to the Sabi River, which they crossed with little trouble. The passage Msimbi chose was only waist deep amid the wide and muddy floodwaters.

The party consisted of Shadrek with his .375 magnum, Msimbi with his gill nets and muzzleloader, and the Chauke brothers, John and Phineas, both armed only with their knives and knobkerrie axes.

As he had planned to do, Shadrek went off on his own just as soon as they reached the far bank. Msimbi, too, planned to go in search of elephant, although he had never shot one before. It is probable that he did not want to be outclassed by his notorious companion. Shadrek had instructed him carefully regarding how to approach his quarry and where to place his lead slug. Finally, he had told Msimbi that elephants were very dangerous and that he must not treat them with disrespect.

John, Phineas, and Msimbi stayed together for a while after Shadrek left, and they talked about how the Chauke brothers should set Msimbi's nets. Eventually John and Phineas took the gill nets and went off to the Lundi, placing them across one of the quieter backwater pools that all four men had agreed to use as a rendezvous.

Shadrek quickly located a herd of cows and calves in which three big bulls were busy servicing a young cow in estrus. He shot two of the three, and the others ran off. Not long after that he came across a lone bull and killed it, too.

At that point Shadrek heard Msimbi's muzzleloader go off. He described the report as: *Qua-fa,fa,fa-Quawaaooow*. This was followed by much trumpeting and screaming from the cowherd that Msimbi had obviously tackled.

The furor died down almost as quickly as it had erupted, and Shadrek gave the matter no further thought. Northeast of Tamboharta he discovered another group of bulls, from which he killed two. Not too far west of there he killed two more. He had not done at all badly. Seven big bull elephants before lunch on the first morning!

Shadrek felt he had killed enough elephants for one day and was conscious of the hours flying by, because he wanted all the ivory cut out before dark. So he returned to the Lundi, to the pool where John and Phineas had said they would be waiting. He knew they would by then have stretched Msimbi's nets across the pool and would be lazing away the day on the bank.

Shadrek called out their names, and they emerged from a hidden level of the riverbank. "How'd you get on?" John Chauke asked Shadrek.

"Seven!" Shadrek replied. "But now we've got to cut out the ivory. Bring your axes. You can leave the nets—you won't be able to pull them up until tomorrow morning."

"Where's Msimbi?" Shadrek asked.

"I thought he had joined up with you," said John Chauke.

"No," Shadrek responded. "I haven't seen him since we crossed the river this morning. But I heard a shot." Shadrek, with his sharply attuned sixth sense, began to feel something was very wrong.

"We did, too, from over that way," Phineas said, pointing east of the pan.

Shadrek nodded and tried to think where the shot had come from when he was at the top end of Tamboharta. He triangulated the positions and worked out in his mind's eye where the two lines crossed.

"I think we'd better go find Msimbi," Shadrek said, his tone of voice reflecting the worry in his mind. John and Phineas, too, were now worried. Shadrek's concern was contagious.

"Where did you last see Msimbi?" Shadrek asked.

John Chauke smirked. "Where the elephants you shot at this morning ran over the top of us."

"What? What happened?"

"Nothing really. After you fired your first shot, a whole herd of elephants ran all around us and right through our position. Then they ran on. After that, Msimbi went off on his own, taking up the elephants' tracks."

"He followed the same elephants?"

"Yes. There was a good bull in the herd, and it seemed the logical thing to do," Chauke replied.

They picked up Msimbi's tracks on top of the elephant spoor and tracked him down as if he were an animal. It did not take them very long to find him.

Msimbi had been killed by a herd of enraged cows and calves. The tracks told the story: After Msimbi had fired his shot—which clearly had resulted in a wounded elephant, for there was no carcass nearby—the animals had run him down, encircled his body, and vented their rage on his carcass. There were two tusk wounds in his left arm and one through his lower left leg. One tusk had passed through his stomach and another right through his chest from armpit to armpit. One elephant seemed to have stood on his left thigh, for the muscles were distorted and the bone was broken, its shattered ends protruding through the flesh. His stomach had burst open, and his intestines were strewn about the body like dirty spaghetti.

The elephant had then covered Msimbi's corpse with tree trunks and leafy branches. It was like a crypt. Shadrek had never seen anything like it, and he wondered at the elephants' reasons for "burying" the man they had just killed. All around were the pungent smell of elephant musth and the sweet gut-stench of a horrible human death.

Shadrek took off the overalls he was wearing, and the three men extracted Msimbi's broken body from the pile of debris, and they manipulated it into the denim suit. They had to split open the fabric of one leg of the overalls to accommodate the shattered left limb. They tied the material closed with bush-string made from the inner bark of a sapling. They then trussed the body onto a pole with bark rope, and, working in pairs, carried it to the banks of the Sabi River, a mile or so to the east.

On the riverbank they put the body down in the shade of some big trees, untied it from the pole, and laid it out in a respectful manner. It was not possible to carry the corpse across the swollen river, for either it or the pallbearers would have been swept away by the heavy current. It would also have placed them all in danger of being taken by crocodiles.

Once the body had been properly arranged, they encircled it with a ring of gunpowder from Msimbi's own muzzleloader pouch and set the gunpowder afire. The smell of the burnt gunpowder, they thought, would ward off any scavenging animals that might come along in their absence. Then they covered the body with leafy branches to hide it from the vultures.

The three men then crossed the river, carrying their important belongings above their heads, and proceeded directly to Msimbi's village to tell his mother the bad news. His father had passed away several years before. Msimbi had three wives and seven children, and there was much crying and wailing in the family village.

"Before his father died," Msimbi's mother lamented, "he told Msimbi that his gun was far too old to be used safely."

"Mama," Shadrek said to her softly. "We don't know if the gun was at fault. Msimbi was hunting on his own, and we really don't know what happened."

The next morning the three hunters took those of Msimbi's relatives who could cross the flooding river back to the corpse. It was still intact. No hyenas or vultures had found it.

It was important to Shadrek that the relatives understood that Msimbi's death had been caused by an elephant, lest he himself be blamed. This they were able to verify by examining the wounds. They also returned to the scene of the encounter, where Shadrek explained what he thought had happened. Then they returned to the riverbank and buried Msimbi in a four-foot-deep grave under the trees.

In deference to the man's death, Shadrek postponed his planned hunting trip in the Gonarezhou and returned to Madjwisanga. But he left his rifle with John Chauke because he intended to return once the commotion over Msimbi's death had died down.

He advised his two brothers-in-law just where to find the elephant he had killed and instructed them to recover the ivory. Shadrek paid John and Phineas handsomely for their work and said he would also pay whomever else they got to help them carry the ivory across the river and into Mozambique.

As it happened, however, the very next night the river came down in the first proper flood of the rainy season. John and Phineas were unable to cross into the Gonarezhou for several months. When they did so, the ivory was gone. The game scouts of the Gonarezhou had discovered the carcasses, and the tusks were taken to Chipinda Pools.

When he returned to Madjwisanga, Shadrek sat down with his father and told him all about the death of Msimbi. Shadrek had been more shaken by Msimbi's death than he cared to admit. It was the first time he had experienced a death from an elephant attack, and in the back of his mind he heard the litany: "There but for the grace of God go I." Muteruko warned Shadrek that the burial of Msimbi on the banks of the Sabi would not be the end of the matter. Muteruko was right.

Tabita was also concerned, for she had long suspected that Shadrek's charmed life could not last forever. Sooner or later an elephant or a buffalo or the game scouts of the Gonarezhou would get him—and that would put her entire family in jeopardy. Life was good for the family just as long as Shadrek continued to provide for them.

She was also concerned for her brothers, John and Phineas, for they, too, had been involved in Msimbi's death. Phineas had been a particularly close friend of the deceased, and she herself had known Msimbi and his family. So Tabita and her young daughter, Alice, visited her paternal family village at Mahenya's to express her sympathies regarding Msimbi's death.

When news of Msimbi's fate reached the district commissioner at Chipinga, he asked the police to investigate and confirm the cause of death. Game Ranger Glen Tatham from Melsetter accompanied a uniformed policeman to Mahenya's to help verify the facts. Glen took along with him a colleague, Game Ranger Graham Hall.

During the investigation it was revealed that Msimbi had been in Shadrek's poaching party when the elephant had killed him. This was all the excuse Glen needed to visit what I had told him was Shadrek's "home" at Mahenya's. I had already furnished Glen with a copy of the photograph that Charles Mackie had taken from Shadrek's home at Madjwisanga.

Once inside the Chauke kraal, Glen and Graham made a thorough search of the village huts. They found Shadrek's .375 magnum hidden away in the thatch of the kitchen hut, and four elephant tusks under a bed. Glen confiscated both the rifle and the ivory and immediately arrested John Chauke. He was subsequently convicted of being in possession of an illegal firearm and illegally possessing four elephant tusks. He spent the next twelve months in Chipinga jail. The tusks, of course, were Shadrek's, but John Chauke could not prove that, so he took the whole rap.

Chauke told Glen that the rifle belonged to Shadrek, but he could not prove that fact, either, although we all knew it was true. Chauke did not tell Glen that the village was his and not Shadrek's. Thus, after Glen's raid on the village, we erroneously continued to believe that Shadrek ran two homes, one in Mozambique at Madjwisanga and one in Rhodesia at Mahenya's.

Shadrek told me quite categorically that his home was and always had been at Madjwisanga and that he never had a second kraal at Mahenya's. But he admitted openly that he regularly stayed at John Chauke's village when operating out of Mahenya's.

I mention all this to reinforce my readers' understanding of the disjointed nature of Shadrek's story. He jumped from one subject to another, with little chronological order. Sometimes he talked so much and so fast he was like the verbal equivalent of a grasshopper on a hot summer's day.

I *sometimes* had to disregard his chronology and piece together the story fragments as they seemed to fit best. Nevertheless, in the process, I have tried to avoid leaving out any part of his story.

As mentioned, there were many discrepancies in different people's accounts of specific incidents. In Glen's report, for example, he clearly states that he encountered Tabita and one of Shadrek's sons at Shadrek's kraal, and that it was this little boy who positively identified his father in the photograph. Yet Shadrek claims it was his daughter, Alice, who accompanied Tabita.

The culmination of this episode is that Shadrek lost his .375 magnum rifle and that John Chauke—who had become a major player in Shadrek's story—went to prison for a year.

Chapter 20

Shadrek went cap in hand to Fror at Espungabera and told him about Msimbi's being killed and about the investigation by the police and the game rangers. He told him, too, about the confiscation of his rifle and John Chauke's arrest. Shadrek expected Fror to be very angry at the loss of the rifle, but he was not. The chief of police was far more concerned that Shadrek no longer had a firearm with which to shoot elephant.

Fror took Shadrek to Alberto, and Shadrek again explained what had happened. Fror persuaded Alberto to give Shadrek back the original .375 magnum, plus five boxes of solid ammunition. So Shadrek was back in business, and his friendship with Fror and with Alberto continued as though the loss of the weapon had never occurred. The only change was that both Fror and Alberto now demanded that Shadrek step up his poaching activities in the Gonarezhou. They seemed almost frantic in their desire for more and more ivory—and they wanted it as soon as possible. They gave Shadrek no hint at all about the reason for these more urgent demands upon him.

A few months later, things changed very suddenly in Mozambique. Without any warning the Portuguese vacated Espungabera, and both Fror and Alberto were en route back to Portugal. In their stead, FRELIMO officials came to live in the town. The Portuguese *chefe de posto's* position was filled by a FRELIMO political commissar, and a FRELIMO policeman took over Fror's job.

The Portuguese had abdicated their position in Mozambique, and overnight FRELIMO had become the new government. There had been no good-byes. No demands were made for Shadrek to return Alberto's rifle. No nothing. One day, Shadrek's Portuguese friends had been at Espungabera; the next day they were gone.

Shadrek was left in a bit of a vacuum. His father still had his old 10.75mm elephant rifle—with no ammunition. Shadrek still had Alberto's .375 magnum, but fewer than fifty rounds of ammunition were left. They also still had Muteruko's old muzzleloader, for which they could make their own gunpowder and shot. But Shadrek knew that with the departure of his Portuguese friends, life would not be the same ever again.

Nevertheless, he realized, his life must go on. One afternoon shortly after the Portuguese departed, Shadrek left Madjwisanga and traveled to Mahenya's on his bicycle, arriving just after dark. John Chauke was still in jail, and Phineas had just left to work a year's contract on the South African gold mines. Shadrek found himself alone with the village womenfolk.

John Chauke's wife was not happy with Shadrek, since she blamed him for her husband's arrest and jailing. She told Shadrek it was *his* rifle the police had found in John's possession, so it was Shadrek who should have gone to jail and not her John. Nevertheless, Shadrek was family, and she grudgingly gave him an evening meal.

It did not take long for Shadrek to grow tired of the tirade to which he was subjected that night, so he decided to cross over into the junction area in the moonlight and camp there. It would give him the opportunity to make an early start in the morning.

The river was down, so Shadrek waded across the shallow water just above the apex of the junction and began making his way through the high-canopy riverine forest toward the Lundi. Suddenly he came across a large group of tents that barred his passage upstream. The whole camp was silvery-silent in the moonlight, so he assumed that everybody was asleep. Curiosity got the better of him, and he decided to wait until morning to see what the unusually big camp was all about.

At the crack of dawn the camp stirred, and many white men wearing Rhodesian army camouflage came out of the tents. They were all fit-looking soldiers, and wherever they went they carried their military rifles with them. This rifle-carrying seemed ominous and threatening to Shadrek.

Shadrek watched for half an hour and saw soldiers move to the outskirts of the camp, where they changed places with others who had clearly been there all during the night. These, he correctly concluded, were the camp guards. One of them was positioned no more than fifty yards from where Shadrek lay. He was very lucky not to have alerted this guard in the night. He might have got himself shot.

It was the first evidence Shadrek had seen that the Rhodesian war effort was about to be extended to the Gonarezhou. He was witnessing an exploratory expedition by the Rhodesian army to familiarize themselves with conditions in the Gonarezhou. Now that FRELIMO had taken over the reins of government in Mozambique, the Rhodesians clearly anticipated ZANLA terrorist incursions all along the border right down to the Limpopo, which eventually did take place.

If the Rhodesian army were about to occupy the Gonarezhou, Shadrek's elephant-poaching activities would be adversely affected. This thought worried him for the next several weeks.

Shadrek backed off slowly from his exposed position and found refuge in the dense undergrowth near the river. Weaving his way through the heavy brush, he quickly made his way back to the Sabi. Then, seeing the wide-open expanse of muddy water and golden sand before him, he decided not to cross the river again at that point in broad daylight. Instead, he moved upstream and crossed onto the top end of Sabi Island, then traveled downstream and crossed the Rio Save, right on the border, onto the south bank at Marhumbini. The heavy reedbeds there hid his crossing from any prying eyes in the soldiers' camp.

From Marhumbini Shadrek quickly made his way to the tsetse department camp at Chitove. He greeted the two cattle guards there and a little later he shot two big elephant bulls not far from their camp. Then he returned to the camp and invited the guards to come and collect some meat. They were frightened at first since they had heard all about the notorious Shadrek. But the poacher was persistent, and in the end they went with him and cut huge bundles of meat from the carcasses while Shadrek chopped out the ivory. When he had removed the tusks he told the men that they should invite their friends to come and get meat, too, thereby befriending these tsetse guards. He carried the tusks off into the bush one at a time, leapfrogging with them as he took them farther and farther from the damning evidence of the butchered carcasses.

They were big tusks, and it took him all that day to get them across the border game fence onto the Mozambican side. Once they were safely hidden in the bush beyond the fence, Shadrek returned to Mahenya's, where he slept the night and recovered his bicycle.

The next day he returned to his ivory cache and was busy loading his bicycle with two tusks when he heard a vehicle approaching along the game fence. It stopped at the exact point where he had yesterday dragged the last of the tusks under the bottom strand of the fence. A white man and two black men emerged from the vehicle to examine Shadrek's tracks. The black men were wearing the uniform of the Rhodesian Tsetse Department.

Shadrek quietly put his cycle flat on the ground and prostrated himself in the wiry grass and short bush —watching. The men were less than fifty yards away, and he could hear them talking quite plainly. They correctly recognized the strange signs in the sandy ground as tusk drag-marks, but they incorrectly interpreted yesterday's spoor as being very fresh. They looked for a moment, penetratingly, into the bush where Shadrek lay. Then the white man instructed one of his two assistants to climb through the fence and see where the tracks led him.

"Maybe it's Shadrek," he heard the white man say. "And maybe he has hidden his tusks in the bush over there."

One of the black men squeezed through the tight steel strands of the high fence and began tracking Shadrek's spoor directly to where he lay in the grass. It soon became obvious that the man would walk right on top of him, so Shadrek rose up out of his scrubby cover and crouched, pointing his rifle. Suddenly their eyes met. The man nearly died of fright. He stood frozen in his shoes.

"What do you want?" Shadrek asked abruptly.

"*Haaaiee*... don't shoot!" the white man shouted at Shadrek. "Don't shoot."

"What do you want?" Shadrek shouted at the white man. "Best you get in your Land Rover and drive away from here."

"No! No!" the white man responded. "I want to talk to you. I want to buy your ivory."

"Who are you?" Shadrek demanded.

"We belong to the tsetse department," the man shouted back. "We're not police or game rangers."

Shadrek looked him over quite openly as he considered the man's suggestion. He already knew they were tsetse department officials. He had seen enough of the black men's uniforms both inside the Gonarezhou

and in the thickets in Mozambique, where they had been spraying DDT for years now, to know that.

"I live at Vila Salazar," the man continued hurriedly. "And we," he gestured at his two assistants, "look after the fence line along the border."

"How much do you offer me for my ivory?" Shadrek asked—always the businessman.

"That depends. How big are the tusks?"

Thus was the ice broken between them. The tusks were very big, and the tsetse department official agreed to buy all four for 250 Rhodesian pounds—but, he said, "I have only fifty pounds on me at this time."

Shadrek did not show any emotion at the high price that the white man offered him. It was many times higher than the best price he had ever been paid for equivalent-size tusks inside Mozambique.

Throughout this discussion, many different thoughts and emotions were playing games with each other in the back of Shadrek's mind. He was acutely conscious of the absence of Fror and Alberto, who until recently had been his biggest and best customers. There were rumours, too, that since FRELIMO had taken over in Mozambique, the South Africans were no longer getting power from Cabora Bassa. That meant the helicopter crews that had maintained the power lines would not be buying ivory off him. So his potential customers were reduced to the few remaining Portuguese storekeepers—and even they were thinking of leaving the country.

The coming of FRELIMO and the departure of the Portuguese had caused Shadrek's ivory markets to suddenly dry up. Perhaps this meeting with the white Rhodesian tsetse department official was fortuitous. Perhaps this white man would be the answer to all Shadrek's problems. It was worth taking a risk with him.

"If you give me the fifty pounds, I will hold these tusks for you," Shadrek offered. "How long will it take you to get the other two hundred pounds?"

"I can meet you here at this exact spot in two weeks," the white man suggested. "I will then have the extra two hundred pounds for you. But we must show our good faith in each other—you let me have these tusks now, and I will give you fifty pounds now."

It was worth the risk. Shadrek needed a new market for his ivory, and this man seemed to have dropped from heaven. They shook hands on the deal. Shadrek received his fifty pounds immediately, and the white man drove off with the four giant tusks. In fact, the deal saved Shadrek a great deal of time and effort because he now had no need to transport the tusks to his home at Madjwisanga and no need to seek a market for them.

That same day, Shadrek returned to the game reserve and stayed the night in the thatched encampment of his newfound tsetse department friends at Chitove. They knew nothing about the soldiers in the junction area and said nothing about any game-ranger contingent in the area, either—although at that time I was culling elephants all over the Lundi sector of the game reserve. Our permanent camp was at Fishans, at the upper end of the Chilojo Cliffs. Chitove is at the bottom end of the cliffs.*

Early that morning Shadrek left the Chitove camp and shot two more big elephant bulls on the southern slopes of Kundani Hill. At eight o'clock he was busy chopping out the tusks when he heard the droning engine of a low-flying aircraft. It was the Piper Super Cub belonging to the Department of National Parks and Wildlife Management. It was busy locating and selecting elephant herds for a cull that was to take place to the north of Kundani Hill that morning.

Shadrek hastily chopped off some mopane branches and scantily covered the carcasses. Then he hid his cycle, climbed, and slid around to the north slope, from where he sat watching the plane circling high up. Below it he could see a large herd of cow elephants in the mopane scrub.

*Shadrek's chronology here was very faulty, since he states that these events took place after the Portuguese had left Mozambique in 1974; in fact, the elephant-culling exercise, about which he had most definitely been talking, took place in 1972.

They seemed undisturbed, for they went about their feeding as if the soft humming of the aircraft engine high above them did not exist.

Then Shadrek saw in the distance a whole convoy of vehicles crawling through the mopane scrub toward the elephants. There were several Land Rovers followed by big lorries and tractors with trailers, which transported a whole herd of black labourers who sat silently and patiently. Presently the vehicles stopped, and a small group of men started walking toward the elephants. The majority of the people stayed with the vehicles.

What happened next shocked Shadrek. He was truly angry when he told me what he had witnessed. Three hunters approached the large breeding herd and at very close quarters began shooting. The fire was rapid and intense, but it lasted only a few minutes. When the shooting stopped, the entire herd of elephants lay dead.

"They shot everything," Shadrek told me. "There were several big cows and one very big bull in the herd, but all the rest were *totos*—juveniles and calves. But they killed everything. There must have been forty or fifty in that group, and they killed every one." Shadrek cast his head down and shook it sadly.

I felt guilty as sin as Shadrek told me that story, for I was the leader of the three game-ranger hunters who shot those elephants. I remember the kill very well because it was the only one we ever conducted in the shadow of Kundani Hill. In retrospect, and in light of my newfound knowledge regarding the true extent of Shadrek's poaching in the area, I am surprised that this was the only time he came across our handiwork.

We shot out several herds in the Marhumbini area, for example, and others near Tamboharta. But I must admit that most of our culls took place on the upper Nyamasikana River above Fishans, and deep in the sandveld area behind the cliffs—all a long way from the junction area. Also, the Lundi cull had lasted only two weeks that year from start to finish. Still, I found it amazing that Shadrek had personal knowledge only of this one cull.

"Why would the white man do such a stupid thing?" Shadrek asked me. "Doesn't he realize that those baby elephants he killed would have grown up into big bulls one day—and that it is only the big bulls that are worth shooting?"

"They tell me they shot out big numbers of elephants in the game reserve some years ago because they were damaging the forest, Shadrek," I told him. "It was to save the big trees that they killed so many elephants."

"Hah!" Shadrek retorted, repudiating my statement immediately. "The white man is stupid. It is not the cows and the babies that do the damage but the big bulls. Have you ever seen a baby elephant knock down a big tree? Or even a cow elephant? No, you haven't," he continued with authority, "because they don't hurt the big trees."

I could not answer Shadrek, for what he said made a lot of sense. In fact, he had echoed my own criticism of the Rhodesian national park policy of shooting out large numbers of cows and calves in the Gonarezhou rather than killing a preponderance of bulls. We had conducted the culling programme principally on the basis of the serious damage being done to the high-canopy trees along the rivers—all of which was carried out by the bulls. Yet our charge was to reduce elephant numbers by knocking out the cow herds, thereby limiting the population's capacity to reproduce quickly.

We were also to eliminate "a proportionate number of bulls"—whatever that meant. On the other hand, we were told to remember that big bull elephants were the tourist draw card, and in the interests of tourism, it would be good for the game reserve to have lots of big bulls running around.

So there was a serious contradiction in all of this official blarney, and here Shadrek, a comparatively ignorant poacher from rural Mozambique, had hit the nail right on the head the very first time we ever discussed the subject.

This brought back to me a lesson that our onetime chief research officer in the department, Roelf Atwell, once gave to an arrogant, know-it-all young research officer at Chipinda Pools. This young man had just lamented the fact that he alone, among all the staff in the game reserve, had had a "proper" university training.

"You see that old man over there?" Roelf replied, pointing to a ragged old tribesman who was still living on the banks of the Lundi River inside the Gonarezhou. "You will learn more about your profession as a wildlife research officer from that old man than you will ever learn from your university professors. I can guarantee you that that old black man has learnt more about wildlife from practical experience than a university will ever be able to teach you in a lifetime. So don't be so quick to criticize people who lack your academic qualifications. Learn a little humility!"

Learn a little humility—indeed! I will never forget those pearls of wisdom, and during my discussion with Shadrek, I was sorry that Roelf Atwell had not had the opportunity to meet my elephant-poacher friend. They would have got on like a house on fire.

Shadrek continued his tale of the cull, describing how a mass of labourers had arrived at the kill site , how they had cut out the ivory and stripped the carcasses of their hides and meat, and how they had loaded it all onto the lorries and tractor-trailers and driven away to the north. Then he told me how a big yellow machine had dug a huge hole in the ground, had shoveled the bones and guts of the elephants into the hole, and had covered all the remains with the soil it had previously excavated. Everything he told me was true to the last detail. I have no doubt in my mind that Shadrek had sat on the side of Kundani Hill that day and watched the entire proceedings.

The tsetse department official from Vila Salazar did not keep his appointment with Shadrek. So Shadrek never received the extra two hundred pounds he had been promised for the four big tusks he had given the white man. This truly infuriated Shadrek, for he put great store in a man keeping his word. He was also very disappointed that he had not opened up a new market for ivory, for he was now genuinely concerned about the loss of his old markets inside Mozambique.

Shadrek fumed for days after the missed appointment and the white man's broken promise. He seethed for revenge, racking his brains for a way to achieve retribution. Finally he came up with a solution that would not only reimburse him handsomely for his loss but also salve his festering anger at the white man.

Accompanied by two friends from Mozambique, Joromea and Petro, Shadrek went one night to the tsetse department camp at Chipote, just above Tamboharta inside the Gonarezhou. They waited in the bush until after midnight. Then Shadrek silently pulled out the gate poles from the cattle kraal and quietly drove the cattle out. Joromea and Petro flanked the herd on either side while Shadrek gently drove the animals on from behind. The tsetse department guards slept on in their huts not fifty yards from the kraal, as Shadrek and his friends drove the thirteen cattle away and over the Sabi River.

On the road through Mahenya's, the cattle rustlers encountered a very drunken man, whom Shadrek knew very well. His name was Mundangandira, and he was wending his way home after what had obviously been a wonderful party. Shadrek told Mundangandira to tell the tsetse department guards at Chipote that it was he, Shadrek, who had stolen the cattle, to compensate himself for the theft of his ivory by the tsetse department white man who looked after the border game fence out of Vila Salazar. Thus, he thought, he would both gain compensation for his stolen ivory and bring justice to the unscrupulous white man who had tricked him out of two hundred pounds.

Shadrek settled down with the cattle at his home at Madjwisanga and was just beginning to think that he had pulled off his feat when he had a visit from the new FRELIMO officials at Espungabera. Mundangandira had clearly passed on Shadrek's message, for an official complaint had been registered against Shadrek by the Rhodesian police.

At this juncture I must say that although I was by then stationed in Salisbury (now Harare) and had been promoted to provincial game warden-in-charge of the Mashonaland South province, I never heard a word about Shadrek's theft of those cattle. And the tsetse department never breathed a word about its official at Vila Salazar being implicated in an illegal trade in ivory with our infamous poacher. But it must have

Chapter 20

known about it all! The truth of Shadrek's story about this cattle theft was later verified by John Davey from police records at Chiredzi.

A FRELIMO police Land Rover arrived at Shadrek's village at Madjwisanga three weeks after the theft of the cattle. The black policeman in charge of the investigation asked Shadrek if he had indeed stolen cattle from the Rhodesian Tsetse Department as the Rhodesian police report had alleged. Shadrek readily admitted that he had stolen the Chipote cattle—and explained why. In the process, he gained the policeman's sympathy.

"You had better come with me to Espungabera," the policeman said. "I can understand why you stole these cattle, but I cannot let you keep them just on the strength of what you have told me. In fact, I have no authority to make any kind of decision on the matter. You will have to explain your case to the FRELIMO commandant."

So Shadrek went to Espungabera with the black policeman and again explained his case to the FRELIMO commandant. The man smiled and shook his head. He had heard all about the infamous elephant poacher named Shadrek, who regularly singed Rhodesian beards in the Gonarezhou. He, too, was sympathetic to Shadrek's case, but the theft of the cattle had placed the commandant in a difficult position.

At that stage of Rhodesian/Mozambican affairs, with FRELIMO having recently taken over in Mozambique, the two countries were trying to behave in a civilized and neighbourly manner toward each other. It was only later, when FRELIMO blatantly supported the ZANLA cause against Rhodesia, that Rhodesia closed its borders with Mozambique and a de facto state of war came into being. At the time of Shadrek's theft of the tsetse department cattle herd, however, the FRELIMO administration at Espungabera was enjoying certain important privileges extended to it by the Rhodesians.

"Shadrek," the FRELIMO commandant explained, "I understand where you are coming from. And quite frankly, anyone who has done so much damage to the white regime in Rhodesia, as you have reportedly done in the Gonarezhou, deserves a bloody medal. If it were up to me,

I'd tell you to keep the damn cattle. Unfortunately, there are other facets to this matter.

"You may not know this, but the Rhodesian government allows us FRELIMO officials to use the Chipinga to Umtali tarmac road inside Rhodesia to get from here to Chimoio and back. If you don't know where Chimoio is, it is inside Mozambique, just across the border and directly opposite the Rhodesian town of Umtali. And from Chimoio there is a tarmac road right down to Beira.

"For us to get to Beira from Espungabera direct requires that we travel on a terrible and very bumpy dirt road for fourteen hours. Using the Umtali to Beira route, it takes us about ten hours and is a comfortable drive all the way."

The commandant looked at Shadrek to see if his visitor understood. Then he continued: "We are afraid the Rhodesians will withdraw this privilege if we fail to return the cattle you 'acquired' in Rhodesia."

Shadrek shook his head in dismay. There was clearly no justice in this world.

"Do you understand the predicament you have placed us in, Shadrek?"

Shadrek nodded. "Yes," he said dismally. "But tell me, commandant, how can I get my money back from the Rhodesian white man who tricked me so badly?"

"I don't know, Shadrek," the FRELIMO official said with a sigh. "But it is better that you, as one man, suffer the consequences of your own actions than that the whole of the government administration here at Espungabera do the suffering for you. Consider yourself lucky that we shall find it impossible to arrest you for the offense and hand you over to the Rhodesians." The threat was not very veiled, and Shadrek understood it implicitly.

He agreed to return the cattle to the Rhodesian Tsetse Department through the good offices of Chief Mahenya, which he did just as soon as he got home—except for one animal slaughtered for his own consumption. He drove the remaining twelve animals back along the path, near the north bank of the Rio Save. At the border he collapsed the cattle fence that separated Mozambique from Mahenya's and drove the cattle through, leaving them to wander while he visited the old chief to tell him where they could be found. It was up to Mahenya then to get word back to the tsetse department cattle guards at Chipote.

When he got back home, he and Tabita began preparing to move from Madjwisanga to a new kraal site at Chiwi on the south bank of the Rio Save. For some time Shadrek and Tabita had been mulling over the changed circumstances that had followed the FRELIMO takeover in Mozambique. Shadrek now had few ivory market options left in Mozambique, and he was astute enough to realize that there was probably going to be a new and perhaps permanent Rhodesian military presence in the Gonarezhou.

It was time for them to make a major career change.

Chapter 21

Shadrek's move to Chiwi was driven by the lack of any worthwhile markets for ivory in Mozambique. He still occasionally hunted elephants in the Gonarezhou, for elephant hunting was in his blood, but his impact on the game reserve's big bulls shriveled away to nothing. His limited stock of ammunition diminished with every hunt, and he did not want to run out of cartridges. The irregular presence of Rhodesian security forces in the game reserve was a constant worry for him. As a result, Shadrek's elephant hunting now tended to be more for sport or for nostalgic reasons than for ivory.

FRELIMO's earlier benevolent compassion for Shadrek's cause evaporated with the appointment of a new political commissar at Espungabera. Now he was just one of the masses and had to follow exactly the same rules and regulations that applied to every other communist "comrade" in Mozambique. He was required to pay an annual personal tax of three pounds seventeen shillings and sixpence a year plus a monthly "hut tax" of one shilling per hut. There were other taxes, too. He was also required to spend one full day every week tending crops on state farms run by FRELIMO. Finally, the new *chefe de posto* sent a personal message to Shadrek warning him that if he were caught crossing the border into Rhodesia for any reason, he would be fined one hundred pounds.

What made it really difficult for everybody on the Rio Save was that FRELIMO refused to allow the men to go to South Africa to work in the gold mines. The periodic disappearance of the menfolk to South Africa, and the money and presents they brought back for their families a year later, had become almost a traditional way of life for the Mhlengwe,

Ndau, and Shangaan people of the Rio Save. Many, however, still sneaked away. The Rhodesian's antitsetse fly campaign also came to a halt, further reducing employment opportunities for the people. The people's plight did not worry FRELIMO. Communist dogma was the force that ruled the country and its international relations in those days.

So Shadrek's move to Chiwi was a matter of survival. He had to do something to earn a living, and he decided he could make a lot of money by opening a store at Chiwi. He also desperately wanted to own and run what he euphemistically referred to as a "hotel." He chose Chiwi as the location of these businesses because FRELIMO had opened up a new

military base there, and there were no store or bar facilities to serve the soldiers and the families of the officer corps.

Let me explain what a "store" comprised in remote parts of the African bush at that time. It was a brick building with a counter and some shelves on the back wall stocked with a few tinned goods, some clothes and fabrics, and sundry other items. Shadrek eventually employed a tailor who sat in the store behind his sewing machine and made clothes for customers who bought material off the shelves. During the Portuguese era, such establishments normally carried a reasonable supply of Portuguese wines. In Shadrek's time there was none.

The "hotel," in Shadrek's case, consisted of one big room with a small bar at one end. There were tables with benches where clients could sit and drink and buy frugal meals. There were no sleeping rooms.

These establishments cost Shadrek fifteen pounds and four pounds per month, respectively, in FRELIMO taxes. Even so, given the reasonably large military establishment at Chiwi, these two simple enterprises quickly paid Shadrek handsome dividends because they had no competition. In the beginning, however, they took up all his savings. Construction was expensive, as was the purchase of furniture and stock. One of his biggest problems, however, was procuring the very meagre goods and liquor that were then available in the still war-torn country.

Chiwi was not far from Massangena, the principal metropolis on the Rio Save, where there was a police *and* a military presence. Chiwi, however, was the biggest military base in the area.

Shortly after Shadrek moved to Chiwi, other developments began to work in his favour. FRELIMO constructed three satellite military base camps along the river upstream from the settlement. They were called Muchele Camps One, Two, and Three, and they were well hidden in the dense riverine bush of the Rio Save. The Muchele camps, although ostensibly run by FRELIMO military personnel, were really ZANLA terrorist bases—springboards for ZANLA freedom fighters entering the lowveld of Rhodesia.

Shadrek's hotel served the soldiers in all these bases, FRELIMO and ZANLA alike, and he did very well for himself financially—so much so that his elephant-hunting adventures fell by the wayside. Every time he left home to hunt elephant, he lost business. Shadrek had by then become something of a living legend on the Rio Save, and the soldiers came to his hotel to meet the intrepid elephant hunter. ZANLA came also to pick his brains regarding the conditions of passage through the game reserve.

The four tusks from the elephants that I had shot with Don Boyd in the Sabi-Lundi junction area—on that very first "poaching" expedition with John Chauke and Josiah—had in fact been taken by John Chauke and Josiah to Shadrek at his hotel in Chiwi.

I learnt from Shadrek that he had not recently gone to South Africa to work in the mines—as Josiah had told Don Boyd and me at the start of the operation. That was just a ploy by Josiah to avoid discussing a sensitive subject.

Neither had Shadrek helped out Chief Mahenya with his elephant problem. Mahenya had not asked him to do so, and Shadrek did not even know that Mahenya had a problem. In any case, Shadrek had no market for ivory in Mozambique and was then husbanding his ammunition. He had also been very busy running his two new businesses.

Shadrek had arranged to sell "our" four tusks to the Portuguese man who ran the sawmills at Sarason, not far from Chiwi. He took the tusks to Sarason to show his buyer their size and quality, and they agreed on a price. But—once bitten, twice shy—Shadrek had not released them to the Portuguese. Instead he brought them back to Chiwi and locked them away in the storeroom of his hotel while he awaited the Portuguese man's return from Lourenço Marques with the money. Lourenço Marques had by then been renamed Maputo by FRELIMO.

At that stage, relations between the Rhodesians and FRELIMO had been reduced to a state of undeclared war. FRELIMO was openly assisting Robert Mugabe's ZANLA freedom fighters in their quest to overthrow the Rhodesian government, and the Rhodesians were making regular cross-border raids into Mozambique to knock out known ZANLA terrorist bases. In the Tete and Manica provinces of Mozambique, the Rhodesians and

ZANLA virtually ran the country. Both had a permanent presence there, and each fought a war of annihilation and attrition against the other.

Both sides were ruthless. The Rhodesians, however, were the better equipped and the more aggressive. They enjoyed the upper hand when contacts were made. But ZANLA persisted, continually entering northeastern and eastern Rhodesia to murder and cause mayhem amid the local black populace and the white farming community alike. By comparison, the war situation on the Rio Save was very low key. Nevertheless, the Rhodesians were not ignorant of the ZANLA presence south of Espungabera, and they bided their time, awaiting the most opportune situation.

Chiwi became an important potential target, for terrorists captured in the Rhodesian lowveld revealed that FRELIMO was helping ZANLA fighters out of Chiwi to enter southeastern Rhodesia. Shadrek's hotel was a major part of that target because it was there that a great many FRELIMO and ZANLA soldiers spent their idle hours. After some horrifyingly successful Rhodesian raids on ZANLA bases in the Tete and Manica provinces, FRELIMO understood that the Chiwi base would soon become an important target for the Rhodesians. So they continually warned the civilians living there to be prepared for possible land and air strikes.

When Shadrek and Tabita heard the drone of engines early one morning, therefore, they rushed outside to see an armada of aircraft converging on Chiwi. Without trying to recover any of their possessions, they grabbed up their children and ran straight into the nearby bush.

They kept moving as, close behind, they heard the shriek of jet engines, the thunder of bombs striking their targets, and the chatter of machine guns strafing the soldiers in the FRELIMO camp. And there was the sound of FRELIMO antiaircraft guns retaliating and of FRELIMO soldiers firing their AK-47s at the diving aircraft.

Five helicopters were holding back from the target area, lighter now that they had dropped their troop payloads. They functioned as airborne gunships, machine-gunning anything that moved on the ground.

Looking back, Shadrek saw two twin-boomed Lynx aircraft screaming down toward the barracks. As they pulled out of their dive, each released two squat canisters from their wings. They contained frantan—Rhodesia's home-brew version of napalm. It was gelatinized gasoline carried in large drumlike containers that detonated the moment they hit the ground, showering everything and everybody within a fifty-yard radius with adhesive globules of burning petrol.

After dropping their bombs, the Lynxes strafed the FRELIMO camp, then rose above the havoc they had created and circled the battle scene.

Shadrek urged Tabita and the children on, wanting to put as much distance as possible between themselves and the battle behind them. A little farther on, Shadrek stopped to look back again. This time he saw two lines of transport aircraft three abreast, arriving over Chiwi. They were DC-3s of the Rhodesian Air Force. Paratroopers were being dropped on both the eastern and western sides of the Chiwi township.

The transports flew on toward them. Shadrek and Tabita resumed their flight, but the heavy droning of aircraft engines drew closer and closer above them. One line of machines was almost overhead when the aircraft turned to the east. Then, just five hundred feet above their heads, there came the repeated crunching sounds of parachutes cracking open. Shadrek looked up in dismay, but quickly realized that the descending paratroopers would land just on the Chiwi side of their position.

The family rushed on as fast as they were able. It was touch and go, but soon they were definitely outside the killing fields. They had been extremely lucky not to have been caught within the encircling net. Still the family ran on.

What Shadrek did not know was that yet more troops had invaded the country in lorries and Land Rovers, crossing the border at Mahenya's and at Marhumbini. They timed their arrival at Chiwi to coincide with the end of the primary air strikes.

The air attack lasted no more than fifteen minutes; a fierce battle on the ground carried on for more than an hour. It was a slaughter. The FRELIMO soldiers, softened up by the aerial bombardment, hadn't a

chance. Then the Rhodesians spent several hours mopping up. Deep in the sandveld bush, Shadrek and Tabita lay in a dense thicket listening fearfully to the not-so-distant sound of sporadic gunfire.

FRELIMO offered comparatively little resistance. Those soldiers who had survived the air bombardment scattered into the nearby bush, and the circling helicopters accounted for most of them. Others hid in whatever cover they could find. These, however, were routed from their retreats by the Rhodesian ground troops and ruthlessly cut down the moment they broke from cover. Few escaped.

Finally, there were loud detonations as Rhodesian sappers demolished key structures in the Chiwi barracks. And all the while there was the banshee screaming of helicopter jet engines and the *whap-whap-whap* of their rotor blades.

For hours thereafter a deathly silence reigned. Shadrek and Tabita and their three quivering children lay hidden in the bush, wondering what was going on. It was late afternoon when Shadrek, on his own, returned cautiously to Chiwi. The Rhodesians had gone, and elements of the FRELIMO army and police had arrived from Massangena and Espungabera to take control of the tiny settlement.

Corpses lay strewn everywhere. Many of the bodies were shattered horribly or burnt to cinders. The smell of burnt and still-burning human flesh curled Shadrek's nostrils. The stench reminded him of scorched roast pork. Soldier-medics tended to the many wounded who lay screaming or groaning all about the small town. Shadrek was warned off and told not to attempt entry into his shattered hotel, for the Rhodesians had left booby traps everywhere.

Before the people of Chiwi were allowed to return to their shattered homes, FRELIMO had the mammoth task of locating and disarming the cleverly hidden explosives. Nearly a hundred vehicle land mines—recovered by the Rhodesians from the sacked FRELIMO magazines—and myriad antipersonnel mines had been laid throughout the town. Not only had these explosives been set underground in the conventional manner but many also had been used, together with some ingenious and innocuous-looking trigger devices, as booby traps within the debris of the town. It took FRELIMO over a week to clear the small town of all these potential death traps.

Shadrek and his family stayed with his parents at Madjwisanga while Chiwi was being cleared. And they stayed on after discovering that nothing was left of Shadrek's hotel. Every single building in the small hamlet had been gutted by fire or blown up by bombs, rocket fire from the aircraft, or explosions detonated by Rhodesian soldiers on the ground.

Shadrek's hotel was a total wreck. His most prized possession, a hi-fi radio, was missing. It had not been destroyed—it had been taken away by either the Rhodesians or FRELIMO. Everything of value had gone, including the four tusks that John Chauke and Josiah Chiranzwa had brought to Shadrek. The soldiers had drunk all of Shadrek's beer and liquor, and what they didn't take they destroyed. Nothing was left that could be salvaged. Four hundred pounds in cash—Shadrek's hard-earned savings—were gone. His sewing machine in the store had been smashed to smithereens.

FRELIMO told the international community that an estimated one thousand civilians had been killed in the raid, and just as many had been wounded or maimed. It had been a senseless attack on innocent people, they claimed, and was an affront to the people of Mozambique. In FRELIMO's press release there was no mention of the number of FRELIMO or ZANLA soldiers that had died in the raid.

Shadrek knew that despite FRELIMO's propaganda, the attack had been a major victory for the Rhodesians and a disaster for FRELIMO and ZANLA. He knew, too, that FRELIMO's huge casualty figures were a complete fabrication. Nowhere near a thousand people had been killed, and although there had been many civilian casualties, the bulk of those killed and wounded had been FRELIMO soldiers.

A number of ZANLA fighters were dead, too—those who had been staying the night in the FRELIMO barracks. But ZANLA got off lightly, since the Rhodesians had completely missed its Muchele camps. They had been too well hidden away in the riverine bush, although not far off the road used by the vehicles that had transported the Rhodesian ground troops into Chiwi. Perhaps, Shadrek surmised when telling me this story, the camps were just too new for the Rhodesians to have known about them.

ZANLA made no attempt to attack the retiring Rhodesian column as it passed by the Muchele camps on its way back to Marhumbini. The freedom fighters had been cowed by the ferocity of the Rhodesian air bombardment and the noise of the ground battle that had followed. Just the sounds of war had caused them to vacate their camps and scatter into the nearby bush, and then to lie low until the battle was over.

Shadrek told me that he believed that his hotel had been singled out as a principal target because it had hosted FRELIMO and ZANLA soldiers. It was not a freebee establishment, however, for every one of the soldiers had paid the going price for anything he bought.

The hotel and store together had been earning Shadrek a reasonable and stable living. After the Rhodesian attack, both were in ruins and all Shadrek's possessions were gone. All his blankets and personal clothing and furniture had been burnt. His pole-and-*dagga* (mud) huts behind the hotel and everything in them had gone up in smoke. This single Rhodesian raid had ruined Shadrek.

After the raid FRELIMO requisitioned the sawmills at nearby Sarason, which became their headquarters as the demolished town was slowly reconstructed. Shadrek and Tabita stayed on at Madjwisanga, where they began picking up the pieces and trying to plan a new life.

Almost in passing, Shadrek told me something of great significance. Only when the FRELIMO military command left Sarason and returned to the battered barracks at Chiwi was Tabita able to return to her job across the river in Chiwi. Her job was the family's saving grace; her small salary was all that kept them going. He traveled across the river with her each day and began to rebuild the pole-and-mud-thatched huts that had been their home. They returned each night to Madjwisanga.

"What job does Tabita have in Chiwi?" I asked Shadrek, wanting to totally understand the family's predicament. I was feeling very sorry for

Shadrek. His situation after the Rhodesian raid clearly had been devastating. I was even beginning to take his side against the terrible Rhodesians.

"She works for the FRELIMO commandant," Shadrek replied.

I could not believe my ears. "She works for the man in charge of the FRELIMO military base at Chiwi?"

"That's right," he said.

"What kind of work does she do, Shadrek?"

"She is the commandant's *mabarant,"* he replied. The native word means "scribe." In other words, she was the commandant's secretary! I could not believe my ears. This was just too good to be true.

"You mean she writes the commandant's letters and keeps his books?"

"Yes," Shadrek said simply. "She is the only woman in Chiwi who can read and write in Portuguese."

"So she will know when senior ZANLA people come to visit Chiwi from Maputo—even before they arrive?"

"Yes!" Shadrek said, smiling shyly at me as he slowly began to understand the implications. Tabita was a potential gold mine of important military intelligence. I looked down toward the river and watched John Davey reel in a nice fat bream. I smiled inwardly. My Special Branch friend was not going to believe this!

"We can discuss Tabita later, Shadrek," I said to change the subject. "Go on with your story."

"Well," Shadrek continued, "I felt very bad at not being able to provide for my family and having to rely on Tabita's small salary. Then I remembered John Chauke's story about you and your suggestion that we go into business together." Shadrek smiled as he recalled how his Chiwi businesses had been flourishing and considered the potential that I represented. "I really had nothing to lose coming to see you," he said, looking me straight in the eye.

Even though Shadrek had started to rebuild his huts at Chiwi, it took some time for the hard truth to sink in—that it would be impossible to rebuild his businesses without money. And he could no longer make any money by shooting elephants and selling their ivory. So he had decided to take the bull by the horns and arrange to meet with me.

"I truly had nothing to lose," Shadrek said again, almost forlornly. "First FRELIMO came into power, then I lost my ivory markets, and then—my whole life was destroyed in the Rhodesian raid. I said to myself that maybe the strange Rhodesian soldier-hunter has something of value to offer me!"

For a long few seconds Shadrek said nothing. He looked up at the sky. He stretched leisurely. I did not interrupt his thoughts.

"I trust John Chauke and Josiah," Shadrek continued. He looked down at Josiah fishing alongside John Davey and John Fynnes-Clinton. "And now John Chauke is lying like a living corpse in his family's hut at Mahenya's."

I, too, thought about John Chauke. We both knew he was dying a slow and agonizing death from the puff-adder bite and gangrene. But he had refused to go to hospital. He did not want his leg to be cut off. He would rather die, he had told Shadrek, than spend the rest of his life as an invalid.

"Both John and Josiah told me we should all work with you." Shadrek paused—then laughed out loud. "But *they* didn't know I had lost all my ivory markets in Mozambique."

Then he smiled at me, knowing that I would understand this part of his reasoning: "And there was the possibility of my getting back into elephant hunting." The melancholy left his voice completely. "That is work I understand. That is work I am good at." The moment was almost poignant.

"Yes," Shadrek said, summing up his thoughts with a big sigh, "it was worth the risk of coming into Rhodesia to meet with you—no matter what you had to offer. I have nothing left in Mozambique."

That was how and why Shadrek came to march into John Davey's office in the Chiredzi police station and announce his preparedness to work with the Rhodesian SB and the white Rhodesian soldier-hunter. His temerity in doing so—particularly given his poaching history in the Gonarezhou and so soon after the Rhodesian attack on Chiwi that destroyed his entire world—is remarkable. Perhaps he was right. Perhaps he really did have nothing at all to lose.

What really amazed me was that Shadrek seemed to have little hatred in his heart for the Rhodesians. Had I been in his shoes, I am sure I would have been beside myself with fury at anything and everything Rhodesian—especially after the Rhodesian security forces had destroyed everything I owned.

But he seemed to have a much deeper and more subtle dislike of FRELIMO. In fact, he blamed FRELIMO much more than he blamed the Rhodesians for the destruction of his once very organized life in Mozambique. Life had been ecstatic for Shadrek when Alberto and Fror had been his guardians and sponsors—and FRELIMO had pushed them out. Life had not been good for Shadrek in many ways under FRELIMO's communistic rule. Deep in his soul, I think he was glad that FRELIMO had been so badly beaten up during the Rhodesian raid on Chiwi.

In reality, Shadrek had been caught between the devil and the deep blue sea, in a conflict he neither understood nor cared to get involved in. The big love in his life had always been, and would always remain, hunting elephants. He resented everything and everybody who had intervened to destroy this all-consuming passion.

In truth, he probably had no love for either FRELIMO or the Rhodesians, but he was pragmatic enough to understand that he had now reached a crossroad in his life. He had to make a choice. He could continue with a life of drudgery in Mozambique under FRELIMO or he could join the Rhodesians and begin to live again. To save his spirit and nurture his soul, he had little choice. Nevertheless, it was a vital decision that would determine not only his survival but his destiny, too.

I now know that Shadrek was searching desperately for some kind of guidance—some direction, a light at the end of a very long and dismally dark tunnel—that would show him a pathway into the future. It was the only thing that could explain his boldness in readily accepting a plan of action that was extremely dangerous for him, but would, if successful, bring him wealth beyond his wildest dreams. Working with the Rhodesian security forces was something he had never thought about or dreamed was possible. The fact that he would thereby be helping to destroy his old ZANLA friends on the Rio Save never caused him to blink an eye. All these considerations—in my analysis—were the reasons Shadrek so readily agreed to join me and the Rhodesian security forces and fulfill the tasks we outlined for him.

In thinking all these facts through—when I first started writing this book—I came to believe that Shadrek would probably never have agreed to work with me except for that Rhodesian raid on Chiwi. All my bright ideas about "getting Shadrek on our side" might never have borne any fruit at all if at that precise point in time the destruction of Chiwi had not ruined him. But once Shadrek decided to meet with me, he was well and truly hooked, for the inducements I was able to offer him were unrejectable by someone in his position.

Consider the facts: I had been authorized to promise Shadrek a farm in Rhodesia that he could occupy after successfully completing his military tasks in Mozambique. He would receive total amnesty for all his poaching in the Gonarezhou. Finally, he would be paid for his services on the basis of the reward posters that were displayed everywhere throughout Rhodesia. It truly was an offer he could not refuse.

Addendum to Part II

Note One

The task that Shadrek agreed to undertake on behalf of the Rhodesian security forces was to work with me inside Mozambique. He was to show me the ZANLA base camps that he knew about that were located between the Rio Save and Espungabera. He was to show me also those FRELIMO bases that were actively engaged in helping ZANLA elements to infiltrate Rhodesia. It was to be my task to pinpoint all these camps with accurate six-figure map references.

A six-figure map reference—for those readers who do not know—pinpoints the location of any position on a map with infallible accuracy. The accuracy with which the chimney on a house can be map-referenced, for example, would be absolute, with a degree of error no greater than fifty metres (not yards) on a map of the world.

As I explained earlier, Shadrek at that time was a celebrity in the region, and he had an open invitation to visit many of these camps without prior notification. With regard to the reputation he enjoyed with both the FRELIMO soldiers and the ZANLA freedom fighters alike, for example, he told me that when they visited his hotel at Chiwi, they often joked about the fact that if he were ever caught poaching elephant in Rhodesia he would never get to court. "You will have your throat cut," they would joke, "long before you ever reach the police station."

They knew, therefore, that Shadrek was a wanted man in Rhodesia, and this made him something of a hero in the eyes of the local people of the Rio Save, especially with the ZANLA terrorists. Furthermore, his bold theft of the tsetse department's cattle at Chipote added to his stature—notwithstanding the fact that FRELIMO had made him hand the cattle back. As a consequence, Shadrek was a most welcome guest whenever he had occasion to visit the Muchele ZANLA camps.

The commanders of other ZANLA camps were jealous of the frequency with which Shadrek visited Muchele Camp One—where he had a particularly close relationship with the camp commander—and they persistently told him that he would be welcome to visit them in their own camps at any time. All this notoriety placed Shadrek in a position that was above suspicion. As long as he kept his cool, therefore, neither ZANLA nor FRELIMO would ever suspect that he was working for the Rhodesians.

After I had finished recording Shadrek's personal life history, he began telling me about his knowledge of ZANLA bases in Mozambique, and I immediately realized that we had hit a gold mine in this intrepid hunter.

There were only three proper ZANLA camps on the Rio Save, he told me, the Muchele Camps One, Two, and Three. There was a fourth ZANLA camp lower down the river. It was again on the south bank, and it was located a hundred metres or so downstream from the Cabhora Bassa power lines. ZANLA called this camp Zambareja—after the pan on the north bank where the first temporary ZANLA base camp on the Rio Save had been located. There was, however, no longer any kind of ZANLA presence at the old site.

Zambareja Camp was a reception centre for black Rhodesian recruits who had elected to train to become ZANLA freedom fighters. The recruits stayed at this camp until their numbers grew large enough to fill a FRELIMO army truck, whereupon they were whisked away to Maputo. From Maputo they were flown to ZANLA training camps in Tanzania.

In the north, near the airfield, there were two military camps at Espungabera. At the southeastern corner of the airfield, farthest from the Rhodesian border, there was a permanent emplacement with three antiaircraft guns, and there was a small but permanent garrison located there to support the weaponry. This was a FRELIMO battery. Then, just south of the airfield, there was a large military base that belonged exclusively to FRELIMO. Not too far away, to the southeast, there was a ZANLA camp known as Mabuane.

Several miles farther south still, and closer to the Rhodesian border, there was yet another camp. This camp, like the Muchele camps, was administered by FRELIMO, but it was used as a major jumping-off point by ZANLA terrorists entering Rhodesia. This camp was called Espungabera. Finally, there was a reportedly very large ZANLA base a few miles north of Espungabera town on the higher slopes of the Chimanimani Mountains. It was from this latter base camp that ZANLA terrorists infiltrated the Chipinga and Melsetter districts of eastern Rhodesia.

Shadrek said he had seen all the camps in the vicinity of Espungabera town—except the northern one—but he had never been into any of them. He was, therefore, not known at all by either the ZANLA or the FRELIMO commanders in these camps.

In the Garawa area there was a FRELIMO base that was being used all the time as a transit camp by ZANLA. It was called Musirizi. Here, because of Shadrek's close family links to the paramount chief, he was well known and accepted. He had been into this camp many times and was able to give me a reasonable picture regarding its size and composition.

Musirizi, Shadrek asserted, together with Mabuane and the Espungabera camp, was used as a feeder camp for a major terrorist base that had been building up for some time in a remote, mountainous region across the border inside Rhodesia. He had not been to the Rhodesian terrorist camp, but he was adamant about its existence.

Farther south from Garawa, on the Rupembi Swamp drainage, there was another FRELIMO base that was used regularly by ZANLA terrorists in transit to Rhodesia. Rhodesia's border with Mozambique ran along the western side of the Rupembi marsh adjacent to Mahenya's. This camp was known as the Honde Camp. Shadrek was known in the Honde Camp and, he said, was able to gain entry to this base at any time.

I counted up the score. Excluding the Chiwi FRELIMO base, Shadrek knew of one camp north of Espungabera; four camps just south of Espungabera; one camp in the Garawa area, and a ZANLA base opposite, inside Rhodesia; one camp on the Honde; three camps near Chiwi, the Muchele camps; and, finally, the Zambareja recruitment centre. There were twelve in all, of which seven could be called entirely ZANLA camps, and three FRELIMO camps, which were used as serious transit stations for ZANLA.

I pointed out to Shadrek the opportunities he had for greatly enriching himself purely by *showing* me all these camps—thereby enabling me to pinpoint them accurately with six-figure map references. He had experienced a Rhodesian military raid on Chiwi, and he had seen the dead and dying people on the ground after the raid. He also knew that the Rhodesians had carted away lorry loads of arms and ammunition from the armouries and the magazines of the FRELIMO camp. What the Rhodesian soldiers did not want they had destroyed.

I went over the details of the reward posters with Shadrek again. There was a $5,000 reward for a ZANLA sectorial commander killed or captured. There were lesser amounts for more junior officers, but even a recently trained cadre was worth $1,000. One land mine would bring him $1,000. An AK-47 assault rifle, $500. As I recited these figures, I could see his eyes rolling in his head like dollar signs on a cash register.

"And all I have to do is to *show* you these camps?"

"That is all." I nodded. "And you already know ten camps that will be of interest to us, Shadrek. I don't think the Rhodesians will want to take out those bases that are purely FRELIMO. But any FRELIMO camp that is actively assisting ZANLA will, I expect, be fair game."

"And Zambareja, the recruitment camp?"

"I don't know, but I'll find out for you. I think, though, we would be happy to pay you a cadre's price for a recruit."

Note Two

On 30 August 1978, I finally completed taking the notes that told Shadrek's story. Clearly, he had given me only a skeleton of his life history up to that time, but it was enough for me to record the most important of his many experiences. He most certainly had had an interesting, adventurous, and very full life.

At that time, Shadrek told me that Tabita and he had three children, and that she was currently pregnant with their fourth child. Their children's names were Johan (fifteen), Alice (ten), and Mishek (three).

Note Three

Shadrek named three other Mozambican hunters who had killed elephants in the Gonarezhou: Tcumani, who lived on the Chefu River, just inside Mozambique on the Rhodesian border; Nyakatche, who lived at Musamani in the big thicket south of the Rio Save (this was the extensive, dense bush area between the Rio Save and the Malvernia-to-Lourenço Marques [Maputo] railway line); and Mchakaema, who lived near Malvernia.

All three of these men had poached elephants in the Guluene-Chefu corridor and near Vila Salazar in the Mabalauta Sector. Shadrek had hunted elephants only in the Lundi Sector, in which, to his knowledge, none of the other three hunters had ever operated. He was, however, derisive of all their efforts, saying that they were too afraid of the game rangers in the Gonarezhou and that they had, consequently, not killed many elephants. This observation amused me. Shadrek was indeed a most unusual character, and, with my inside knowledge, I enjoyed recording what he had to say immensely.

We had, in fact, attributed all the elephant poaching in the Guluene-Chefu and at Mabalauta to Shadrek, but clearly we had been wrong. He said the elephants the other hunters had killed in those areas were very few in number, and in that respect he was right. Shadrek's revelations in this regard, therefore, tied in with our own records.

Note Four

Shadrek had discovered a hollow baobab tree off the flood plain in the Tamboharta region of the Sabi-Lundi junction area. He used this tree as a refuge in time of inclement weather, or as a hiding place for his tusks. He even sometimes left his rifle there, propped on a gun rack made of two wooden pegs hammered into the soft inside trunk.

He took me to that tree and I climbed inside. I saw the wooden pegs for the gun rack. For anyone who might be interested in locating this tree, it can be found at map reference VM 430312.

The two elephants that Shadrek and I shot together on the occasion of our poaching trip to the Gonarezhou were killed at location VM 444341 and VM 443352.

Note Five

While Shadrek was hunting elephants for Fror and Alberto in Gorongoza, he saw his first black rhino. It had come down to a water hole to drink. Having never seen such an animal before, he cautiously approached it along the riverbank from above. He shot it in the back of the neck. This gave him an opportunity to examine the dead beast at close quarters.

On another occasion in Gorongoza, he was mock-charged by a black rhino, and on that occasion, when it blunderingly stopped just short of him in a cloud of dust, he shot it dead with a bullet through the earhole. He did not like the way black rhinos behaved, he said, and so he did not like them.

Despite our having stocked the game reserve with eighty-one black rhinos between 1969 and 1972, however, Shadrek said that, although he came across rhinos and saw their spoor quite often, he never shot a rhino in the Gonarezhou. I believed him because he had no reason to lie to me and had been open and honest in everything else he told me. Indeed, I am surprised that he did not boast of having shot many rhinos in the Gonarezhou because he was a very egotistical person who, I felt, may have exaggerated many of his hunting exploits. The truth of the matter was probably that he had no interest in black rhinos. Elephants were the only animals for which he had any real affinity.

Shadrek never recovered the horns of the two rhinos he had killed in Gorongoza, since he had no idea of their value. He left them with the carcasses, a waste of resources, as was his killing of the two animals in the first place.

Other poachers in the 1980s—when Robert Mugabe's government in the new Zimbabwe was in power and when civil discipline had collapsed throughout the country as a consequence—wiped out the game reserve's black rhino population to the last animal. I think that the rhinos we had introduced with so much blood, sweat, and tears had probably increased to about two hundred animals during the 1970s and early 1980s before they were whittled away to nothing in the latter part of the 1980s. This fact has been the most devastating and soul-destroying truth about Robert Mugabe's Zimbabwe!

Note Six

FRELIMO, knowing about Shadrek's prowess as an elephant hunter, sometimes used him to deal with problem animals. On one occasion, a number of elephant bulls were raiding the people's crops not far from Chiwi. In telling this story Shadrek derisively mimicked FRELIMO's communistic jargon, which he hated. On this occasion, FRELIMO pressured Shadrek into accompanying a militiaman to track the elephants down. A militiaman was a "trustee"—a local person who had been armed by FRELIMO with a .303 rifle to support FRELIMO's socialistic cause among the people. This meant, of course, keeping the people in line.

When they caught up with the animals, the militiaman had handed his .303 rifle to Shadrek, who then shot two of the offending bulls. He was then required to immediately hand the weapon back to his black shadow.

Shadrek complained to me that having done FRELIMO's bidding, and despite Tabita's working for the man, the commandant at Chiwi had not even had the courtesy to acknowledge the service Shadrek had rendered him.

On another occasion, "Fire," the Portuguese *msote kambate* (veterinary officer) at Massangena, asked one of his government hunters to shoot a hippo that had killed a local farmer. The hunter had wounded the animal but then failed to find it and kill it. Recognizing the even greater danger the wounded hippo now posed to the people, FRELIMO tasked Shadrek to kill the beast. For this job, Fire gave Shadrek his .375 magnum, and he instructed Shadrek to kill all the hippos he could find.

In telling me this story, Shadrek informed me that the game rangers in the Gonarezhou had just completed a hippo-culling exercise on the Lundi River and that this had pushed many hippos downstream into Mozambique. This information was of interest to me because I myself had conducted that hippo-culling exercise, during which I had killed 160 hippos. I cannot now remember the exact number of hippos the Gonarezhou had been carrying at that time, but the Nyahungwe Pool herd alone had numbered well over one hundred animals.

All along the Lundi, the hippos had eaten off the grass up to five miles from the river. When I say they had "eaten off" the grass, I mean they had cropped the grass as short as a very bare turf-wicket cricket pitch. As a consequence, many species of riverine grazing animals, such as waterbuck, were dying of starvation in droves all along the riverbank.

The hippo-culling was necessary to create a balance between the game reserve's grazing animals. The game reserve was, after all, not an elephant or hippo zoo, in which these two abundant species could be allowed to proliferate ad infinitum. The Gonarezhou had been created as a national park in order to preserve an across-the-board spectrum of wild animals and plants indigenous to the area. The fact that the disturbance caused by the culling had pushed hippos out of the game reserve into Mozambique, therefore, was of considerable interest to me since I'm also a biologist and ecologist.

The hippos at Massangena that had been harassed by Fire's hunter were reluctant to reveal themselves during the day. So Shadrek had followed them to their grazing areas in the bush at night and, in the moonlight, had shot four animals on the first night out. All four ran back to the river, where they died in the water. The next morning the local people pulled out the carcasses and chopped them up for meat. By complete chance, one of the hippos Shadrek killed that night was the wounded one. Shadrek was paid five pounds by the veterinarian for successfully completing this job.

Below Massangena, right on the Rio Save, FRELIMO tasked Shadrek with shooting two lions that had been killing the people's cattle. He was told that the lions came nightly to the kraal and tried to get the cattle to break out of their enclosure. They did this by urinating just upwind of the corral. When the cattle panicked and broke out, the lions killed whatever animals they wanted in the nearby bush.

Shadrek said that he had sat in the middle of the kraal and waited. When the lions came in the night, the cattle began to mill around, bellowing and lowing loudly. He then moved to the edge of the kraal and waited and watched through the pole fence. When a big female lion walked past him, he shot her in the heart at point-blank range. The male, which had been walking just behind the female, ran off a short distance and looked back at the kraal, growling. Shadrek could see it quite plainly in the moonlight, so he shot that animal, too. With the first shot, the big male lion had fallen over, but it did not die instantly like the lioness. It roared and writhed and tumbled about, and Shadrek was obliged to shoot it two more times.

Note Seven

Shadrek demanded absolute perfection from his rifle. When he wounded an elephant, for example, he never ever attributed the wounding to his poor marksmanship. It was always the rifle's fault. It was too weak, or it had lost power because of long use, or whatever. And when he wounded an elephant he never followed it. This was the advice that his father had given him many years before, and he followed that advice all his life.

One day, for example, he shot an elephant at Machaniwa and it ran off. He was most disappointed, he told me, because it had very big tusks. He immediately abandoned the hunt and proceeded by bicycle directly to Fror at Espungabera. There he requested a new rifle because the one he had was worn out. This was a pattern that he repeated several times. His Portuguese colleagues never challenged his assertions. They merely arranged to get a new weapon for him.

On this occasion, the big bull he had wounded died at Lisodo. The game scouts found it, and they proceeded to Mahenya's and enquired after Shadrek, telling the old chief that Shadrek had shot an elephant in the game reserve and that he had not recovered the tusks. The tusks, they said, were in the back of their Land Rover. It was a puerile ploy to get Shadrek to reveal himself, and, of course, it did not work.

Immediately after obtaining another rifle, Shadrek returned to the Gonarezhou, where he shot and wounded another elephant bull northeast of Tamboharta. This animal the game rangers also found, and this time they visited the tsetse cattle guards on the Sabi and enquired after Shadrek. The guards denied any knowledge of Shadrek, although by this time he was already a legend in the area. Nevertheless, this was the kind of intangible support Shadrek enjoyed among the local people, and it was one of the reasons why he was never caught.

Shadrek returned to Espungabera, and Fror again changed the rifle for him. Shadrek's Portuguese colleagues were clearly very long-suffering, but they endured Shadrek's whims because he produced the ivory they wanted.

Note Eight

Nothing yet has been said of Shadrek's proficiency with a muzzleloader, the ancient Tower Muskets that many poachers in Africa still use to this day. Shadrek's father, Chief Muteruko Kumbuya, owned a musket, and he taught Shadrek not only how to use it but also how to make his own lead bullets (in an old original bullet mold) and how to make his own gunpowder. He made gunpowder from charcoal and natural sulphur that he obtained from sulphur springs along the Rio Save. To this mixture, in the right proportions, he added salt peter, which he obtained by shaving the centuries-old crystalline dassie (hyrax) urine deposits that abound wherever stony hills are found in Africa.

Sometimes Shadrek used a trick he had learned from the miners in South Africa. He made gunpowder by roasting granulated ammonium nitrate fertilizer in a dry tin can over a hot fire. When he ran short of lead, he used a hacksaw to cut two-inch-long sections of rusty reinforcing rod, which he obtained from demolished concrete slabs at an old bridge site near Massangena. All the old-time African poachers were ingenious in meeting their needs. Shadrek was clearly no different. He was, in fact, better than the best of them even at the ancient arts and crafts of their trade.

Shadrek, as a young man, shot many buffaloes with his father's muzzleloader, and a goodly number of elephants, too. He was prepared to use any weapon to continue with his only enduring love in life, hunting elephants. Nevertheless, he told me very little about his killing of buffalo and elephant with his father's muzzleloader, except that he had done so. Even before he had killed his first elephant, he told me, he had killed two buffaloes on two consecutive days with the family musket.

Note Nine

Shadrek told me the story of what happened, from his point of view, when, on the occasion of my first visit to the lower Lundi, John Osborne and I came across a big elephant bull that Shadrek had shot at Nyahungwe. He told me he found the big bull early in the morning at Tamboharta, but on his initial approach, the wind had changed and the elephant got a whiff of his scent. There followed a cat-and-mouse game that lasted all day as Shadrek, determined to get the big bull, doggedly remained on its tracks. Tired of being pushed from pillar to post, the big elephant moved out of the junction area and into the Chihunja Hills. Later in the day it gravitated down to Nyahungwe Pool on the Lundi.

Shadrek shot the animal on the edge of the woodland, and it ran off toward the river, something he had not expected. Nevertheless, he watched the elephant closely and saw it collapse in the open. He then walked down toward the now-dead elephant, stepping on rocks and whatever hard ground he could find, until he came to the dirt track that ran parallel with the river. On the road he discovered very fresh Land Rover tracks, and he immediately knew that the senior game ranger from Chipinda Pools was on tour in the area.

Resorting to his Kruger National Park tactics, Shadrek retired to a nearby rocky ridge to wait out the day. He had seen our vehicle approach, and he watched the game scouts canvassing for spoor. He remained in his hiding place, and, unperturbed, he watched our attempts to locate his tracks. He later described our every action in minute detail, just as I remembered it. Finally he watched us drive off. He then set about cutting out the tusks.

Shadrek walked back in the bright moonlight to the Sabi, with one tusk over his shoulder, as he followed the vehicle tracks we had left behind. The second tusk he buried in the river sands in the shallow waters of the Lundi. He returned two days later to collect it.

"Weren't you afraid they would find you and arrest you?" I asked Shadrek.

He laughed. "No, why should I be? There were only ten black scouts at Chipinda Pools, and they had a huge area to patrol. They couldn't be everywhere at the same time, so I went about my business as if they did not exist. Anyway, I knew their timetable like the back of my hand. They were as regular as clockwork. They were very rarely on patrol at the end of the month, for that is when they received their pay. They would then all go to Chiredzi to do their monthly shopping."

"How did you know that?"

Shadrek laughed. "My brother-in-law, Phineas—John Chauke's brother—worked at Chipinda Pools for about six months. I asked him to go there and find out how the white man at Chipinda organized his game-scout patrols. The Rhodesian government paid him a salary while he was working there for me." Shadrek's face nearly split as he grinned. "So I did most of my serious hunting at month's end."

"Also," he continued almost gleefully, "whenever someone at Mahenya's was arrested for poaching, I knew the game scouts would be tied up with the police for at least the next week. If you kept your ear to the ground, you could work out when it was safest to go hunting. Sometimes, of course, you just had to go hunting. . . ." He laughed uproariously.

"And the white men? The white game rangers?"

"They were worse than useless," Shadrek opined with a smirk. "I often sat and watched them as they caught fish in the river. They always came in Land Rovers—very rarely on foot—so I was able to avoid them quite easily. They depended on the black game scouts to do all the foot-slogging patrol work."

All that Shadrek told me was true. We always had far too much administration and development work to do. We were always understaffed. We nearly always had to keep to the civil service schedule that required the men to be paid at the end of every month. Then we had, also, to prepare our monthly returns and reports, and many of these required contributions from the game scouts. Finally, we most certainly relied heavily on game-scout foot patrols to keep us informed about what was going on in the game reserve.

So we were "worse than useless"! I turned Shadrek's words round and round in my head with some degree of amusement. *If only you knew to whom you are speaking,* I thought. I could feel the fixed smile on my face, and Shadrek watched it in puzzlement. I was thankful he could not read my mind.

Note Ten

About a week after the Rhodesian raid on Chiwi, I was called to the Rhodesian Light Infantry barracks in Salisbury to collect four tusks that the commanding officer said had been recovered by his soldiers on a raid in Mozambique. You can imagine my surprise when I saw those four tusks lying on the floor of the CO's office, for I immediately recognized them as the four tusks that Don Boyd and I had sent to Shadrek with Josiah and John Chauke.

"These tusks come from the Rio Save," I told the officer with complete authority.

The soldier was taken aback. At that moment there was suddenly a gremlin sitting on my shoulder urging me to do some mischief.

"How do you know that?" he enquired with obvious bewilderment.

"Oh, I know the type of ivory that comes from that part of the world," I said, maintaining a straight face. "These tusks come from the Sabi-Lundi junction area of the Gonarezhou, or from the adjacent area inside Mozambique."

I felt sure that when I departed from his office that afternoon, the commanding officer of the RLI thought I was a wizard. I did not enlighten the man regarding my knowledge about the origin of those four tusks. He also never told me where his men had recovered them. But we both knew I was right.

So it was, therefore, that Shadrek's ivory came home to roost.

* * * * * *

This, then, is Shadrek's own story, complete at last, as best I can tell it.

And so the stage was set for Shadrek to enter the last phase of his exciting life. On the occasion of his hunting elephants with me in the Sabi-Lundi River junction area of the Gonarezhou, in August 1978, he made a momentous decision. He committed himself through me to working with the Rhodesian Security forces against ZANLA, thereby to make his fortune. The elephant poacher was about to become something else. He was about to become a secret military agent for the Rhodesians inside Mozambique.

John Davey's job was now complete. It was now necessary for him to pass control of Operation Poacher to an officer of Special Branch (External). I was sorry to lose contact with him, but that was the way the cookie crumbled.

PART III

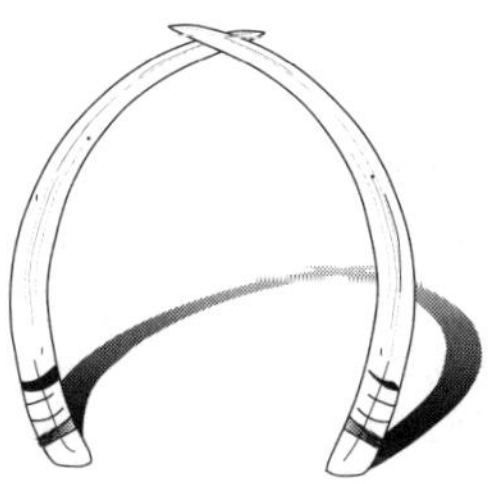

Chapter 22

Sometime in mid-October 1978, an Allouette III helicopter of the Rhodesian Air Force dropped me off just below the old Marhumbini mission station at 4 PM. Shadrek was there waiting for me. We crossed the border into Mozambique at Marhumbini, under a bright full moon. It was just six weeks after our elephant "poaching" trip in the Gonarezhou.

I was dressed, as I usually was in my role as a combat soldier, in khaki shorts and a camouflage army shirt and floppy hat. Across my chest I wore webbing with four spare magazines for my military FN 7.62mm rifle. On my back I wore a pack jacket, a heavy canvas waistcoat with padded shoulders and lots of pockets.

In the main back pocket across my shoulders I carried, among other things, a TR 48 single-sideband radio, the channels of which were different from those used by normal army units. This was a precaution in case the radio should fall into enemy hands. I was not to use the radio except under conditions of extreme emergency—such as the need for a hot extraction by helicopter. Four rifle grenades were also in that pocket, two on either side of the radio, their fins protruding menacingly above and behind my ears.

In the side pockets I had rations for one week. Other pockets held two hundred spare tracer rounds of 7.62mm NATO, a compass, and folded 1:50,000-scale military maps of the Rio Save region. Two water bottles fitted snugly into pockets on either side above my waist. Finally, my rolled-up, lightweight, silk sleeping bag was secured to the big shoulder-pocket ties below the fins of the rifle grenades.

The beauty of using a pack jacket is that everything is carried above the waistline. Conventional army webbing requires that certain items, such as water bottles and ration packs, be carried on the waist belt, where they interfere with running. Although it is a very heavy weight at shoulder height, the pack jacket gives you complete freedom of movement.

Finally, for use under severe battle conditions, a single heavy metal zipper up the full length of the front allows you to free yourself quickly from the impediment of the heavy pack jacket. This leaves you with just your rifle and chest webbing—the minimal essentials that a soldier needs to wage war.

In my hands I carried my tried and tested army-issue FN 7.62mm NATO military rifle, an old friend that I knew inside and out. It had brought me safely through many battles with ZANLA during the previous five or six years. The rifle carried a magazine with twenty rounds and was capable of fully automatic fire. However, I had never fired this or any other weapon in the fully automatic mode during my entire sixteen years of warring against the Zimbabwe freedom fighters. The weapon was painted in camouflage patterns of brown and dark green.

The final touch was that my bare legs, arms, and face (and fair hair) were all smothered in "black-is-beautiful" camo-cream. In the beginning, my eyes and my lips were untouched, giving me that old Al Jolson look. Within a day, however, everything would be smudged black—except those parts of my body covered by clothing.

I had brought along a nondescript nonmilitary shoulder pack filled with rations for Shadrek. If we were to share the same dangers over the next few days, he, too, would have to be provided for. The Rhodesian army had not been inconsiderate of that fact.

When he saw me in my military fighting gear, Shadrek burst out laughing—but he sobered up quickly when I rebuked him for not taking our mission seriously enough. Whereas he would be on home territory and be able to walk about as any other black civilian could, I would have to remain hidden and be prepared to defend myself should I be discovered. Our roles in this exercise were to be very different, and we each had to dress and play our respective parts carefully.

Once the helicopter had departed, Shadrek and I got down to business. In the comparative shelter of the tattered walls of the old church, I drew out my maps. We discussed our options and finalized our strategies. He was to lead me, at night, right up within sight of each of the Muchele camps on the river. Our approach was to be from the south, and we were to retreat to high ground, to the south, after each mission was accomplished.

"I would be happy just to get into the general area of the Muchele camps tonight," I told Shadrek. "We can begin checking them out tomorrow night."

From our daytime high ground it would be my task to locate and identify a prominent physical feature, such as a high hill on the horizon—preferably two high hills spaced well apart—or a river junction below us. These features had to be recognizable on my maps. Then I would obtain a magnetic compass bearing on each feature. The Rio Save itself, of course, provided the most important baseline feature for our first four objectives.

By taking one compass bearing at a time, subtracting the reading from 360 (the number of degrees in a full circle), and making allowance for the magnetic declination, I would be able to calculate a backbearing from each feature. Then, using a protractor, I could draw a pencil line back from each one. The lines would intersect at my exact position on the map. This fix would enable me to accurately determine a six-figure map reference for each of the ZANLA camps that Shadrek would show me.

At least, that was the theory.

I had chosen our moon-phase period carefully. The evening we crossed the border into Mozambique was the third night before full moon. That meant we would have virtually all night to walk under a bright moon. The following night we would have nearly an additional hour of moonlight time, and on the night of the full moon itself we would have twelve hours of moonlight. On the night following the full moon we would have nearly one hour of darkness between sunset and moonrise. The following night we would have two hours of darkness, and so on. So we would have about one week of bright moonlight—assuming clear skies—to aid us in our nocturnal activities.

I was petrified when I crossed the border that night with Shadrek. I wondered just how mad-in-the-head I was to follow this known scoundrel so deep into enemy territory—*at my own instigation.* I remembered the fear I had felt the night Don Boyd and I, together with Josiah and John Chauke, had crossed the Sabi with elephant tusks over our shoulders—tusks literally still dripping with blood. That night, I had been afraid of crocodiles. This fear was different, yet it left me with the same tingling love/hate conflict within my soul and my adrenaline running high. I had asked for this. I had planned for this. Now I had it, and I knew I had to make the best of it.

At the back of my mind was the possibility that Shadrek could simply walk into a ZANLA camp on the morrow and announce my whereabouts. Then I would be a sitting duck. Shadrek, after all, had very recently had his whole world shattered by a Rhodesian raid, and what better way was there to get some revenge than by simply betraying me to the enemy?

Against this fear I had to weigh another Shadrek—a Shadrek who was a capitalist, who understood just how rich his simple cooperation with me could make him. And I just knew that my instincts were right about this man. Nevertheless, he was still, then, an unknown quantity.

We marched on in the moonlight. The die, in any case, was now well and truly cast. What would be would be!

Over the first part of our journey, Shadrek took a devious route until he found what he was looking for—an old elephant path that ran through heavy thickets of the sandveld. This path, he said, led directly to Chiwi and would enable us to keep off the open lines cut by the Rhodesian Tsetse Department. We would be vulnerable, he said, if we used the tsetse tracks.

Shadrek's plan was a survival tactic. It was the poacher-hunter instinct in him coming out. It made me feel more comfortable about the man. What he said made total sense and I followed him more faithfully, putting my trust more confidently in his experience and in his intimate knowledge of the country.

Nevertheless, I constantly glanced up at the moon to make sure our direction was correct. We were three days away from full moon, which meant that the moon's curvature was still facing west. After the night of the full moon, the curvature would be facing east. Using the moon as a rough compass check was much easier than using the stars. Watching the moon enabled me to ascertain that we continued to travel in the planned direction—east-northeast—and my raw and quaking nerves slowly settled down.

Every hour or so I called a halt, and we had a five-minute break. During those breaks I removed my heavy pack jacket and worked the cramps out of my shoulders. Getting that weight off was a luxurious relief.

It was after three in the morning when we emerged from the sandveld thickets onto an old road. On our left side I could see that the countryside dipped sharply away from the road, and I recognized the trees about me as being riverine forest. We had reached the banks of the Rio Save. By then the moon was setting on the western horizon. Had it been higher in the sky, the golden sands of the nearly dry riverbed would have reflected the moon's bright light through the trees. The stars sparkled overhead in a blue-black sky. The effect was ethereal and mystical, and it suited my mood.

Presently Shadrek stopped and turned to face me. "Muchele Three is about a mile farther along the road," he said. "We've got time to do Muchele Three tonight. What do you think?"

I looked at my watch. It was 3:20 AM. We did have time, and it was a good time because at that hour the ZANLA soldiers in the camp would be submerged in a dead-to-the-world sleep. However, we might make mistakes if we were too hasty. Shadrek must have read my mind, for he said encouragingly: "I know the country. We can get in and out of Muchele Three easily before dawn."

But the moon was down. I weighed the odds carefully.

"OK," I replied. "Let's do it." I knew that my best course of action would be to give Shadrek his head and allow him to follow his instincts. We were, after all, in *his* territory, and I should have the common sense to allow him to call most of the shots. Nevertheless, fear and uncertainty continued to nag at my gut, and I detected a faint quivering in my hands. This was not like hunting elephants. Elephants did not retaliate in the middle of the night with machine guns.

Twenty minutes later Shadrek led us off the road, and we wound our way quietly through the heavy riverine bush. The lack of moonlight was an impediment, but the bright stars gave us enough light to see where we had to go.

"There is a guard at the camp entrance," Shadrek whispered, "but I think he'll be asleep now. ZANLA doesn't get many visitors in the middle of the night!"

"OK," I replied hoarsely. "But remember—we don't have to go *into* the camp. I just have to see it."

"And there are dogs."

Sh--! I said to myself and stopped dead in my tracks. *Why the hell didn't I think about that?* I had done enough night work in and around native villages to understand that barking dogs were a dead giveaway. It was unforgivable that I hadn't considered the possibility of dogs in the camps. It would severely restrict our movements and our achievements, for I had hoped to get a good close-up view to ascertain what was in the camps.

Damn. Damn. Damn!

Calming down after my little fit of pique, I asked Shadrek quietly, "What kind of dogs? Are they trained guard dogs or just village curs?"

"They are pets that ZANLA fighters pick up as puppies in the local villages."

I sighed with relief. Village strays were one thing; trained guard dogs would have been quite another. But even pavement-specials would alert the devil himself if they heard us on the outskirts of the camp—or even if they just smelled us. I placed my finger in my mouth to wet it and held it up in the air. I could detect no breeze at all.

"The wind down here runs upriver at night nearly all the time," Shadrek assured me. "It blows from the cool sea in the east toward the hot hinterland in the west. It is the same tonight."

We were four hundred miles from the Indian Ocean, but my five-odd years of living in the Gonarezhou had taught me that the sea definitely influenced the game reserve's weather. Shadrek had lived here nearly all his life. I would have to trust his knowledge about these little niceties.

"OK," I said at last, "but the presence of the dogs means that we can't go right to the edge of the camp. If the dogs wake up and start barking, we may well start something we cannot control."

I had visions of a pack of mangy dogs coming after us, yelping and snapping at our heels as we tried to run through the dense bush in the darkness. A follow-up by ZANLA in the morning would most certainly put a permanent end to our mission.

Shadrek turned to go. "Just be careful," I cautioned him. "Keep to the upstream side of the camp, and don't get in too close."

We approached the outskirts of what was clearly an extensive series of large thatched huts, but I could see very little even though we went in closer than was really prudent. All I could see in the starlight were vague hut shapes amid the heavy shadows cast by the towering riverine trees. The atmosphere was eerie. Absolute silence reigned except for the deep and resonant hooting of a pair of Pels fishing owls down at the river's edge.

"Let's get out of here," I whispered. "We can't see a damn thing, so we'll have to come back when the moon is higher in the sky."

Shadrek led me directly away from the camp. We moved due south as planned. When we crossed the dirt track, we were very careful not to leave footprints in the soft sand. I did not have to tell Shadrek anything about antitracking tactics, for he was a past master and knew almost instinctively how to minimize the chances of our tracks being picked up in the morning. But ZANLA was not expecting a clandestine visit from a mad-in-the-head Rhodesian, so it would not be looking for evidence of our visit in the night. That thought tempered my many anxieties.

The ground rose sharply to the south of the camp, and Shadrek led me to a small patch of *panga-panga* trees growing on the upper edge of a sandy incline. Amid the little thicket was a small pod mahogany tree in full leaf. It would give us shelter in the heat of the day. The site looked perfect.

I looked out over the valley of the Rio Save, and in the starlight I could see there was an extensive view to the horizon. There would be features out there that, come morning, I would be able to pick up on the map and upon which I could get a compass bearing. Getting a Loc Stat—a map reference—on Muchele Three was going to be a piece of cake.

It was a great relief to finally unburden myself from my heavy pack jacket and arrange myself on the soft sand beneath the spreading pod mahogany. I unfurled my silk sleeping bag and lay down to rest.

It was then that Shadrek announced he was leaving.

"My home is not far from here," he said. "It's about five miles away downstream on the other side of the river. I'll spend the day there and come back here this evening."

I was stunned. I had expected Shadrek to remain with me throughout the operation, but he had other ideas. My silence must have spoken eloquently, for he laughed softly and said, "Don't worry. I'll be back—tonight at sunset."

I lay on my sleeping bag and listened to the fading noise of his departure as he shuffled through the dry leaf litter underfoot. Then he was gone. I was left with a very active mind and a high degree of uncertainty. Tomorrow would be the big testing day. If Shadrek was going to betray me, it would come in the morning, and if he did, by midday I would be fleeing back toward the Rhodesian border, without my pack jacket, as fast as my legs could carry me.

While I lay there, my rifle was loaded and cocked at my side. I kept my chest webbing in place, just in case I had to make a quick getaway. And I kept my light canvas hunting boots on. I was a bag of nerves—nerves under control but taut enough to keep my body atingle during the last hour of darkness before the dawn. But I was dead tired and I dozed off listening to the *burrrpp . . . burrrpp . . . burrrpp* of a scops owlet as it sang away the rest of the night. Each burp was separated from the next by an exact five-second interval. It was the last thing I remembered about that first night in Mozambique.

Chapter 23

The first rays of the sun struck my face at the crack of dawn. There was a briskness in the air as I sat up and rubbed the sleep from my eyes. It was decidedly chilly, but I knew the heat would be very real come midday.

October in the Gonarezhou is always unbearable, with temperatures rising to over 120 degrees Fahrenheit. The worst I ever experienced was 128 degrees. That was at Mabalauta in 1969, when all fourteen of our black-headed Persian sheep died, all our chickens died, and the pregnant wife of one of my black staffers died. We had worked then from dawn to just after 8 AM and from 4 PM until dusk. The rest of the day we had just languished in the shade, the sweat pouring from our bodies, replenishing our fluids with anything that was liquid. The heat had ruled the land, scorching off whatever green vegetation had survived the dry season up till that time. Today, I knew, was going to be another one of those days.

I was totally alone in the territory of the enemy and nervous because Shadrek was still an unknown quantity. Muchele Three camp was less than a mile from my position.

The campsite we had chosen in the darkness was probably the best we could have found. It was on high ground above the river, and I could see clearly to the far northern horizon. The mahogany tree made the position ideal for surviving the heat of the day, but I immediately realized it would also be a magnet for every ZANLA cadre who might be sent out to patrol the area. When hunting elephant in the dry, hot months of September and October, I had myself sought out the heavy shade of the pod mahoganies, there to search for my quarry at midday.

These mahoganies are the only trees with green leaves at the height of the dry season, and they draw elephants to their deep shade like bees swarming around an open honey pot.

In addition to the fact that the tree above me would make me vulnerable to ZANLA, there was Shadrek to consider. If he was going to betray me, today would be the day. All he had to do was tell the ZANLA commander in Muchele Three that I was sitting under what appeared to be the only pod mahogany tree on the hillside. I would then be surrounded and in ZANLA hands in next to no time. All things considered, therefore, I knew I would have to move.

But first I had to locate myself on the map. My position was elevated only in relation to the nearby riverbank. I was, in fact, not much higher than the treetops on the Rio Save a mile away below me. That meant I could not see much of the river itself. Nevertheless, the snaking meanders of the river were clearly delineated by the ribbon of green trees growing on its banks. Every now and then I could see stretches of bright yellow river sand, and there were reedbeds all along the far bank.

There were also an alarming number of thatched villages on the far bank, stretching upriver and down as far as I could see. There were open lands, plowed and bare, waiting for the rains. Already people were walking about the villages preparing for the day as I scanned the scene with my seven-power pocket hunting binoculars. The Rio Save was much more populated than I had ever imagined.

In every family manage, smoke from cooking fires was filtering through the thatched roofs of the kitchen huts. It snaked into the still morning air in slow, lazy spirals, adding to the blue-gray haze that already covered the land.

There was a lot of mopane scrub behind the villages, but it was sparse and devoid of leaves. All the grass had been burnt off. It was not the kind of countryside in which a fugitive could seek refuge.

Far to the northwest I could make out a broad swath of open, uninhabited countryside that swept down to the river from the north. It, too, had been burnt off, but there were patches of bright yellow grass at various places along its length. And smudges of greenness amid the black indicated grass regenerating in the damp black soil of the *vlei*. Even at that early hour, cattle were grazing on the greenery. This, I surmised, was the Rupembi drainage line that ran along the Rhodesian border parallel to Mahenya's. It was a heavy marsh during the rains, but during the dry season it clearly represented a valuable grazing ground.

Away in the hazy distance, far up the Rupembi drainage, I could make out a solitary high hill. It rose to a peak and would be easily discernible on the map. I didn't even bother to check its existence on the map but took a compass bearing, recording the figure in my notebook.

Then I rolled up my sleeping bag tightly and fastened it onto the back of my pack jacket. That's all I had to do to pack up my frugal camp. I propped my rifle against the mahogany and lifted my pack jacket from the ground. It was so heavy I could not get it above my head with one hand, but when I slipped my arms through the armholes, its quilted lining fitted snugly against my shoulders. Yes, the pack jacket was heavy, but I had no complaint about its comfortable fit.

I picked up my rifle, wiped away the butt-mark in the sand below the tree trunk, and scuffed away all ground evidence that might indicate that I had been carrying a military pack or a firearm. My light, civilian-type canvas boots were well worn, so they left no army tread that would betray my military connection. I myself had discovered far too much incriminating evidence on the tracks of terrorists that I had followed, both in the Zambezi Valley and in northeast Rhodesia, to be so foolish myself.

This was Africa, and African bush wars are often fought on sign left behind by the enemy. I had at that stage been engaged in fighting ZIPRA and ZANLA freedom fighters for some fifteen years, and in my role as a combat-tracker it was my job to use my hunting and tracking skills to follow and interpret the sign left by the enemy. So it had become a sixth-sense activity to leave no unavoidable signs behind me when the roles were reversed.

I looked about me and, fifty yards away, noticed a heavier than normal patch of Mellitia thicket that would afford me a good view of the pod mahogany tree. The thicket would also provide some shelter from the scorching sun that was to come. And it was located west of the mahogany—that is, on the side closer to the Rhodesian border. If Shadrek betrayed me and armed ZANLA fighters came to the tree, I could immediately scuttle away backward and head for the border while they sorted out my spoor.

I headed south from the mahogany, leaving distinct footprints leading away from the tree, and traveled south for some fifteen minutes before doubling back on the western side of my outgoing tracks. The heavy green foliage of the tree guided me back without too much trouble. I came in cautiously. After careful observation for fifteen minutes, I began to relax. Nothing seemed to have changed under the pod mahogany, so I settled down into my new hideaway to wait and watch, and to endure the blistering heat that would come.

I lay on my sleeping bag on my stomach and withdrew my maps from their pocket in the pack jacket. I penciled in the line denoting the backbearing from the pointed hill up the Rupembi valley. I didn't need a second bearing because the river itself was a known feature on the map. It was an easy matter to pinpoint the position of Muchele Camp Three. I worked out the six-figure map coordinates and wrote the numbers down in my pocket notebook, thereby completing one of my mission objectives.

As the sun moved across the sky, I shifted the position of my sleeping bag from time to time to make the best of the available meagre shade. Each time I moved, I dug a new hip-hole in the sand beneath the silken groundsheet. If I was to spend the day in this position, there was no need to be uncomfortable. After each move I propped my rifle in the low fork of a bush next to me, lay down, and snuggled my hip into the new hole.

That first day in Mozambique was a long, long wait. And I had a lot of time to think! I thought of the changed circumstances through which Operation Poacher had passed. I was now under the command of a special branch (external) officer. My new superior was Peter Dewes—whom I had never met. I took my direct orders from Inspector Michael Shannon.

Shannon was a very different kettle of fish from John Davey. His approach was very businesslike, and although he was helpful and not unfriendly, the honest camaraderie that I had shared with John Davey was absent. Shannon let me know, in no uncertain terms, that I was now in the big leagues and, as a newcomer to the brigade, was an untried entity.

Nevertheless, Dewes and Shannon must have seen the potential in my link with Shadrek. For my first excursion into Mozambique they had prepared the ground well—through, I was led to believe, John Davey's connection with Josiah. I could not fault their logistical support at all. Nevertheless, their cool acceptance of my self-imposed task left my spirits jaded.

Maybe "acceptance" wasn't the right word, I thought sadly. Maybe the word should be "acquiescence." Maybe Dewes and Shannon had just acceded to a superior command—the imperative to control the last phases of Operation Poacher. Maybe they felt my intrusion into their busy schedules was an imposition.

Certainly I had not felt any exuberance from anyone in SB (External) for the task at hand. This left me with an empty feeling. I so much wanted everybody to be just as enthusiastic as I was about my mission. Finding myself under the control of people with so little emotion was very disconcerting.

Maj. Garth Barrett, of the elite Special Air Services unit, arranged the air-force helicopter. He had been much more friendly and helpful. He had told me to ignore Shannon's coolness and to get on with the job at hand.

"Shannon's a bit of an arse hole," Barrett had told me, "but when you need help in a hurry, he'll see that you get all you need. So don't be too hard on him. Think positive." I met Garth Barrett only on that one occasion, but I liked him. He gave my fuzzy spirits the boost they needed, and his little pep talk had enabled me to cross the border into Mozambique with greater confidence.

Midmorning I opened a tin of baked beans and ate them with the hard dog biscuits that were standard issue in the army ration pack. Like every other soldier in the army, I had discarded the six cardboard "rat pack" containers I had been issued and had stuffed their contents into the many pockets of my pack jacket. I washed this simple meal down with some "jungle juice"—lemon-flavoured sugar that I mixed with water from one of my two bottles. Getting my water bottles replenished, I realized, was going to be a priority task every night.

The terrorists did not find me during that long, hot day, but the mopane flies sure did. Just as soon as the heat began—around 9 AM—the tiny, stingless bees of the African bushveld began to swarm about my head. They tried to enter my eyes to suck up the liquid of my tears. They tried to get into my ears to remove the wax, and they flew up my nostrils to harvest mucus. Thirty . . . forty . . . fifty of the little critters buzzed about my head all day long. They were an absolute pest. Even covering my head in an army-issue camouflage head-net did not help, for they got in under the folds, attracted by the scent of my heavy sweat.

One thing that would have driven them away was citronella oil. Rubbing the oil over your face and into your ears certainly did drive mopane flies away, but that was not an option on a mission such as this.

My tracker unit and I had once lain at night in ambush, intending to kill a group of ZANLA terrorists. We had information that the terrorists were due to cross the Pungwe River from Mozambique into Rhodesia on a particular path. We had prepared the killing ground well with two mini-Claymore mines set on tiny wire tripods on either side of the path. The eight of us—four national park trackers and our four-man protection stick of soldiers—lay to one side of the path with our rifles at the ready. We were on a long, low ridge, and our field of fire covered about one hundred yards of the path, which lay to our left front and slightly below us. The ambush position was perfect.

About ten that night our guard-duty soldier alerted us to the fact that the ZANLA fighters were crossing the river. We awoke from our fitful slumbers and prepared for battle. The bright moon was high in the sky, and the ghostly figures of the heavily laden terrorists were very clear in the dip below us. I counted fourteen dark moving forms as they waded alone and in pairs across the thigh-deep crossing. They regrouped on the Rhodesian side and began their ascent of the riverbank into our killing field.

The lead group stopped once it reached the top of the high bank. An order was barked to those still at the river's edge. A full minute of silence reigned. Through my binoculars I could see the terrorists looking searchingly into the pale moonlight ahead of them. They began muttering softly. Then suddenly—unexpectedly—they dropped their heavy packs and began running back to the river.

Something had seriously alarmed them.

They were out of range of the Claymores, so we opened fire on them with our rifles as they reentered the river. I always used tracer bullets in my army weapon. Seeing the red globes of hot steel flying about their ears demoralized inexperienced troops like you can't imagine. And that night the tracers paid off handsomely, for I was able to see where my bullets were flying and thus could better direct my fire.

Despite the heavy rifle fire, we had only limited success. In the morning we found two men dead and one other wounded. The wounded man had a horrifying bullet-smashed thighbone. We had no idea, of course, how many others were wounded or how many later died and perhaps were washed downriver into Mozambican territory. We could claim only those we found on our side of the river.

The ambush, however, was not a complete failure. We recovered the entire heavy shipment of arms, ammunition, and land mines that the ZANLA fighters had been carrying over the border.

We had lain that night in our ambush positions and listened to the wailing of the wounded man. There was no way we were going to break our cover, for we had no idea how many unwounded terrorists might be lying in wait for us to approach their wounded comrade. So we waited out the night, and in the morning we swept through the position in a professional military manner and secured the area. Only then had we attended to our wounded victim.

Clearly, something had given us away that night. No group of trained soldiers would ever abandon their equipment and their mission in such

a precipitous manner without good cause. Later we discovered that the wounded man had told the interrogating SB officer that the terrorists had picked up the strong smell of citronella oil after crossing the river. We later ascertained that two of our soldiers had used citronella oil to ward off mosquitoes. The gooks had smelled the oil at a distance of over one hundred yards!

We all learned a lesson that night. And that was by no means the only occasion when citronella oil foiled an ambush during the Rhodesian bush war. Indeed, the problem gave rise to a standard warning that all Rhodesian soldiers were given by military intelligence officers. The use of citronella oil was verboten.

And so all that long day I lay and suffered the attentions of the mopane flies—and drank mug after mug of jungle juice to maintain my body's hydration. And still I sweated and I sweated until my body ran dry. When I pinched the skin on the back of my hand, it took several seconds to flatten out. I was suffering from the first pangs of dehydration. And the sun scorched my blackened arms and the backs of my legs. Indeed, the sunburning became so bad that I was forced to lie on the bare ground with the sleeping bag, zipped open flat, on top of me.

By 2 PM all my water was gone. My throat began to dry out, and it ached and burnt continuously. It was a day of purgatory. The heavy shade of the nearby pod mahogany tree was a constant and tantalizing attraction—but I did not succumb.

My decision to move from the shade of the tree to the more exposed position was the correct one for that particular day. It was a necessary survival tactic. Had Shadrek betrayed me that day, I would almost certainly have reached the Rhodesian border without being caught, for my antitracking hike that morning had given me half an hour's start on any search party that might have arrived at the mahogany tree. They would have had to unravel my devious tracks leading south from the tree—then back again. Thereafter, they could never have followed my fresh tracks at the same speed I would be leaving them behind me. I had done more than enough tracking myself to understand that much.

But Shadrek did not betray me. He arrived at the mahogany tree just at sunset, as he had said he would. He was perplexed by my absence and cast around looking for some sign that I might have left behind. I let him be for a while and watched his back trail carefully lest there was a ZANLA group following.

Sensing that I was somewhere nearby, he whistled penetratingly, but my dry mouth could not respond. Instead, I simply rose to my feet and emerged from my hideaway. I carried my gear to where Shadrek stood waiting under the canopy of the tree.

We smiled at each other and shook hands. He had brought with him a canvas bag full of cool, clear water. Almost snatching it from his hands, I took a long drink of the deliciously cold fluid. Immediately I could feel the coolness coursing through my veins as my body began to rehydrate.

"How is Tabita?" I asked him, wiping my mouth with the back of my hand.

"She is fine, thank you," Shadrek responded.

"She still doesn't know about me or what we are doing?"

"No!" Shadrek looked me over. "You look like hell. How was your day?"

"Whew!" I blew the expletive out of my now-moist mouth. "It *was* hell."

"Hot?"

"You can't imagine how hot . . . and the *mgogo-mchanees,* the mopane flies, they were hell, too."

He did not question why I had chosen to abandon the shade of the mahogany tree, and I did not offer an explanation. The sun was setting, so we had little time to prepare for the night. First we had to have food in our stomachs, so we set about preparing dinner from the one-meal tins and packets I had brought along. We buried all the debris deep in the sand. My final act before leaving our mahogany-tree camp was to refill my water bottles from Shadrek's bag. We drank the dregs dry between us.

In the light from the bright, high moon, Muchele Three camp was an eye-opener. It was much bigger than I had ever imagined. Camouflage netting hung from the trees above the more exposed huts and broke up the outlines of others. There were lots of young men in the camp, which was a hive of humming voices. There was a low brush wall along the side of the camp farthest from the river. Shadrek told me there was no similar brush wall on the riverside. I took his word for it. From what I could see, very few of the men were carrying firearms. Those that were seemed to have AK-47s. My little hunting binoculars were not light-intensifiers, but they did the trick in the bright moonlight. It did not take me long to see what I had come to see. Then we backed off quietly and retraced our steps almost to the mahogany tree.

Muchele Two was about two miles downstream. It was almost a replica of Muchele Three—roughly the same size, huts arranged similarly and positioned under the canopies of the bigger trees. None of the open areas between the trees had been used for any kind of buildings, but they were clear of underbrush. A wall of cut brush ran along one side of the camp, and there was a guard post of sorts at the entrance to the camp. It did not seem to be manned, but there could have been no other purpose for the small thatched hut that stood in the gap in the brushline where the vehicle track entered the camp. Muchele Three had had a similar hut at the brushline entrance, and it, too, had been unmanned.

The night was still young when we finished with Muchele Two, and I was tempted to go on to the third of the three camps. Shadrek said it was not too far down the river, and we could easily examine it before the moon had fallen too far into the west. I liked the idea of killing the last two of the Muchele camps in one night, since it would reduce my time in Mozambique by one day. But I still had to lock in the position of Muchele Two. That, after all, was the principal objective of my mission. Reluctantly, and hating the thought of the coming day, I told Shadrek that we would have to pull back and wait out another day.

The land behind Muchele Two was much flatter than behind Muchele Three, so we located a suitable site near some very big trees that I could climb in the morning. I would need elevation to obtain an accurate map reference for the second camp. I could probably have guessed that Muchele Two was two or three kilometres downriver from Muchele Three (all the map grids were in kilometres), but I wanted to present my new SB colleagues with as accurate a report as I could manage. I had gone to a lot of trouble to reach this stage in the operation, and there was no point in skimping on the details now. I had to admit to myself that it was not really the extra day in Mozambique that bothered me so much as the extra day of terrible heat I would have to endure.

Shadrek left me at around midnight and made his way back to Madjwisanga in the moonlight. He promised to bring more water the next evening since I was already down to one and a half bottles. When he had gone, I stripped off all my gear and my boots and slipped contentedly into my silk sleeping bag—keeping the side zip open for ventilation and easy egress. The night was delightfully cool in the river valley, and I was soon lost to the world.

This time I was awakened before dawn when a crested francolin blasted its frightful reveille almost in my ear: *Beer-and-cognac . . . Beer-and-cognac . . . Beer-and-cognac.* It was a litany with which I was extremely familiar.

I lay in my sleeping bag and thought about the other partridge-type francolins that I knew. They all had similar onomatopoeic translations of their calls. Shelley's francolin sang *I'll drink your beer . . . I'll drink your beer.* The diminutive Coqui recited *Swempie . . . Swempie . . .*, which had no real meaning but gave the bird its familiar colloquial name. I love birds. They fascinate me. I can never understand why some people can see nothing in them.

When dawn broke, I was still lying comfortably in my sleeping bag, listening to the world awaken all around me. I watched a party of white-eyes, tiny green-and-yellow birds, rummaging about in the leaves of the tree above my head, and I listened to the distant booming of the giant ground hornbills.

My Bushmen trackers used to tell me that the ground hornbills talked to each other. One bird would say, "*Nanso ifudu*—look, here is a tortoise."

A second bird would answer, "Where . . . Where are you?" Then the first bird would respond, "*Bwiya lapa, tina puza*—come here, we will eat it."

I missed having my tracker, Ben, with me on this exercise. He had been my right-hand man since I was twenty-one years old. We had shared everything together. But he was never included in my association with Shadrek. It was probably a wise decision because Shadrek's potential was just too good to be compromised by a simple slip of the tongue by Ben or anybody else.

Across the river the faint sounds of people shouting to each other drifted across the cold, still air, reminding me of my mission today. There was also the resonant clanging of neck bells as cattle were released from their corrals.

I sat up and slipped on my canvas hunting boots, double-knotting the laces. Then I rose and stretched, and squatted down again to roll up my sleeping bag. When it was secured to the pack jacket, I was ready for whatever the day had to offer. I opened a tin of bully beef and gobbled the contents down, washing away the taste with a swig of precious water. I buried the bully-beef tin deep in the sand.

By then the sun was casting long rays across the treetops, and I looked about to see which tree was the most climbable. Soon I was scrambling into the upper branches of one to look for a suitable physical feature on the north side of the river.

As high as I climbed, however, I could see very little of the north bank of the Rio Save. I looked for yesterday's feature—the peaked hill far up the Rupembi drainage—and was able just to pick it out through the top leaves of the river's forest canopy. The rising sun helped, sculpting the peak in bright yellow sunlight against a dreary background of distant hills still in shadow. With some difficulty I was able to get a compass bearing on that pinprick of light without falling out of the tree and breaking my neck. I recorded the bearing in my pocket notebook, then descended to ground level.

As I had done yesterday, I geared up and set off in a southerly direction, purposely meandering through the dense undergrowth and then doubling back after perhaps half an hour's walk. I had some difficulty relocating the group of tall trees in the amorphous dry woodland, and I stumbled onto my outgoing tracks twice before coming home to roost. This necessitated erasing my intruding spoor, lest a tracking party find it later in the day. Finally, I settled down in the shade of a dead and recumbent tree trunk that gave me a good view of the trees under which I had slept the night.

The day was a repeat of the previous day—hot, dry, and unbearable, and the mopane flies were no less a nuisance. I lay in the shade of the tree trunk all day long, moving as the sun shifted the shade. The only improvement over yesterday was that I did not have to endure the direct rays of the sun.

Shadrek arrived at sunset and brought two waterbags along. I noticed they were Rhodesian made and pointed this out to him. "They're from Mahenya's," he said. "Everybody around here has Rhodesian waterbags from Mahenya's. You can't get anything like that in Mozambique anymore—not since FRELIMO took over."

"What does FRELIMO say about that?"

"Nothing," Shadrek replied. "They turn a blind eye to many things like that. I think they are embarrassed by the fact they are not running the country as well as the Portuguese did before them."

That night we reconnoitred Muchele One camp. Again Shadrek went home about midnight, and again the next morning I was forced to climb a tree to get my bearings. Again the peak at the upper end of the Rupembi valley provided me with a perfect reference. And again the day's heat nearly killed me.

The next night Shadrek took me to the outskirts of Chiwi, which we quietly circumvented. He pointed out to me the rebuilt FRELIMO army barracks and explained how they had been all but destroyed by the Rhodesian soldiers. A goodly number of FRELIMO soldiers were walking about—all armed with AK-47s, which made me anxious to move on. However, Shadrek wanted to point out to me the ruins of his store and hotel. He was still very upset by the destruction of his businesses.

"Never mind," I whispered to him encouragingly. "When the Rhodesians come here again to take out the Muchele camps, you can think of all the good money they will be making for you." I clapped him on the shoulder and added, "Then you will have your own farm in Rhodesia, too."

He shrugged eloquently and said, "Maybe." Seeing his destroyed properties in the moonlight had depressed him. Obviously, he had pinned great hopes for his future on developing those two businesses.

For the first time, it seemed, the Shadrek of old had changed. He had grown tired of his wild, youthful peregrinations, and the excitement he had once felt for elephant hunting had become somewhat muted. His interest was still there, but it was not the same. Now all he wanted—and he wanted it desperately—was to settle down in a more sedentary and productive life with Tabita and his children.

This was a Shadrek I did not know and did not understand, for the elephant-hunting bug was still strong in my own soul. Many years were still to pass before I would accept that a spirited man like Shadrek—who truly had elephant hunting in his blood—could ever desire peace and quiet and inner contentment more than he needed the adrenaline rush and the fear and the excitement that came with hunting elephant.

"Let's go," I urged Shadrek quietly. "We'll have to discuss your options. Maybe you'll be able to use the Rhodesian money to rebuild your Chiwi businesses. Maybe the Rhodesian government will be able to pay some of your reward money in Portuguese escudos rather than Rhodesian dollars. Then you'll have enough money to build a much better store and hotel here at Chiwi."

"Do you think that will be possible?" Shadrek asked, a renewed excitement ringing in his voice.

He was no longer enamoured of the idea of living on a strange farm in a foreign country—even if the farm were his own. My turning around his options—to include the possibility of his remaining on his home ground—was clearly much more appealing to him. At the same time, I was concerned for Shadrek should my suggestion become a reality. If he started displaying new wealth on the Rio Save after the camps that he was showing me were raided, I was sure FRELIMO would smell a rat. And it would not go well for Shadrek in war-torn Mozambique if he were ever suspected of aiding and abetting the Rhodesian war effort.

"Yes, it's possible," I assured Shadrek. "But let's talk about it some other time. Maybe tomorrow. You will be staying with me during the day tomorrow?" I had noticed that this time Shadrek had brought an old blanket along with him.

"Yes," Shadrek replied.

The moon was very bright that night, and we walked along an old track on the high bank that followed the river. Once our eyes adjusted to the monochromatic light, we could see everything about us almost as if it were daylight. Some time after midnight we walked under the hydroelectric power lines that had once taken electricity from Cabora Bassa to South Africa. As we passed the two giant pylons on the south bank, I stopped and looked up at the heavy cables that ran off into the gloom to the north and south. There was no ozonic hum from the heavy wires. Now they were stone dead.

We were still within sight of the last pylon when Shadrek pointed out to me the village called Zambareja—the ZANLA recruitment camp. It was tiny by comparison to the Muchele camps, comprising only ten thatched huts. It was, in fact, an old village that ZANLA had commandeered and improved upon, and it sat out in the open on the riverbank like all the other villages in the area. There was no military aura about the camp whatsoever.

By the time we reached it, everyone had gone to bed. The huts brooded in their sombre black-and-gray colours in the moonlight. I was disappointed, for I had expected something quite different. I doubted Shadrek's word that it was a ZANLA camp at all.

I did not voice my suspicions but sat on a stump in the adjacent open lands and made a rough sketch of the village layout. It was very rough, because my only illumination was the light of the moon. My silence or lack of enthusiasm must have been eloquent, for Shadrek seemed to settle into a state of melancholic detachment.

There was a faint glow in the sky far away downriver, and I pointed this out to Shadrek. "Massangena," he announced. "It's about twenty miles from here."

Massangena! It must have streetlights, I thought, *or there must be some big security light burning.* Whatever the source of the light, it was a perfect feature for taking a compass bearing. I maneuvered into a position that brought the sky glow directly over the village and, taking out my compass, fixed the bearing on the centre of the halo. I checked and verified the bearing with the aid of a tiny pocket torch, and recorded the coordinates in my notebook. I then took a second compass reading off the nearest pylon that we had just passed. That done, we quietly visited the river and filled both my water bottles and Shadrek's two canvas waterbags.

It was two in the morning when we settled down for the night in a convenient green-leafed thicket. Shadrek had taken me several miles inland because the whole region here was far too populated for us to risk staying close to the river. It did not matter to me—I had got an exact compass bearing for Zambareja and did not need to be near the river the next day anyway.

Chapter 24

The next day, as we lounged about trying to minimize the terrible heat deep in the bushveld, Shadrek and I discussed all his options. I learned all about his fears and aspirations about working with me and the Rhodesian security forces. I had been correct in my earlier assumption that he really did not want to leave the Rio Save area. Since our initial discussions, he had had time to think about what he really wanted to do and had come to a decision. He much preferred to stay and rebuild his small businesses at Chiwi than to leave the country and live in a strange land, even on a small farm of his own. He was also concerned about the uncertain outcome of the continuing war in Rhodesia. He had no wish to move to Rhodesia and then have ZANLA win the war there, as FRELIMO had done in Mozambique. The outcome of the war was an equally uncertain factor in both our lives. Shadrek understood that; nevertheless, he also recognized the huge window of opportunity that existed in his working with me.

Shadrek was no fool. He had very carefully worked out all the possible scenarios. Furthermore, he had already considered the dangers of flashing around too much money in Mozambique after the Rhodesian raids. But he could still use the money, he said, especially if the rewards were paid in Portuguese escudos, to slowly rebuild what he had lost. Thereafter he could gradually develop a sound and prosperous business. His perspicacity in all these matters took a weight off my shoulders, for I had come to like Shadrek very much and did not want any harm to befall him.

The heat beat down on us all day long, drying up our mouths as well as our conversation. The only way to survive the day was to estivate—to

slow down to a state of torpor, the way a crocodile does during periods of severe drought. When river pools dry out, crocodiles creep into holes in the bank or under logs or some other cover away from the sun and wait out the dry season. They do not move until the rains break and revive the river. We had to wait in a similar fashion that day until the evening coolness made life bearable once again.

The moon rose an hour after sunset that night. We waited another hour for it to rise above the treetops before we broke camp and wended our way back to Zambareja. I had openly questioned Shadrek about the authenticity of the recruitment centre, and he had insisted that we return to the village so that I could see its purpose for myself.

We reached the village about nine o'clock that night and, using the riverbank for cover, were able to approach quite close without fear of being detected. On my belly, I watched through binoculars as sixteen young black men sat about their campfire making conversation. There were two older men dressed in dark military fatigues—clearly the supervisors. These two carried AK-47 assault rifles whenever they moved from one place to another. There was no doubt Zambareja was a ZANLA recruitment centre, just as Shadrek had told me. The young men were obviously waiting patiently for their numbers to build up before being shipped off for training.

"How many men do you see?" Shadrek asked me in a whisper.

"Sixteen recruits and two older armed terrorists. Eighteen."

"Then it's worth eighteen thousand dollars to me—nine thousand pounds—if you Rhodesian soldiers do your job properly."

I chuckled quietly to myself and thought: *You're a hard-arsed, mercenary little bastard, Shadrek. You really don't give a damn about who is killed in the process just so long as you get your reward.*

But then, that's what our agreement had been all about from the very beginning. That had been the incentive I had offered him. It was good to hear that the idea I had planted in Shadrek's mind had taken such a firm root. After that remark, I lost all fear that Shadrek would ever betray me.

Eighteen thousand dollars for knocking out a recruitment camp! *It is a hell of a lot of money,* I thought. Add to that the numbers of trained fighters I had seen in the Muchele camps, plus those in the camps yet to come! For the first time I began to wonder if the Rhodesians would ever pay Shadrek the rewards that they had promised him through me! It was entirely conceivable that Shadrek could earn himself well over a million dollars in dead and captured ZANLA terrorists alone—not to mention the rewards he could get from the recovery of the arms from the sacked camps!

I began to realize that Shadrek probably would not be paid his full reward. That possibility began to worry me, but I did not voice my thoughts. The matter of rewards was really far above my head, and it was beyond my status to intervene. I just hoped for Shadrek's sake that he would be given his just rewards. He was most certainly earning them.

We took off our boots and crossed the wide but shallow river just upstream from Zambareja. After rebooting on the other side, we headed westward toward the Rhodesian border. We passed through or skirted village after village but encountered not a single person out and about. Everyone by that time had gone to bed, and the villages were all silent—except for the dogs!

Every time we passed a group of huts, dogs ran out barking. And they continued to bark as long as they could hear our footsteps receding into the distance. But by then we were passing another village and another set of dogs emerged to take up the challenge. Everyone within hearing distance must have known that someone was walking through the villages, and they would have known, too, our exact location at any given time.

I hoped fervently that no FRELIMO elements were sleeping in the villages that night, and that no overzealous militiaman might want to gain kudos from his new masters by coming out to challenge our passage. I had no yen to kill anybody that night, for it would have compromised our errand.

After about an hour's walking, Shadrek suddenly changed direction and began traveling northwestward. Even so, it took us the better part of another hour to pass through the inhabited area on the rich soils of the river flatlands. When we passed the last village, we abruptly entered terrain that was more familiar to me—the gravel-based, undulating, open country of mixed mopane scrub that lay beyond. We had neither seen nor heard a soul during our nerve-racking forced march through the villages.

No sooner had we entered the open mopane veld than Shadrek turned to the left and maintained a westward course until well after midnight. When we reached the edge of the wide Rupembi drainage, we moved north and meandered along the edge between the mopane scrub and the *vlei*, seemingly with no purpose. I was about to protest when Shadrek suddenly stopped.

"Can we take a break, Shadrek?" I asked. "My pack jacket is killing me."

I had already unzipped its front when he answered me in the negative: "Not yet. *Nanso.*" (There) He pointed to the bare top of a distant baobab tree deeper in the mopane scrub. "We are going to that *sibuyu* over there." It looked to be another mile away at least.

"Even so," I said, peeling off my pack jacket, "I need a break." I dropped my *katoonda* onto the ground and laid my rifle over the bundle. "*Whew* . . ." It was great to relieve myself of the heavy load. I worked my arms to ease the stiffness in my back and shoulders. This had been our first stop since crossing the Rio Save, and it was long overdue.

Shadrek leant his two waterbags against my pack and dropped his blanket and the army shoulder pack I had given him to the ground next to my equipment.

It's all right for you to keep going, I thought. *All you've got to carry are two waterbags, one blanket, and a light shoulder pack.*

"Is your pack heavy?" Shadrek asked me. This was the first time he had shown any interest in, or concern for, the weight of the equipment I was carrying. I picked up my rifle and indicated the pack jacket. "Pick it up and put it on," I said.

He moved over to my pack and lifted it laboriously from the ground. "Sh--!" The expletive burst from his lips almost unconsciously. It was the first time I had heard him swear with any degree of sincerity.

"And you've been carrying this all night?"

"Not just all *this* night, Shadrek," I replied. "Every night since we left Marhumbini."

"*Hauw* . . ."

"Put it on. Here, I'll help you." I helped him lift the heavy burden above his head and guided his arms through the armholes. Then I zipped up the front with one smooth pull. The pack jacket was much too big for him. I laughed softly because he looked something like a tortoise in a shell that was much too large.

"*Hauw* . . ." Shadrek exclaimed again in typical native fashion. He did not need to say another word.

"OK," I said then, picking up Shadrek's blanket, waterbags, and shoulder pack. "Let's go to your *sibuyu*." And without another word I set off in the direction of the distant baobab tree. Shadrek tagged on behind me, moaning and grunting like a junior schoolboy grudgingly doing his prefect's bidding.

Fifteen minutes later we dropped our kits at the base of the baobab. I helped remove Shadrek's heavy armoured cocoon and laughed at his antics when the burden was taken from his shoulders.

"*Hauw* . . . You must be very strong to carry that weight all night long," Shadrek said sincerely, a clear respect in his voice. I think he understood now why I called regular halts to ease my shoulders of the heavy burden.

"You just get used to it," I said, deflecting the compliment.

After that little exercise, however, Shadrek showed a lot more respect for me, and sympathy for the heavy burden I had to carry. The little game cemented even further the strong bond that we had been forging over the last several days.

The baobab was hollow, but the tiny entrance to its cavity was at least ten feet above the ground. Shadrek had clearly used this hideaway often, since foot-long mopane stakes were driven into the soft flesh of the trunk right up to the opening. Inside, more pegs led down into the cavern. It was story-book stuff but very real.

We slept away the rest of the night at the foot of the tree and were awakened come dawn by the drumming and resonant calls of ground hornbills. After a breakfast extracted from the tins of our ratpacks, plus many of the hard dog biscuits, we ascended the tree and transported all our *katoonda* inside.

There was ample room for both of us inside the big tree, but it stank of bat droppings and the decaying stench of ammonia from their urine. Above our heads, a swarm of bats hung by their feet from the roof, twittering and squirming and looking for all the world like a pack of maggots on a rotting carcass.

Shadrek struck a match and set alight a ball of dry elephant dung, one of several that were lying on the floor. I watched him blow into the smouldering excrement and wondered at his purpose. But I said nothing. The pungent smell of the burning dung soon permeated our little cave. As it rose to the roof, the bats began to vacate their lofty perch. At first they piddled on us, then a few flew out through the opening. Suddenly, we were showered with a deluge of urine droplets as the remainder swarmed from their diurnal retreat. I marveled at this new evidence of Shadrek's seemingly inexhaustible repertoire of bush craft.

After the bats were gone, silence reigned inside. And it was cool. In fact, it was cold—even at midday—despite the terrible heat outside. Looking outside, I could see the sweltering mirage of heat waves rising from the naked and baked ground. Yet inside it was so cold I had to wrap my sleeping bag about my shoulders to ward off the damp chill.

"I often stay in hollow baobabs during the heat of the day when I hunt elephants at this time of the year," Shadrek explained, snuggling into his blanket. "Only a fool will endure the terrible heat out there when he can stay in here." He was dead right.

This tree was but one of many hollow baobabs Shadrek knew about, and used, in the region of the Rio Save and the Gonarezhou. The two he used most often were one in the Gonarezhou near Tamboharta and another near his home at Madjwisanga, where he often hid his rifles, tusks, and ammunition. Then there was the Rupembi baobab in which we now lay.

"There is another one," he told me, "high up in the Chihunja Hills of the Gonarezhou, and another in the big thicket between the Rio Save and the Malvernia railway line."

He knew of five baobabs in this region of African bush that had hollow centres big enough to accommodate a man comfortably. I have seen tens of thousands of baobabs in my lifetime, all over Africa, but have not found one with a hollow centre. Yet Shadrek had found five within a hundred-mile half-circle to the west of his home. This was an indication to me of the extent of Shadrek's exploration and hunting activities in the region. To find that many hollow baobabs in such a relatively small area meant that he must have visited every single big baobab tree. And to have done that, he must have walked the country flat. My admiration for the man seemed to grow and grow with every such revelation.

"How far is the Honde camp from here?" I asked Shadrek, for that was our next destination.

"Not far. About five or six miles," he answered. "But we are going to have to watch it. There is a hill overlooking the camp, and FRELIMO has a guard post on top of the hill that is manned twenty-four hours a day."

"When you say a guard post, what do you mean?"

"Well, there is a thatched hut and an open thatched shelter on top of the hill that the guards use. From there you can see for miles and miles all around."

"So it's an observation post?"

"If that is what you'd like to call it, yes. There are always FRELIMO guards up there."

"So what is the problem? We're going in there tonight, and I doubt any guards on the hill will see anything of us in the moonlight."

"Except they've got special eyeglasses that see in the night."

I raised my eyebrows: light-intensifying scopes?

"Have you seen these things—these special eyeglasses?"

"Yes!" Shadrek replied, almost laughing. "I know the FRELIMO commandant in this camp quite well. I often spend the night at Honde when I travel between Madjwisanga and Espungabera. He invited me once to go up the hill and see for myself how the magic glasses work."

"And what did you see?"

"Everything. It was a dark night, but you could see just as well as you can during the day—except that the colours were all black and yellowish-green."

It's a light-intensifying scope, all right! I thought. *Thank God Shadrek has told me about it. And thank God he knows about it and understands its danger to our mission.*

I thought deeply about the coming night. Our job was to pinpoint the Honde camp with a six-figure map reference. And because the camp was used as a transit station for ZANLA groups entering Rhodesia, maybe . . . just maybe . . . the Rhodesian SF would want to take it out. If FRELIMO were indeed aiding and abetting the ZANLA terrorist cause out of the Honde camp, maybe FRELIMO *did* need a lesson. But such decisions were not matters I needed to worry about. All I had to think about was my own task at hand.

It was my job to obtain a bearing to the camp and, if possible, sketch a layout of the huts. Shadrek had told me that the camp was similar to the Muchele camps, so I knew it was not a sophisticated military base. It was nothing more than a temporary military outpost near the Rhodesian border, and I suspected that it had been constructed solely to support ZANLA terrorists entering Rhodesia. I had no doubt that the Rhodesian SF would decide to take it out.

For that reason, Shadrek had agreed to take on extended responsibilities. It did not surprise me, because he was bursting with bravado. His self-appointed job was to enter the camp and find out which huts were used for what purposes. In other words, he was to determine which hut was the commandant's personal quarters, which was the officers' mess, the kitchen, an armoury or magazine, barracks for the troops, toilets, etc.

"How do you think we should tackle our task tonight?" I asked Shadrek. "You know the lay of the land and how FRELIMO operates in this camp. What do you think we should do?"

"We're going to have to get you up on the hill," Shadrek said. "And you are going to have to stay there the whole of tomorrow."

"On my own?"

"That's right." He looked me straight in the eye, challenging me to trust him. He smiled, knowing that my mistrust of him was now in the past.

I held his stare, smiled, and nodded my head. "I have no problem with that."

"I'll take you up the hill. I know of a place where you'll be able to stay out of sight and, for most of the day, out of the sun, too. It's a place where I think you will also be able to see the camp clearly."

"You think?"

"Yes. I haven't been to this place myself. It's a small overhanging rock face that—if I remember it correctly—looks right down on the Honde camp. If it doesn't, we'll have to find you another place."

"OK. So we'll play that by ear."

Shadrek nodded. "Then I'll have to come down the hill and return here to the baobab tree." I nodded, understanding his strategy up to that point. So far, so good. "Then, about two o'clock tomorrow afternoon, I'll go to the camp gate and pay my respects to the commandant. He'll invite me to stay the night, but I won't accept. What I will do is talk about how nice his camp is looking and get him to begin boasting about it. That is the best way to get him to tell me what you want to find out." He looked at me to see if I approved. I shrugged and nodded. *Sounds good to me,* I thought.

"I'll leave the camp before dark and head north toward Garawa," he continued, "telling the commandant that I am going to see my uncle there. Then I'll double back to where you are hiding and we'll go down the hill together—or I can meet you at the bottom of the hill.

"That would be better. I think I can climb down the hill on my own."

"Then," Shadrek concluded, "we can cross over to Mahenya's. We'll be back across the border before the sun comes up. The border is not very far from here."

"And what about the magic eyeglasses?" I asked. His plan was perfect except for the complicating factor of the light-intensifying scope.

"Agh," he said, shrugging the matter off. "We'll just have to risk it."

"No!" I said strongly. "We take no chances, Shadrek."

"But the guards sleep most of the time anyway," he said, probably the honest truth. "And they won't be sitting with their eyes glued to the eyepieces. They won't use the glasses unless there is a big noise in the middle of the night—something that attracts their attention. If all is quiet, most of them will be sleeping, with only one guard staying awake."

"How many guards go on duty up on the hill?"

"I don't know, but there were four of them together when I was up there."

And that is probably how many they will have at night, too, I thought. *Shadrek is probably quite right. Three of them will be asleep most of the night and one will be on duty. They'll have a roster.*

"We'll have to climb the hill sometime after midnight," I said after I had thought the problem through. "I think you are right, Shadrek. If they have a night scope up there on the hill, it is most unlikely that they will be looking through it all night long."

"So . . . we'll have to take a chance?"

"Yes, dammit!" I said, smiling at Shadrek. He was clearly pleased that I had to accede to his way of thinking.

"And you'll have all the time in the world to draw a plan of the camp tomorrow," he said.

"Yes. Then, when we get together later, you can tell me which hut is which. As long as we get the general layout and function of the camp, that is all we need."

There was nothing at all wrong with Shadrek's plan of action. I could not have worked out a better scheme myself. And although we would be working separately during the hours of daylight, we would both be working toward the same objective. I realized that I was enjoying myself despite the dangers involved. This was much like hunting big elephant bulls in thick bush, and I think Shadrek felt the same. I was again reminded that I liked this little black man. I liked him immensely. And I enjoyed working with him.

Chapter 25

We began scaling the hill at 1 AM. The moon was high in a cloudless sky. Visibility was excellent, and we were able to pick our way soundlessly through and over the rocks with little difficulty. It took us an hour, however, to reach the rock overhang that Shadrek had remembered—not because the hill was high but because we had to move with great care so as not to awaken the FRELIMO guards above us.

The rock shelter near the top of the hill was no more than ten feet high. It faced northeast. That meant I would be exposed to the sun until about 11 AM. Then I would be in full shade for the rest of the day.

Using my hunting binoculars, I looked down on FRELIMO's Honde camp, which was clearly visible in the stark light of the moon. Every hut stood out as a black mass against the pale soil beneath, despite the shade of the many trees under which the huts stood. Some huts, I noticed, were very large. Others were just thatched roofs with no solid walling underneath. Those, I figured, would be the dining huts. Looking down, I realized that I would be able to see every movement inside the camp come daylight. The position Shadrek had selected seemed perfect.

"*Shuuuuushhh,*" Shadrek cautioned me quietly. "The guards are not very far above us. You will have to remain very quiet all the time you are here."

I hadn't forgotten about the guards, but I had no idea where they were positioned.

"How far up the hill are they?"

Shadrek looked down and indicated a *sterculia* tree no more than thirty feet away. "About that distance above us," he hissed.

Thirty feet! The FRELIMO guards were only thirty feet above us? What the hell was Shadrek thinking about, placing me here?

"There is no other place where you can hide so well on this hill and see the camp at the same time," Shadrek said, as if reading my mind. "If you remain still and don't make any noise, you'll be OK. Just think about how a kudu hides itself when standing out in the open. It becomes a statue. Nobody will see you if you don't move about."

Sh--! And if I sneeze? Or let gas? They'll smell my bloody gas!

"One other thing," Shadrek continued, unfazed by the danger. "The path the guards use to get to and from the camp is about twenty yards in front of us around the edge of the hill." He pointed in that direction. "They won't see you if you lie still. But you will hear them walking past." I could hear him softly chortling behind the cupped hand that he suddenly threw over his mouth. He was enjoying himself immensely at my discomfort.

Then he said, "Give me your water bottles." He began topping up my bottles from his waterbag. "I can get more water down at the camp tomorrow, but you need to have full containers now." I had not thought that he might be able to get water from the camp, but it made sense. I had had visions of having to nurse my meagre supply until we got back to Mahenya's. Shadrek's idea was brilliant. I was surprised that I had not thought of it myself, and I was pleased to see that Shadrek's brains had not been addled by the heat.

"I'll be off now," he said abruptly. "I'll see you at the big *mtswiri* tree at the bottom of the hill at one o'clock tomorrow night."

I held out my hand and he took it firmly in his own. We shook hands. "Good luck," I said.

"Good luck to you, too," he said. "Just remember to keep still—like a kudu—and everything will be all right."

I watched Shadrek's progress down the hillside. He was like a silver wraith fading into the black and gray of the night. He left no sound at all behind him. Then he was gone.

Now that I was standing still and alone, I began to feel cold. A gentle breeze was attacking the copious sweat that I had worked up during my strenuous climb up the hill. I would have to make myself comfortable for what remained of the night.

I looked about me and saw that the open area under the overhang was used by dassies as an early morning sunning area. The tiny rabbitlike droppings of hyraxes lay in abundance everywhere. There was a strong stench from them and the pungent, musty aroma of the animals' urine. This familiar smell was identical to the musk scent given off by bull elephant. It reminded me that the two animals, so different in size and shape, are in fact distant cousins.

The dassies will have to move over for one morning, I thought as I ungraciously commandeered their sunbed.

I thankfully shed my pack jacket and laid out my sleeping bag next to the rock, atop a carpet of dry dassie droppings. Next I removed my chest webbing and laid it alongside my bed. My rifle I placed on top of the chest webbing. I then positioned the pack jacket so that it would be next to my head. Finally, I shed my boots and climbed into the sleeping bag. I was dead to the world inside five minutes.

I was awakened by the raucous screeching of a dassie not four feet from the end of my bed. I was not sure whether it was celebrating the coming of dawn or protesting my intrusion into its privacy. Whatever the reason, its hoarse and strident alarm shocked me into instant wakefulness. I sat bolt upright and banged my forehead against the rock above me. I cursed volubly—until I remembered the FRELIMO guards on the rock just above me.

Rubbing my bruised head, I listened to the animal's scuttling progress as it ran off round the side of the hill. There was no sound from above, so I guessed the guards were used to dassies sounding their reveille.

My first thoughts of the day involved my safety. I was almost in a state of funk. *I must be crazy to have contrived to get myself into this situation,* I thought to myself almost desperately. *I really must be mad in the head.* But as the minutes ticked by and nothing threatening happened, my composure returned and I began to enjoy myself.

For perhaps an hour I stayed in my sleeping bag—but opened the side zipper fully. I pulled myself up against the pack jacket, which I used as a backrest, and lazily watched the sun rise above the eastern skyline.

To the south the wide Rupembi marshland was a patchwork of black, burnt ground powdered here and there with a green blush of regenerating grass. There were extensive stands of tall yellow grass, too—grass that had been too wet to burn when the local people had set fire to the veld. From my position at the head of the drainage line, the cattle were now much bigger and closer than when I had last viewed them from south of the Rio Save. I could see no villages at all, however, and I wondered where the cattle had come from so early in the morning. I concluded that they must have been left out all night, and I guessed that a fair number must be killed by lion and hyena each year—for there were many of those predators at Mahenya's, not very far away. *They must surely cross the border from time to time,* I thought, *to sample steak "a la Portuguese."*

In the distance I could see the high ground of Marhumbini hill. So the border was really not far away at all. And when I leaned out from my rock shelter, I was able to locate the lone pointed hillock called Kundani, to the right of Marhumbini. If I had taken the trouble to move round the side of the hill I was on, I would have been able to see the eastern end of the Chilojo Cliffs, too. But I heeded Shadrek's advice about staying put.

I drew a compass bearing on Marhumbini and worked out the backbearing. Then I obtained a backbearing on Kundani, too. They were very close together and not ideal for my purpose, but they were the best I had. As far as the eye could see to the south, the land seemed to be as flat as a pancake. As it turned out, however, it did not matter. On the map, the backbearing line from Marhumbini cut right across the very first hill feature on the upper Honde drainage, so it was a dead cinch to work out my position. As a check, the nearly parallel line from Kundani also cut through the same hill, so I knew I had identified my position accurately. Marking the position of the Honde camp at the base of the hill made working out the six-figure map reference for the camp an easy task. Mission five had been accomplished.

I heard mumbled conversation from the hill above me, so I decided to prepare for war—if such should ever happen. I pulled on my boots, then strapped on the chest webbing. Finally, I tightly wrapped up my sleeping bag and tied the roll to the back pocket of my pack jacket. My rifle lay nearly flat, its muzzle propped in the fork of a small bush. I was ready to move at a moment's notice.

I drew my camouflage net scarf over my head, draping the ends over my shoulders. This broke up my head-and-shoulders profile and made me feel more confident about moving forward from my sleeping place to a position where I could look down into the camp.

There were a lot of soldiers here. My first count was fifty-three men. All were dressed in FRELIMO camouflage. Few carried firearms, however, which meant they were lax. All those who did carried the infamous AK-47 assault rifle. I searched for a ZANLA presence but saw none. Today there seemed to be only FRELIMO soldiers in the camp.

I drew out my notebook and, with the help of frequent scans with my binoculars, was able to sketch the entire camp. Despite all my doubts, the observation point that Shadrek had chosen for me was absolutely perfect. Indeed, except for Shadrek's extra task, our final mission on this trip was complete. All that remained, after Shadrek had done his work, was for me to extricate myself safely from the hilltop and for Shadrek and me to escape across the border back into Rhodesia.

The moon phases were now not so much to our advantage: Tonight the moon would not rise until nine o'clock. Tomorrow night it would be nearly ten o'clock. We had almost overstayed our welcome. From now on we would have less and less moon time to use, so it was appropriate that Shadrek and I go back to our respective homes. Our reconnoitring of the Garawa and Espungabera camps would have to wait for the next full moon.

The morning sun was very hot, and I was fully exposed to its stinging rays. But, as Shadrek had predicted, the rock overhang gave me full shade from eleven o'clock onward. My situation thereafter was idyllic compared with what I had endured on the Rio Save. High up on the hillside, I was above the sweltering midday heat in the valley below, and the deep shade from the rock overhang was a joy. During midday and throughout the afternoon, my situation was truly comfortable. Now that I had pinpointed the Honde camp's position and sketched the disposition of the huts, there was nothing left for me to do but wait for the night—except that I wanted to witness Shadrek's visitation.

There was one interlude in an otherwise uneventful midday. It was vulgar, but it broke the monotony for a brief spell. On the rock above me I heard two FRELIMO soldiers in conversation. Then I heard and then saw one and then two thin columns of water falling just out of my reach across the face of the rock overhang. There was laughter above me, and the columns of fluid wavered and reached farther and farther out, in spasms, from the vertical. The soldiers were standing on the edge of the cliff and having a peeing competition! I do not know who won, but when they ran dry the two men retired from the cliff top and tranquillity returned.

Shadrek strolled up to the camp gate at precisely two in the afternoon. Over his shoulder he carried his blanket, and in one hand he held two empty canvas waterbags. He was greeted like a long-lost friend by the camp guard, who directed him to the commandant's hut. A pompous-looking fat black man bedecked in a crumpled FRELIMO uniform emerged from the hut when Shadrek knocked. He shook Shadrek's hand and then stretched his arms and upper body luxuriously. Shadrek had obviously disturbed his siesta.

No other life was visible in the camp—the heat down there must have been oppressive. All the soldiers were no doubt sleeping the hot hours away in their huts.

The commandant called to someone in one of the open huts. A junior soldier came running at the command, and Shadrek spoke to him directly. Shadrek turned and thanked the commandant, then followed the other man back to the open hut and disappeared inside. Shortly he reappeared with both canvas bags full of water.

The commandant strolled over to meet Shadrek, slapped an arm about his visitor's shoulders, and turned him around. The two of them reentered the hut, and all activity in the compound seemed to stop once again. Just

what Shadrek and the commandant were doing inside the open hut was anybody's guess. Mine was that they were sharing Portuguese beer—one of the few alcoholic beverages that Shadrek really enjoyed.

I waited and watched for half an hour, but nothing else happened. I decided that there was really no need for me to keep a watch on Shadrek's activities, so I retired to my rock shelter and lay down amid the dry dassie droppings and rested my back against my pack jacket.

I was just dozing off when the sound of distant gunfire brought me to instant wakefulness. My immediate thought was that something had happened to Shadrek in the camp, but as I listened I realized that the gunfire was coming from much farther away, to the southeast.

Above me I could hear the guards shouting excitedly. I presumed they were talking loudly into a radio. I rose slowly to my feet and rearranged the camo scarf about my head. Then I moved along the rock face and looked down into the camp again. Pandemonium reigned among the huts, with soldiers running hither and thither. The commandant stood in the middle of it all shouting instructions, seemingly to anybody and everybody. I saw Shadrek sidling quietly through the melee, making for the camp gate.

The gunfire seemed to be getting closer and closer Presently, I saw a scattered group of four figures running through the short mopane scrub about two miles from my position. One Allouette helicopter stick, I thought immediately. That meant they were probably Rhodesians. They regrouped on the edge of the *vlei*. I could see lumps on their backs, which told me they were carrying heavy backpacks.

Then they were running determinedly across the wide-open, blackened surface of the marsh. It was not a marsh at this time of the year, of course, for the water had dried out and the surface was hard. The men made good progress, using the small stands of tall yellow grass canes to maximum advantage. The unburned grass was the only cover they had.

About twenty other figures were in hot pursuit. I recognized their camouflage—they were FRELIMO soldiers. When they emerged onto the edge of the *vlei*, I saw that they had dogs with them, held on long leashes. As they ran they fired their rifles into the air.

I focused my binoculars on the running fugitives but could not identify them. They were not dressed in uniform, and all were blackened from head to foot. I guessed they were Selous Scouts, which meant there would be both black and white troops in the contingent. The whites would have smeared black camo-cream over their legs and arms and faces. They made no attempt to fire back but kept running as fast as they could go.

The FRELIMO soldiers suddenly released their four dogs, which tore off running across the burnt flats in pursuit of the fleeing Rhodesians. I could hear their excited yowlings despite the great distance that separated me from them.

A good four hundred yards separated the two groups, but the dogs closed the gap in next to no time, their barking ever more excited as they got closer. The handlers ran after their dogs as fast as their legs could carry them, and behind them ran the supporting FRELIMO soldiers.

On the hill above me I heard mortar bombs being fired. The guards were lobbing them two at a time, which meant they had at least two mortar tubes. I counted the detonations. They had six bombs in the air before the first ones struck the ground.

I kept my binoculars focused on the fleeing Rhodesians and wished them well. I need not have bothered: All four of them dropped to the ground and turned to face the dogs. One at a time I heard their rifles firing, and one at a time the dogs collapsed in their tracks.

Then the bombs began hitting the ground. The explosions—showering the countryside with dried mud and leaving a pall of black smoke—were over a hundred yards behind their target.

The bombing had little effect on the Rhodesians. Although they were running from an enemy, they seemed to have everything under control. I had no doubt that the FRELIMO soldiers would have suffered a fate much like that of their dogs if they had dared to close the gap too much. The FRELIMO soldiers probably knew that, too.

In contrast to the minimal concern shown by the Rhodesians, the mortar bombing had a great effect on the pursuing soldiers. Although the strikes were way off target, they were still between the pursuers and their quarry, which caused the FRELIMO soldiers to stop immediately, turn, and scamper back toward the *vlei* edge behind them. Undeterred, the guards above me fired another salvo of six bombs, two at a time. A stream of FRELIMO soldiers ran around the base of my hill and out onto the flats, obviously intent on cutting the Rhodesians off from the border. Still the Rhodesians seemed quite unconcerned by the forces ranged against them.

The next bomb strikes were better placed, but still hopelessly short. The mortar crews were not giving their rounds enough lead. The runners were seemingly moving too fast for the bombs to catch up.

They should practice with shotguns on flying ducks, I thought ungraciously of the guards above me. Of course, I was rooting for my own countrymen in the chase.

The pursuing soldiers were now standing about on the edge of the mopane scrub, watching the performance of the mortar bombs in the *vlei* in front of them. They had clearly given up the pursuit, unwilling to risk being killed by their own hardware. Below me the soldiers from Honde camp also appeared unwilling to make contact, for they were shuffling along in a desultory manner, though still moving in the direction of the Rhodesian border. In the distance, the blackened figures of the running Rhodesians slowly became absorbed into the burnt-out *vlei*. The guards above me fired another futile salvo, and that was the end of the battle.

The FRELIMO soldiers far down the *vlei* regrouped and began returning to the place from whence they had come. Below me the Honde soldiers dejectedly returned to their camp. This exciting interlude had broken the monotony of my afternoon, and the only casualties were four dogs.

I met Shadrek at the *mtswiri* tree at the bottom of the hill at 1 AM as planned. The first thing I did was refill my water bottles from his FRELIMO supply. That act amused me to no end.

"What was all the excitement about this afternoon?" I asked Shadrek, for I knew he would have been told the story.

"Skuzapo!" he announced. *Skuzapo* was the slang name that black people throughout the region used to describe the Selous Scouts. It alluded to the sly manner in which they operated—like Johannesburg pickpockets, who shared the same notoriety.

So they *had* been Selous Scouts.

"And?"

"A FRELIMO patrol came across them resting in the shade of a baobab tree," he explained. "The *Skuzapo* ran away and the soldiers gave chase. You saw what happened from up on the hill?"

"I saw it all."

"That's all I know."

"OK, then. Let's go."

We skirted the bottom of the hill and kept to the tree line on the edge of the hills. There was no way I was going to be caught out in the open the way the Skuzapo had that afternoon. Keeping north of the Rupembi marsh, however, meant that we had a much longer distance to travel to reach Mahenya's. The trees here were the kind associated with the Chihunja Hill complex of the Gonarezhou. Once we had distanced ourselves from the Honde camp, we found ourselves walking through a tall woodland set amid a jumble of black granifyre rocks. Every now and then we bumped into a thicket of *mzimbiti*—the ironwoods of the Sabi-Lundi Valley—much battered by elephant in the past. These we circumvented.

Using the now east-facing curvature of the high moon as our compass, we reached the cattle fence that demarcated the border by four o'clock in the morning. We crossed the fence and traveled another fifteen minutes before finding a spot to spend the rest of the night. I was dog-tired and so quickly arranged my sleeping bag on the ground and climbed inside. Shadrek wrapped his single blanket about his shoulders and, sitting straight-legged, leant his back against the trunk of a tree.

Before dropping off to sleep, I thought back on our little adventure. It had been as exciting as it had been successful, but I was pleased to be back on Rhodesian soil. In fact, we were almost right back to the place where it had all begun. I judged we couldn't be much more than a mile or two from the place where our lorries had bogged down so badly when Don Boyd and I had come to Mahenya's on that military "hearts-and-minds" exercise—really not so long ago. We had come almost full circle. Certainly the chain of events that Don and I had set in motion was coming to fruition. Everything was working out according to plan.

Shadrek had been a star, and I was drawn to this little black man as I have been drawn to no other—except my two Bushmen trackers, Ben and Mbuyotsi. Thinking of them, I realized that I had not missed my trackers nearly as much as I had expected—Shadrek had adequately filled their places.

The next morning Shadrek and I had a breakfast fit for a king—all drawn from the tins and other supplies of our army ratpacks. Here we were to part company until the full-moon period of the following month, when we planned to tackle the Garawa-to-Espungabera part of Shadrek's domain. There were still four of Shadrek's camps that I wanted to locate and observe, and these we could easily cover over the next full moon.

Shadrek wanted to visit John Chauke at Mahenya's before returning to Madjwisanga, and I had to find a suitable landing zone—an LZ in military terms—an open piece of grassland big enough to allow a helicopter to land amid the tall woodland we were in. I broke out the TR 48 radio set and called the security force base at Buffalo Range airport. The end of our little excursion, for me, would be a cold extraction by helicopter.

After breakfast Shadrek and I shook hands and I gave my newfound black friend a big hug. I really did like this little man. We wished each other luck and promised to meet again come the next full moon. Then Shadrek set off for Mahenya's. Before donning my pack jacket, I stood and watched him walk away amid the trees and rocks. He looked back once and I waved to him. He waved back. Then he was gone.

I never saw Shadrek again.

Chapter 26

The air photography section at the Rhodesian Air Force headquarters had been greatly enlarged since the advent of the war. I had completed my military training as a pilot officer in the air force in 1957–58 and had known the New Sarum Air Force Base quite well. The photographic section then was minuscule by comparison. Now I was led into what amounted to a large barn where several different groups of air force and army personnel were working on projects. Nobody gave me so much as a second glance.

Using the coordinates that I had provided, a Canberra jet bomber had flown over the Rio Save and photographed Shadrek's ZANLA camps from a great height. From the aerial photographs thus obtained, stereo-paired photos had been printed of the sites. Now it was my job to positively identify the camps and help a photographic expert to sketch out a plan of the structures. I saw from the insignia on his shoulders that he was a flying officer. He told me to call him Sam. Although the work we were doing was very important and required intense concentration, it was all carried out in a relaxed atmosphere.

Not counting Zambareja—which was considered an incidental bonus—the only camp I was able to provide any detailed information about was FRELIMO's Honde camp, where I'd had a good high-elevation view and Shadrek had provided me with inside information. My knowledge of the Muchele camps, by comparison, was very poor.

"What was the problem with the Muchele camps?" Sam asked.

"The country was flat, and the best we could do was to get an accurate bearing," I replied. "I could get only a superficial look at the camps in the moonlight. Even then we couldn't get in too close. The gooks in the camps have dogs, and had they smelled us they'd have alerted the whole caboodle."

Sam nodded. "So we'll just have to see what we can do with the photographs," he said sagely. He pulled over a large stereoscope set on a stout frame and pushed the first pair of photographs beneath it, arranging them so that he obtained the required 3-D effect.

After some thought, I said, "Once we have a mapped layout of the camps, I am sure that my Mozambican friend will be able to tell us what each of the huts represents. He has an open entree to all three of the Muchele camps."

We disposed of the Zambareja and Honde camps first, for they were the easiest, then concentrated on the Muchele camps. These were much more difficult to interpret, not only because the huts had been secreted under the forest canopy but also because FRELIMO had used camouflage netting to further break up and disguise their outlines.

"It's not too difficult," Sam said almost casually as, with a white pen, he began to draw in the outlines of the huts that he could see through the dense leaf cover. He marked only the right-hand member of the pair of black-and-white photographs. "See here," he said, indicating a dark blob. He dotted the four corners of the oblong hut that he had seen. "Here is the outline of the thatch. . . ." He moved the point of his white pen over the lines that he could see, showing me what to look for. Then he marked in the lines permanently. "See . . . here's another one." And he marked that one on the photograph, too. Slowly the camp began to take shape before my eyes.

"What's this here?" Sam asked suddenly, pointing his pen at a tiny square mark on the photograph. I carefully looked through the 3-D lenses. It just looked like a dark blob. Then I saw twin vehicle tracks leading from there into the camp.

"It's the guard hut at the camp entrance," I said, happy at last to make a contribution.

"There we go," Sam smiled up at me.

"You can see the vehicle track passing right past the guard hut," I said, explaining my reasoning.

"See . . . it's not difficult at all. It just takes time and patience."

In less than two hours we had completed our mapping of the Zambareja and Honde camps. It took us the rest of the day to attend to the Muchele camps. It was laborious work, but, by the time we finished, even the thin line of brush fence that ran along the side of the camps farthest from the river had been demarcated. We had also sketched in most of the camouflage netting. And when I saw the final products, I could visualize each of the three camps as I had seen them in the moonlight.

Michael Shannon arrived just before five that afternoon, just as Sam and I were putting the finishing touches to the Muchele camps. "How're you getting on?" he asked after shaking our hands.

"We're finished," Sam announced cheerfully. "Or rather I am finished with Ron. It'll take me a few more days to draw up the maps you'll want, based on the photographic interpretation."

"That's great," Shannon said. Then, turning to me, he uttered the only compliment that I ever heard pass his lips: "You've done a good job—both you and Shadrek."

"Thank you," I replied. "But really it's Shadrek you should be complimenting. None of this would have been possible without his help."

"We know that—and I want to talk to you about that. Can I come and see you in your office tomorrow morning?"

"Sure!"

"Nine o'clock all right?"

"No problem."

* * * * * *

"We're taking you off Operation Poacher," Shannon announced to me flatly the next morning. He was sitting opposite my desk sipping tea that my secretary had prepared for us. I was stunned.

"Taking me off Poacher! What the hell for?"

"Now that Operation Poacher is getting talked about at COMOPs, SB has had a bollocking for letting you go into Mozambique on your own. It has been decided that because you have not been properly trained by military intelligence or by the army, you are a danger to yourself and a risk to the operation. In a nutshell, the army believes you are not properly equipped to complete the exercise as we would like it to be done, and Poacher has too much potential to risk failure."

"I don't understand," I said. "You said we had done a good job, Shadrek and I, and that you were pleased with the results of our first trip into Mozambique."

"We are, but there is much more to it than you can even begin to imagine. I'm sorry, but I can't tell you any more than that. What you have started fits into a much bigger regional military strategy that I am not at liberty to discuss with you. It's all on a 'need-to-know' basis."

"And I don't need to know?"

Shannon nodded, putting down his empty cup on my desk.

"And Shadrek? What is going to happen to him?"

"We're going to take him over. He'll be given another man to work with, and he'll operate with a four-man stick in the future."

"Can I not be part of that four-man stick?"

"No."

"This is crazy!" I almost shouted at Shannon. "I have a very personal relationship with Shadrek, and our success on this trip was based on mutual trust. A new man will not have that . . . that 'togetherness' Shadrek and I share."

"I'm sorry—the powers that be have already made their decision."

"And who the hell are these 'powers that be'?" I asked angrily.

"You have no need to know," Shannon replied, smiling weakly at me across the table. "Look," he continued, relenting, "I understand your position. And I sympathize with your anger . . . really I do. But I also know that COMOPs is planning a very big effort in the southeast and you cannot be a part of that. You have neither the background nor the professional military training. Operation Poacher is being integrated into this bigger exercise—and I shouldn't even have told you that! So you'll have to keep your mouth shut on that issue."

"OK, OK. You don't have to worry about that. But for God's sake, can't I just finish the task I started? We've got just four camps to reconnoitre, dammit. It'll take us less than a week to finish off."

"Nope. Sorry!"

"Does Peter Dewes know about this?"

Shannon nodded. "He's part of it." Shannon rose to leave.

"Wait! Wait!" I urged him quickly. "Please sit down for just a few more minutes."

Shannon resumed his seat and looked at me like an impatient but crestfallen bloodhound.

"What about the promises I've made to Shadrek on behalf of the Rhodesian government?"

"A farm in Rhodesia? That he will be rewarded after we have hit the ZANLA camps he has shown us according to the conditions laid out on the government reward posters?"

"Yes!"

"What about it? We'll work out a deal with him after the raids, and he'll be paid according to the results, just as you promised him."

"Do you promise me the government will fulfill those obligations?" I was very anxious that Shadrek receive his just compensation.

"Certainly. It will be worth every penny." Shannon's face was deadpan. It reminded me of my bank manager's face when he had refused me an extension to my housing loan.

"One thing more. Shadrek and I had time to talk on this trip. He doesn't want a farm in Rhodesia. After the raids he wants to stay on in the Rio Save area in Mozambique. He has asked me to find out if he can be paid in Portuguese escudos rather than Rhodesian dollars."

Shannon shrugged. "I suppose that will be possible."

"Will you see to it?"

"Of course. In time I'll have a chat with Shadrek myself." Shannon's face was still devoid of any expression. He clearly wanted to leave my office now that he had dropped the bombshell that his superiors had instructed him to explode.

"You'll give me your word that you'll look after him? I don't want anything happening to Shadrek now that I will not be there to look after his interests."

"Of course."

"I have your word on that?" I persisted.

"Yes. You have my word on that!"

"Finally . . ." I suddenly decided that I needed something back from these sanctimonious bastards. "When you hit these camps, can I be in on the kill? I started it, and I would like to be there when it comes to an end."

"I think that can be arranged. I'll pass on your request to Mr. Dewes."

When Shannon had gone I sat staring down at my desk pad in total disbelief. To say that I was stunned would be a monumental understatement. In just one short sentence Shannon had shattered my world, because my work with Shadrek had become the central and most important issue in my life. One moment I was basking in the euphoria of a successful mission accomplished and looking forward to the coming of the November full moon—the next my soul lay in pieces on the ground.

I thought about what I might do to reverse the decision that Shannon had dropped so precipitously into my lap. But in my heart I knew that I would be reaching for moonbeams. Shannon must have come at Peter Dewes's instructions, and Peter Dewes was head of SB External. I put my elbows on the table and dropped my head into my hands. I felt like crying.

The rest of Shadrek's story is based on hearsay—for I could get no direct answer to my questions. Information was available from the military hierarchy only on a "need-to-know" basis, and there was no reason I could think of why I should need to know.

Chapter 27

The next bit of positive information I had about Operation Poacher I gleaned from the newspapers. Several months after Shannon's visit to my office—which must have been sometime early in 1979—I collected the Sunday newspaper from the gate of my suburban home, unfolded it, and there, blazoned across the front page, was the headline: Security Forces Hit ZANLA Bases on the Rio Save. There was a big map, too. It showed the Sabi-Lundi junction area of the Gonarezhou, Mahenya's, and the Rio Save region from Massangena up to and beyond Espungabera in Mozambique. Ten large red stars on the map showed where ten camps had been hit simultaneously early the previous morning.

It seemed the whole of both the Rhodesian Air Force and Army had been involved. There was mention of the bombing of the camps first, to soften up the enemy. Then the paratroopers had gone in. The Special Air Services had been involved, and the Rhodesian Light Infantry, and the Selous Scouts. Even the Terries—the Rhodesian Army's part-time Territorial Force—had got a look in.

The supporting text told me unequivocally that the attack was the conclusion of Operation Poacher, the foundations of which I had laid more than a year before with Don Boyd and Josiah Chiranzwa and John Chauke—and later with John Davey. This was what I had hoped for when Shadrek and I carried out our reconnoitre of his first five camps. And those camps were all there, marked clearly on the map with five big red stars. The five other stars represented other camps that Shadrek had told me about.

My immediate reaction was anger because my request to be in on the kill had been ignored. But I was not really surprised. There was no "need for me to know" when the raids were going to take place, and there was really no dire "need for me to be involved," either.

I looked at the stars on the map and identified every one. Muchele One, Two, and Three were there, and Zambareja. And the FRELIMO Honde camp. Above Honde there was a star denoting the FRELIMO Musirizi camp. Opposite it, inside Rhodesia, was another star—the Rhodesian ZANLA base that Shadrek had told me was linked to Musirizi. There were two stars below Espungabera. One was undoubtedly ZANLA's Mabuane camp. The next, below Mabuane, was the mixed FRELIMO/ZANLA camp, which Shadrek had said was called Espungabera. Above the Mozambican town of Espungabera there was another star indicating ZANLA's Chimanimani camp, which Shadrek had said he knew about but had not visited. They were all there. Not one less and not one more. This was definitely the ultimate result of Operation Poacher.

Soon my anger left me and a happy glow spread through my soul. Sure, I had not been in on the kill, but I had started it all. I didn't doubt that the Rhodesian security forces eventually would have discovered the location of all these camps in some other way, and that they would have knocked them out with equal ruthlessness and efficiency. But they hadn't. Shadrek and I had hastened the day.

Then I began to think about Shadrek and to wonder what had become of him. What part had he played in all this? Where was he now? Was he safe? And would he be getting his just reward? He'd be like a pig in thick slop when the money was handed over to him.

The next morning I contacted Shannon and hit a brick wall. There was "no need for me to know" the answer to any of my questions. He did tell me, however, that Shadrek was all right and that they were busy working out his reward.

The following week I again phoned Shannon and asked if he had any more information. This time he was totally noncommittal. There was no need for me to know the details. He told me not to phone him again since he was under instructions not to communicate with me regarding any aspect of Operation Poacher.

I must admit that the Rhodesian security forces hit other targets in the area over the period of several months during which the Operation Poacher targets were destroyed. These targets, I believe, were much more important than any single ZANLA camp that Shadrek had exposed for us. Several major ZANLA bases between the Malvernia to Maputo railway line and the Limpopo River were destroyed, as were several road and railway bridges. And other missions were successful as well. All were a part of the overall strategic plan that Shannon had alluded to when he dismissed me from Operation Poacher. In my opinion, however, the ten smaller targets that Shadrek had revealed to us were, collectively, every bit as important as any of these others. It is true that Operation Poacher became part of a much bigger war action against ZANLA and FRELIMO.

Nevertheless, I was puzzled and very hurt by the abruptness of my dismissal from Operation Poacher. It had been my idea, dammit, to bring Shadrek into the picture and to get him on the side of the Rhodesian security forces. I did not deserve this kind of graceless brush-off.

I complained to Graham Child, but he was unable to help me. I phoned John Davey in Chiredzi. Same story. In fact, John was even more in the dark than I was. He said he didn't even know that I had been into Mozambique with Shadrek. *So,* I thought with surprise, *he hadn't acted as a bridge between SB Internal and SB External for my visit to Mozambique with Shadrek. How, then, had SB External arranged it?*

John, in fact, hadn't heard anything at all about what had happened since he'd last seen me. I did not elaborate for fear of breaching security. There was "no need for him to know!" This thought slammed me like a fistful of hard fingers. I was getting as bad as Shannon!

"What about Josiah?" I asked John hopefully. "Can you get hold of him and find out what has happened to Shadrek?"

"He's gone," the SB man replied.

"Gone?"

"Yes, SB External took him under its wing. The next thing I knew, he'd moved his whole family out. I haven't a clue where he's gone to."

I believed him. So my only link with Shadrek had gone. There was no way I could even get a message to him.

I fumed and I cursed—and I worried. I felt responsible for Shadrek. It was I, after all, who had inveigled him into getting involved with the damned Rhodesians in the first place. My frustration was so strong that I had even begun to think of my countrymen as "damned" Rhodesians. But there was absolutely nothing I could do. I had exhausted all avenues of inquiry. I would just have to wait. Something, I hoped, would come up—sometime.

A few months after the Rhodesian raids, Graham Child walked into my office and announced, "Shadrek's at it again."

"He's poaching elephants in the Gonarezhou?"

He nodded. "This time with an AK-47."

"Damn!" I said. "Those bastards in SB External haven't paid him his reward money. It's the only reason he would go back to hunting elephants in the Gonarezhou."

"How do you know that?" Graham, ever the scientist, never committed himself to anything unless the proof lay before his eyes.

"Because he wanted to use the reward money to build up his businesses at Chiwi on the Rio Save," I said. "You know that the earlier attack on Chiwi destroyed his businesses there?"

"So you told me."

"Well, the Shadrek we once knew—the inveterate elephant poacher—has been changing over the years. Since FRELIMO took over in Mozambique and buggered up his ivory markets, Shadrek turned his attention to building up what he likes to think of as a hotel and a store at Chiwi. The Rhodesian raid destroyed all that, and he told me he wanted to rebuild at Chiwi with the reward money that he expected from us. If he'd got his reward money from SB External, that is what he'd be doing right now."

"It makes sense," Graham said, nodding. "I'll see what I can find out from my contacts in SB."

"How many jumbos has he killed?"

"They've found nine in the last month."

"And there will be another nine that the warden down there hasn't found. Shadrek's angry. And he wants us to know it!" I sighed. "He hasn't even got a market for his bloody ivory anymore."

"We don't know that," Graham said firmly. Here was the scientist coming out in him again. "He may well have discovered a conduit into South Africa."

"I doubt it." I shook my head, thinking deeply. "Can I go down there and try to make contact with him? I did it before. I can do it again."

"No! Absolutely—*No!*" Graham Child was clearly adamant. "You've done enough down there, and there is no need to risk your life on a lost cause. Who knows—you may be on the top of his hit list! Anyway, let me have a talk to SB and see what I can find out. I'll come back to you as soon as I know anything."

"Are you sure it's Shadrek?" I asked thoughtfully—hopefully. "There are other Mozambican Africans who've poached in the Gonarezhou, you know."

"Oh, it's Shadrek, all right," Graham said, smiling. "The elephants he has killed are all in the junction area, and he's been flaunting his presence at Mahenya's. He's not trying to hide the fact that he's been the one killing the elephants."

I fretted for a week, wondering what the hell had happened to make Shadrek so angry. I just knew that something was amiss because there was no point in his shooting so many elephants. He had no market for the ivory. But I also knew that killing elephants in the Gonarezhou was the only way he could express his fury at the Rhodesians.

Good for him, I thought. *I'd be bloody angry, too, if I hadn't been paid for the work I had done. And it was damn dangerous work, too. Who could possibly have decided not to pay him? And I just knew that he had not been paid. I could feel it in my bones. Damn them!*

Had he received any kind of reasonable reward money from the Rhodesians, he would right away have begun rebuilding his beloved little hotel and his damned excuse for a store. They were his symbols of an independent future.

There could be no other explanation: Shadrek was angry with the Rhodesians and expressing his anger at their betrayal. Maybe Graham Child was right. Maybe he would try to kill me if we met during his present rage. He must include me among the people who had led him up the garden path.

I felt sick in my heart, and in my stomach. I had not wanted anything like this to happen. Damn those bastards in SB External! But there was more to come.

My director returned from a meeting with SB External early the following week. I must say that he had not let the dust settle before trying to find some answers for me. But what he had to tell me was not good. When he walked into my office and sat down in front of my desk, I knew that something was wrong.

"I don't know what happened between Shadrek and SB External," Graham said carefully. "They won't tell me a thing. . . ."

"Because the information is on a 'need-to-know' basis? I know all about that!"

"Yes," he continued after my interruption. "That's how it is, I'm afraid." I could tell from the way Graham looked that he was sympathetic. I think he really understood how I felt. "But there's more. They now believe that Shadrek is expendable."

"Expendable! After what he has done for them? The bastards!"

"Well . . . I suppose we'll never know the whole truth about what happened between Shadrek and SB External in Mozambique, but something has gone sour. And now *we* have to bear the consequences."

"How come?"

"Well, he's shooting all *our* big bull elephants in the Gonarezhou, isn't he?"

I took a deep breath. *Yes*, I thought, *Graham is right. Now the department has to bear the consequences.*

"And in his present mood—for I believe what you tell me, that he is in a towering rage at the moment—there is no telling what he will do if our game scouts confront him."

"Oh, sh--!" I said under my breath. I hadn't thought about that. "He'll shoot them," I said aloud. "He'll kill them sure as eggs are eggs." Now I began to feel desperate. I began to sweat.

"You know Shadrek better than anyone, Ron," Graham Child said to me softly. "And I know that you and he got on well together. But tell me now—do you really believe, in your heart of hearts, that Shadrek will shoot to kill our game scouts if they confront him?"

"Yes," I said immediately. "Under our war conditions, and in his present state of mind, he may even seek them out and kill them in their sleep. Wouldn't you, if you were in his shoes?" Dammit. I could feel my heart pounding furiously in my breast. I knew my face was flushed. I was angry as all hell and beside myself with worry.

"Dammit, Graham, he stuck his neck out for us. Why the hell are they treating him like this?"

"Ron," he said to me softly, clearly trying to pacify me, "just remember, we don't know what happened between Shadrek and the SB. He may have brought it all on himself."

"Balls!" I exploded. "The bastards never paid him. That's all there is to it."

"Maybe . . . but there's not much we can do about that now. They're not telling us anything about the matter, and they have washed their hands of Shadrek and whatever he is doing to our elephants in the Gonarezhou. They've passed the buck. They've passed on the baby."

"Damn them to hell!" I exploded, frustrated to the screaming point.

"But now I have to find a solution to all this," Graham said calmly. "And I'm going to need your help."

"How? What can I do to help?"

"Mister Shannon . . ."

"*MISTER* Shannon!" I exploded. "Damn him to hell. He's worse than the damn gooks! I wonder if he ever gets his hands dirty?"

"Ron, stop it!" Graham Child retorted. "Look, I know you are angry, and I share your frustrations, but we can't solve our problem unless you calm down and stop running your mouth off."

I sighed and nodded my head. "You're right. I'm sorry, Graham, but . . . I . . . am . . . just . . . so . . . bloody . . . angry!" I replied.

"I know, but let's put that behind us—please?" I did not understand how Graham Child could always remain so outwardly calm when everything around him seemed to be going wrong. I had seen this quality in him many times. It was a part of his personality that I greatly admired.

"OK," I responded more soberly. "I'll try to behave."

"Good! Now, have you got any photographs of you and Shadrek together, with you dressed in military camouflage?"

"Yes," I replied. "But they're not prints—they are colour slides."

"That's OK. We can get black-and-white prints made."

"What is your idea?" I asked, intrigued now.

"It's not my idea. It's . . . Shannon's idea." He had left out the "mister" with some difficulty. Graham Child was always the gentleman.

"Huh! So what is Shannon's idea?"

"He says," Graham picked his words carefully, "that if you have the kind of pictures we can use, he'll have copies made. Then he'll drop a bunch of them over Massangena by air, together with a report in Portuguese explaining how Shadrek had worked with Rhodesian intelligence and that's how we were able to knock out those ten camps the other day."

I sat up straight in my chair. "They'll kill him!" I said, horrified at the prospect. If I agreed to that, I'd be just as bad as Shannon and all his cronies.

"Yes, FRELIMO may well do that. But it will also stop Shadrek from killing our game scouts—not to mention more elephants." I hadn't seen Graham Child in such a cold and mercenary frame of mind before.

"I couldn't do that, Graham. It would be like stabbing my best friend in the back."

"And if he kills a game scout? Could you live with that? You know all those game scouts down in the Gonarezhou personally. You worked with them for five years. You know their wives and their children."

I sighed deeply and dropped my head into my hands. I stared at the writing on the notepad in front of me, seeing nothing and caring less. Never before had I been caught between such a big rock and such a hard place.

"Think about it, Ron," Graham said. "Think about it. I don't expect you to make a hasty decision, but we'll have to talk again tomorrow morning. We can't let this thing hang in the air."

"I really don't have to think about it at all, Graham," I said, straightening up. "There really isn't very much to think about, is there? You may not believe it, but I do have my priorities pretty well straight and correct—and clear—in my head."

"OK, then. So you'll do it. You'll let me have the colour slides?"

"No! I won't let Shannon have a damn thing. I'll get prints made myself—on government requisition, if I may?"

"Of course. And if they need more, I suppose they can make copies of the copies. All the same, I think you should get a hundred or so printed of half-a-dozen of the best photographs that you have."

"In black-and-white?"

"In black-and-white."

"This is all part of their plan, isn't it?" I said angrily. "Shannon and company are using us to get rid of Shadrek. They said he was expendable! Besides that, it'll save them one hell of a lot of money. When Shadrek is dead, they won't have anybody they have to pay reward money to!"

"Yes, they said he is now expendable. But I don't know if they consciously planned this. Probably not. They could not have anticipated Shadrek's rage."

Graham shook his head despondently and added, "This is a damn filthy war all-round, Ron, and I'm sick of it." It was the first chink in Graham Child's armour that I had ever seen. "We all seem to get sucked into the dirty-tricks game one way or another. Don't tell anybody I said that," he added, smiling weakly.

I had one hundred and ten black-and-white photographs printed of ten different colour slides in which Shadrek and I appeared together. The McGeorge Brothers' photographic studio in central Salisbury prepared them. The twin McGeorge brothers were personal friends of mine, and

I knew they would not let me down. When I told them it had to do with national security and the protection of the Gonarezhou's elephant bulls, they treated my order as a priority. Consequently, I was able to hand one hundred copies of each photograph to Graham Child the very next afternoon. I kept ten copies of each for myself. They appear in this book.

I had many sleepless nights over this development, but, as Graham had said to me, my hands were tied. My priorities were the safety of the game scouts in the Gonarezhou and the protection of the national park's elephant bulls.

The rest is history.

Chapter 28

Shortly after I released the photographs to Shannon, Shadrek's killing of elephant bulls in the Gonarezhou ceased altogether. Then John Davey phoned me from Chiredzi to say that he had heard through the "grapevine" that FRELIMO had arrested Shadrek and taken him to Maputo. I knew then that SB External had done its dirty deed. My photographs of Shadrek, showing him sitting alongside the elephants we had shot together, me next to him in Rhodesian army camouflage, had been delivered by "special" airmail to Massangena. No doubt Shannon's Portuguese message that accompanied the photographs had sealed Shadrek's fate.

My heart cried out for Shadrek, and my body began to quiver at the thought of his treatment at the hands of FRELIMO. They would not handle him lightly under the circumstances and would beat the truth out of him eventually. A man had only so much endurance under the pressure of torture.

And so the final parts of Shadrek's story came to me in dribs and drabs. Most of it was hearsay. Some of it was fact. Some may have been fabrication.

Some six months later I was surprised to hear that Shadrek had been released from prison and had returned to Madjwisanga. This information came to me, again, from John Davey. He also told me that Shadrek had been severely tortured—including being subjected to the terrible Portuguese beating called the *bastinado.*

The *bastinado* is applied to a victim lying on his back on the floor, with his ankles tied to thongs suspended from a pole. The soles of his feet, held conveniently three feet above the ground, are continuously beaten with a perforated wooden paddle. The treatment is carried out continuously and seemingly forever. The constant abuse slowly separates the hard skin on the soles of the victim's feet from the flesh beneath, and the feet swell up with fluid like balloons. Those who survive the *bastinado* are unable to walk, even on crutches, for months and months. The *bastinado* was once used by the Portuguese not just as a torture to extract information but also as a punishment.

Shadrek had returned to the care of his father, Muteruko Kumbuya, who, it was said, had intervened to save his son's life. The chief was now an old man but still held great sway among the Ndau peoples of the Rio Save. The local FRELIMO military commanders, who relied upon his control of the people to maintain civil discipline in the region, also respected him. The Shadrek who returned to Madjwisanga was a total wreck—a cripple who could get around only on his hands and knees.

Early the next year—1980, I think—I received more news of Shadrek. By then Rhodesia had capitulated politically, and Ian Smith had agreed to a "democratic" election. Everybody was to get the vote—including the primitive Ba Tonka tribespeople who were still living in the Stone Age. Robert Mugabe and his Mashona ZANU party, and Joshua Nkomo and his Matabele ZAPU party, and all their guerrillas in the ZANLA and ZIPRA armies, were allowed to participate. It was the beginning of the end for Rhodesia.

Shadrek, I was told, had been arrested by one of the department's first black game rangers, Jeremiah, at the Mahenya tsetse fly control gate. This was the manned control point on the tsetse game fence that bridged the short gap between the Sabi River and the Mozambique border. This game fence was in the hills north of the Mahenya settlements, near where I had last seen Shadrek and not far from where Don Boyd and I had bogged down our army vehicles on that seemingly long-ago "hearts-and-minds" exercise at Mahenya's that had set the stage for this story.

No sooner was the word out about Shadrek's arrest than Phil Evans, the department's deputy director, came charging down to my office.

"Have you heard the news?" he blustered eagerly. "Jeremiah has arrested Shadrek."

"Yes," I answered calmly. "I got a phone call from Chiredzi yesterday."

"And it took a black ranger to arrest him," he crowed. "For how long did you white game wardens try to catch him?"

Phil Evans and I had had a love-hate relationship going on for years. There had always been respect, but neither had ever given any quarter to the other. Now, it seemed he was delighted to rub salt into what he presumed was an old wound.

I said nothing but smiled inwardly. *If only you knew,* I thought with some pleasure. But I did not illuminate the man.

Evans's attitude was strange, coming from a man who had already arranged to leave the country and take up employment with the Natal Parks Board in South Africa. He did so, in fact, before the election that put Robert Mugabe into power and changed Rhodesia into Zimbabwe. He was leaving the country, he said, because he had no faith in the coming black majority government under Mugabe. In retrospect, I now know that he was right. Later many people in the department said of him, ungraciously, that he must have had a crystal ball.

It took just two years for Mugabe to force most of the department's white staff out of employment. I was one of those who started the slide—because my life was threatened. So perhaps I was too hard on Phil Evans when I criticized him for leaving the country's national parks in the lurch. But then, I was a fanatic. Throughout my service, right up to the end, I believed that anybody who left the national parks for greener pastures was a heretic. That's how I thought of Phil Evans. My attitude toward him has mellowed with the wisdom that comes with age and experience. In all his projections, Phil Evans had been absolutely right. We should all have heeded his advice and left when the going was good. Had we done so, we would have been much better off in our old age.

Nevertheless, I was surprised by Evans's lack of knowledge of Shadrek's and my working together. For all of what I viewed as his faults, Evans was a good second-in-command for Graham Child. He was also not the kind of person who betrayed confidences. I was surprised, therefore, that Graham Child had not made him privy to what Shadrek and I had been doing. It also elevated my respect for Graham, for clearly he had advised only those people in the department who had the "need to know." And nobody really had that need except Graham and myself.

Jeremiah's so-called arrest of Shadrek was not your classic collar. Here is the story:

Shadrek had fretted under FRELIMO after his release from the Maputo jail. Incapacitated as he was, he was helpless to retaliate. But it was an important part of Shadrek's mentality that he needed to settle scores for perceived wrongs perpetrated against him. For example, it was in revenge for the tsetse official's theft of his ivory that he had stolen the cattle herd in the Gonarezhou and taken it into Mozambique. It was his anger at the Rhodesians for not keeping their bargain and (presumably) not paying him his reward that drove him to begin shooting the Gonarezhou's bull elephants again, even though he had no market for the ivory. Squaring accounts was part of Shadrek's psyche.

After being uncovered as a Rhodesian agent, Shadrek had undoubtedly lost all credibility with FRELIMO—and had probably tarnished his stature as a legendary elephant poacher among the people, too. Shadrek, therefore, became a nobody—a person who did not count even within his own community. And that would not have been acceptable to the Shadrek I knew. It was inevitable, therefore, that when his torture wounds healed, Shadrek would again assert himself. He was someone who just had to be somebody.

So it was that when he felt well enough to test his wings again, Shadrek had moved Tabita and his four children to Mahenya's, where they took up residence in her father's old village. Shadrek had then rounded up all FRELIMO's cattle in the vicinity of Chiwi and Madjwisanga and driven them over the border into Mahenya's. I was not told the exact number of the cattle that he thus acquired, only that it was substantial.

Shadrek had not dallied at Mahenya's but had driven the cattle directly up the road that Don Boyd and I had traveled at the start of our "hearts-and-minds" exercise, intending to take them to Josiah's relatives who lived in the Sangwe Tribal Trust Land. From there he planned to go to John Davey in Chiredzi and demand retribution for his treatment by SB. Apparently he still had some trust in and respect for John Davey. And he had decided that he would rather live with the Rhodesians, despite their sometime duplicity, than endure a lingering living death under FRELIMO's yoke.

When Shadrek hit the game fence, however, the two tsetse department gate guards there refused to let him pass through. After all, the whole purpose of the expensive game fence and gate was to prevent game and cattle from crossing from the once tsetse-infested area inside the fence to the tsetse-free area on the other side. This upset all Shadrek's plans and infuriated him.

The guards were from the Gokwe district far to the northwest and had no idea who Shadrek was. So he told them who he was—with due pomp and ceremony, no doubt, if I know Shadrek—and he told them, too, what his mission was. The Rhodesians had promised him a farm, he declared, and owed him a lot of money. He was coming to collect his reward for services rendered.

The guards were totally out of their depth now, but one of them suddenly had a brilliant idea. "There is a government officer staying at the DC's Chiribira Falls camp," he said. "I'll go and see if he can give permission for you and your cattle to cross through the barrier." He cycled off to find Game Ranger Jeremiah, the National Parks Department's very first black officer, at the DC's reconstructed camp. About an hour later Jeremiah drove up in his government Land Rover and promptly arrested Shadrek for poaching elephants in the Gonarezhou.

Jeremiah drove Shadrek to Chiredzi in handcuffs. There the poacher was formally charged and thrown into the remand prison at nearby Buffalo Range to await trial. Jeremiah left the cattle in the custody of the tsetse gate guards at Mahenya's. Shortly thereafter, the Rhodesian government officially confiscated them.

About this time, John Davey was transferred out of Chiredzi, so I did not learn about all that took place after Shadrek's arrest until very recently—almost twenty years after the fact. I am now about to relate what Koos Herbst told me only a few months ago.

Game Ranger Koos Herbst had served in the police during the war. After independence he left the police and joined national parks. At the time of Shadrek's arrest, he was stationed in the Bulawayo area but was called upon by an old police colleague at Chiredzi to take charge of Shadrek's case. Subsequently, Shadrek took Koos to the sites of many of his most recent kills—all elephants taken with his AK-47. What Shadrek showed Koos ensured that he would be convicted for poaching.

Had Shadrek said nothing, I seriously doubt the police could have made a poaching case against him. It was only Koos's affable manner that persuaded Shadrek to provide the hard evidence needed to secure a conviction in court. Shadrek was formally sentenced to eight and a half years in jail, the heaviest punishment ever given for a poaching offense in Rhodesia. And because of Shadrek's history, he was committed to the Chikurubi High Security Prison on the outskirts of Salisbury.

Koos had no knowledge of my involvement with Shadrek during the war, and Shadrek did not enlighten him. Indeed, Shadrek still had no knowledge of my connection with national parks. Had he known who I really was, he might have asked Koos to get in touch with me. And had I become involved in his court case, I would most certainly have given evidence in mitigation. Shadrek's destiny might then have been very different. As it was, however, none of his work for the Rhodesian security forces during the war was ever revealed. The court heard only the bold facts of his most recent elephant killings. I was told nothing of Shadrek's court case. It was all over before I knew that it was happening, and the first thing I heard about it was after his sentence had been passed.

I then lived in the Salisbury suburb of Mandara, and the Chikurubi prison was only five miles from my home. In fact, I used to visit the prison sewage ponds very early every morning before I went to work to collect live zooplankton to feed the tropical fish that I then used to breed.

I was not allowed to see Shadrek in prison, however, although I tried everything in my power to do so. Very few visitors were allowed into the country's highest security penitentiary. It was ironic that every morning I netted water fleas for my fish within sight of the prison walls, yet I was not allowed to visit one of its celebrated inmates.

In April 1980 the country passed into Robert Mugabe's hands. Rhodesia became Zimbabwe. One of the first things the new Zimbabwe government did was to review the cases of inmates in all of the country's prisons. There were thousands of prisoners who had been incarcerated for crimes against the state (of Rhodesia)—which meant, in the minds of the new ZANU government, resistance against the illegal rebel regime. Shortly after Zimbabwe's world-recognized independence, therefore, all these prisoners went free.

I cannot say whether Shadrek's case was reviewed or not. But since Mugabe's security people carefully scrutinized the record of every inmate in every jail in the country, certainly Shadrek's Mozambican connection was not overlooked. And it would have been a miracle if the investigators had not also realized that this was the Shadrek who had worked with the Rhodesians to knock out the ten ZANLA guerrilla camps on the Rio Save—a man who had been responsible, therefore, for the deaths of hundreds of ZANLA comrades, maybe several thousand! Thanks to myself and SB, confirmation of that fact was then freely available in Mozambique. And once that knowledge was in the hands of Robert Mugabe's new-style central intelligence organization, Shadrek's life would have been in very serious jeopardy.

After Mugabe's takeover of power, no Rhodesian European who remained in the country was allowed any kind of "inside" political, military, or security information at all. Consequently, it was impossible to find out what happened to Shadrek after April 1980. Rumour had it that by August 1980 he was no longer in the Chikurubi prison. ZANU advised those who enquired that he had been among the many political prisoners released shortly after Zimbabwe's independence. But there was no proof of that fact. Indeed, nobody in authority would tell me anything about

Shadrek at all, and everybody who cared about him or who thought about his fate believed that Mugabe's people had had his throat cut.

I continue to hope and pray that Shadrek was not murdered and that he was indeed released. And I hope and pray that he was able to return to Tabita and his children, and to his home at Madjwisanga on the Rio Save. I believe, however, that the chances of that having happened are remote.

If Mugabe's people killed my friend Shadrek—and I feel sure that they did—then I hope that my readers will accept this book as a suitable and worthy epitaph, for Shadrek must surely rank as one of Africa's greatest elephant poachers of all time.

Annex

Twenty-three years have passed since I last saw Shadrek. Thirty-three years have gone by since I first heard of him. That is a lot of water under the bridges of time.

The reason I mention this, to be honest, is that when I sat down to write this story I discovered that I could not remember all the finer details. I cannot, for example, now recall many of my conversations with pertinent people, or who told me what. One or two names I have forgotten entirely, so I have invented substitutes. One or two other names I have changed purposely to maintain anonymity. And the sequences of some events that I relate are now just hazy memories.

Dates, particularly, presented a major problem. Shadrek's telling of his own story to me was very disjointed, and he, too, sometimes got his chronology terribly mixed up. Another factor is that he told me only those of his adventures that he felt were the most important, or that happened to come into his mind when he opened up his heart to me. Therefore, I have written just a brief reflection of Shadrek's real and very full life. What he did tell me, however, I recorded faithfully in a small black notebook that is still in my possession. The information it contains is the foundation upon which Shadrek's personal history is based.

I have also invoked some measure of poetic license. For example, I have had to reconstruct, in a somewhat fictional and sometimes dramatic manner, many of the conversations and some of the events. I have embellished some of Shadrek's stories, using my own experience of big-game hunting, to make them more interesting. I have done this because during the few short days that I had to record his life's story,

Shadrek often gave me but a mundane catalogue of his adventures. The gist of the story, however, remains correct in all its dimensions. Shadrek and all the people I mention are, or were, very real.

I regret that I cannot conclude that Shadrek was the illegitimate son of Bvekenya Barnard of *The Ivory Trail* fame. That is what everybody once thought, and what many people still think. Such a fact would have rounded off this story beautifully. This rumour, however, is totally without foundation. Nevertheless, Shadrek in his time was every bit as big in legendary stature as his notorious predecessor was in his day. Indeed, I sincerely believe Shadrek is the greater of the two.

In view of the military circumstances of the Rhodesian bush war, and because of the life-and-death realities that still influence the lives of all Zimbabwe's citizens since the country's independence in 1980, very few Zimbabweans today are prepared to talk very much about their involvement in Zimbabwe's War of Liberation. To maintain a peaceful existence, the ex-combatant white Rhodesians who are still there keep a low profile and let the rest of the world go by. So it is difficult to pick up many of the still-missing pieces of the jigsaw puzzle that comprise Shadrek's life and eventual fate.

In addition, those who really know what happened to Shadrek, especially in the last period of his life, are now scattered to the four winds—the result of the grand exodus of white Rhodesians just before and immediately following Zimbabwe's independence. Most of the prominent members of the Rhodesian security forces, for example, no longer live in Zimbabwe. The minds and hearts of some of those scattered people hold the most important missing pieces of the puzzle.

Another "truth-hider" was the need-to-know policy that restricted the dissemination of information within the Rhodesian military. It will now be impossible to locate the pertinent people and extract from them the missing bits of information that could complete Shadrek's story.

The late Lieutenant (later Captain) Don Boyd of the Rhodesian Intelligence Corps could have verified the first part of the story up to the point where Don and I sent ivory to Shadrek in Mozambique. Detective

Inspector John Davey of the police Special Branch (internal) knows about the events that took place up to the time Shadrek and I were ready to begin operating inside Mozambique. Inspector Mike Shannon of the police Special Branch (external) knows what Shadrek and I did in Mozambique—and he presumably knows what happened after the police took Shadrek over from me.

Who knows, SB may also have recruited Tabita. Shadrek's wife, as secretary to the FRELIMO commandant at Chiwi, must have represented a veritable treasure trove of military intelligence for the Rhodesians. And it is most unlikely that Tabita's potential intelligence value escaped the likes of Peter Dewes and Michael Shannon. Indeed, this fact may have been the real reason that Operation Poacher was taken out of my hands. Certainly, I was not properly trained to "control" such a military intelligence prize.

Dr. Graham Child, the director at that time of the Rhodesian Department of National Parks and Wildlife Management, knows that I worked with Shadrek during the war since he helped facilitate the operation. Beyond that, he knows little about what really happened between Shadrek and me and the work we did together.

Only Shadrek himself knows the whole story—*if* he is still alive. And Shadrek—*if* he is still alive—may not want to talk about his involvement in Operation Poacher because of its ultimate success. Indeed, despite his egotistical nature, this is one story that he would be well advised not to boast about in present-day Zimbabwe. If the facts were to become common knowledge, he might yet be made to pay the ultimate price for assisting the Rhodesian security forces the way he did—*if* he were alive.

There are some sublime fabrications in this story. For example, I have allowed my imagination to run especially when I was not present during certain events—as when Shadrek was working with his Portuguese friends. What he actually told me about many events was a mere compendium of the facts. It would have been impossible to tell this story if I had denied myself the right to manufacture, for example, Shadrek's conversations with Fror and Alberto. Nevertheless, nothing has been added or omitted that twists the historical facts. Whatever embroidery I have included is designed purely to make the story more readable.

This recounting is the true story of Shadrek and my short personal involvement with him. In my opinion Shadrek was the greatest black elephant poacher the continent of Africa has ever known. It is fitting, therefore, that his story—despite the many shortcomings that might have crept in during my telling of it—be recorded for posterity.

SAFARI PRESS